HAPPY
NOT
PERFECT

HAPPY
NOT
PERFECT

**Upgrade Your Mind, Challenge Your Thoughts,
and Free Yourself from Anxiety**

Poppy Jamie

HARMONY
BOOKS

Library of Congress Cataloging-in-Publication Data is available upon request.

ISBN 978-0-593-23168-5
eBook ISBN 978-0-593-23169-2

Printed in the United States of America

Editor: Matthew Benjamin
Assistant Editor: Danielle Curtis
Designer: Jan Derevjanik
Production Editor: Serena Wang
Production Manager: Kelli Tokos
Composition: North Market Street Graphics
Copy Editor: Robin Slutzky

10 9 8 7 6 5 4 3 2 1

First Edition

To my parents, Pippa and Ian,
who really are the souls behind *Happy Not Perfect.*
You taught me that no matter what,
there is always light to find in the seemingly dark.

CONTENTS

FOREWORD . . . ix

INTRODUCTION:
Getting Bendy . . . xi

PART ONE:
FUCK MY LIFE . . . 1

CHAPTER ONE

My Toxic Core Beliefs . . . 3

CHAPTER TWO

Cold Shower Reality Checks . . . 35

CHAPTER THREE

Why Your Brain Is So Bitchy . . . 51

PART TWO:
FLEX YOUR LIFE . . . 79

CHAPTER FOUR

What Is Flexible Thinking? . . . 81

CHAPTER FIVE

Connection . . . 95

CHAPTER SIX

Curiosity . . . 119

CHAPTER SEVEN

Choice . . . 135

CHAPTER EIGHT

Commitment . . . 151

**PART THREE:
THE FLEX IN REAL LIFE** . . . 169

CHAPTER NINE

Flex the Past . . . 171

CHAPTER TEN

Flex Culture . . . 201

CHAPTER ELEVEN

Flex Confidence . . . 233

CHAPTER TWELVE

Flex the Future . . . 261

ENDNOTES . . . 291

FOREWORD

Like all humans, each of us strives to be happy. The problem is that for most of us we don't know what makes us happy...we just think that we do. As a result, we spend immense amounts of time not understanding that many of the actions we are engaged in to be happy are actually demonstrations of proving one's self-worth by seeking the approval of others and believing that such approval will make us happy. Whether it's the next promotion, the new car or accessory, or a larger house, each of these things only results in a transitory feeling of being happy. Why? Because we don't understand that happiness does not occur because of the external but the internal. Happiness isn't a manifestation of what one has but who one is. So many people run around attempting to demonstrate that everything is fine with them by the appearance of material success. Such an illusion for many comes at a very high cost resulting in worsening self-esteem, insecurity, and anxiety...presenting a smile to the outside world while being profoundly unhappy.

Happy Not Perfect tells the story of Poppy Jamie's journey to understand this reality. By every measure, Poppy appeared to "have it all," yet deep down she struggled with insecurity, anxiety, and the fear that others would find out that she's an imposter. All the work that she had done to be successful only led to further unhappiness. What she realized was that the wounds of her childhood in great part contributed to her unhappiness. Wounds that she had never dealt with, feelings that she didn't understand...she was an actor in another person's reality, smiling, successful...being perfect but not being happy.

What Poppy does in *Happy Not Perfect* is to marshal the evidence from a legion of world-renowned thinkers, living and dead, to demonstrate the reality that striving for perfection is counter-productive, that before we can be happy we must offer ourselves compassion and ultimately that the solution to our own happiness is not external but internal. She offers innumerable examples and practical techniques that give us the tools necessary to be the architects of our own happiness and recognize to be happy one doesn't have to be perfect.

James R. Doty, MD
International and *New York Times* bestselling author of *Into the Magic Shop: A Neurosurgeon's Quest to Discover the Mysteries of the Brain and the Secrets of the Heart*, senior editor of the *Oxford Handbook of Compassion Science,* and founder and director of the Center for Compassion and Altruism Research and Education at Stanford University.

Introduction
GETTING BENDY

We are often most terrified of the thing that makes us the most human: our ability to feel.

Our feelings, like the underswell of the sea, can be unpredictable, vast, wild, still, and engulfing. We fear the things that make us vulnerable yet make us powerful. But who can blame us? Emotions can be painful little buggers.

Just when we're getting in the groove and life seems good, confidence is rising, and it's like an excited orchestra is about to play... we're suddenly *wallop bang bosh*, hit with a nasty one. Surges of anger, frustration, anxiety, regret, shame, embarrassment (among others) can pop our balloon out of nowhere, leaving us scrambling.

Can you remember the first time you were deflated by a powerful emotion? Or remember someone telling you to *stop crying*? *Stop being so angry? Just calm down!* We learn that strong emotions are impolite, distasteful, wrong, or ugly. We're told to *just be ourselves* but in the same breath reminded, *don't be too sensitive.* I tried endlessly to find the perfect balance of "just the right emotion" but "not too much." Unsurprisingly I failed, and instead grew scared of my feelings, praying they wouldn't rear their ugly and inconvenient heads—which they inevitably did, countless times.

Ever since I can remember, my emotions have been what I imagine a group of very naughty schoolchildren must be like. They escape when you don't want them to. They're loud when you don't want them to be. They can be obnoxious, they don't stop talking, they have an attitude and barely listen. They have gotten me into obscene amounts of trouble over the years and left me uncontrollably laughing and/or crying at the most inappropriate moments. (Just google "reporter falls off chair laughing Jude Law" and you'll witness a very public attempt of me at twenty-one desperately trying to keep it together while hysterically giggling on television.)

After years of emotional warfare, I began to consider: What if we took advantage of our biochemical reactions—what feelings actually are—and used them as keys to our liberation? Imagine what would happen if we stopped wrestling with them and instead extracted their wisdom to: (1) understand ourselves better, (2) unshackle from the wounds of the past, and (3) heal our toxic core beliefs to create new future possibilities. I'm talking about becoming a connoisseur of feelings.

We live in a culture that seemingly ranks emotions. *Happy* is celebrated as this optimum state we should all be aiming for, the place where we have *no worries and things are great*. I quickly learned to live performatively. Desperately trying to do and say the so-called right things to fit in and appear nice, happy, and smiling *always*—everything I was told a polite girl should be. But by not allowing myself to feel and express honestly, I was unconsciously cutting myself off from the greatest source of guidance we all have: honest, unfiltered emotion.

Many of us step away from our integrity to perform identities given to us and, in the separation, we begin to lose understanding of what our deepest desires, longings, and passions are. What really lights our soul up. Instead we look to other people, and tune in to their ideas of how to do life. We rely on external sources to validate us, and popular opinion to guide us.

The day I began learning to accept my emotions and challenging what happiness really meant for me was the day I experienced a clarity like no other. Contrary to what I'd thought, happiness didn't reside in the perfect moments I so desperately craved, or in external approval, but rather in the beauty within the mess, the strength that arises from challenges, the ability to value myself before needing others to, and the willingness to see things differently. Happiness can be as painful as it

I was trying anything and everything to make the thoughts stop so I could stay in the moment and concentrate on actually doing my job. *Now is not the time, shut up and PLEASE let me prepare for this talk in peace,* I hissed back to my meanie inside. But nothing seemed to control my pulsating anxiety.

This day could have been one of my most proud memories, but my mind ruined it. I wasn't able to admire the hard work I'd put in or appreciate the challenges and rough years I'd gone through to get here. It didn't matter what I did, the words "You're an insignificant nobody" felt tattooed on my brain and I was lost in that narrative. Our brains are the most convincing storytellers and when they're stuck repeating tales of our fears, they can be difficult to break away from.

In the end, the talk went fine. I had no reason to worry. But like always, my brain spun itself into chaos for nothing.

From career-defining moments to dating, nearly every experience caused a feeling of painful self-consciousness and a sense of harrowing inadequacy. Not for one moment did I feel the confidence anyone thought I had; underneath the smiley self was someone stuck at war with their insecurities.

My quest for #happiness, #success, and to finally feel good enough caused my mind, heart, and soul to collapse on the journey. It was only when I was lying in a hospital bed due to exhaustion, broken by chronic anxiety, and feeling like I was wrapped in an iron blanket, that I reluctantly considered whether my need for perfection had actually led me straight to discontentment, stress, fear, self-rejection, and illness.

Only then did I start to realize my mind was the sole culprit. The time had come for me to confront my cruel inner critic and open up the dungeon of emotions I'd kept locked away for so many years. Not knowing what I would find, I was petrified to do so. I knew I had a clear and important choice to make: I could continue abusing myself, blaming other people for making me feel less-than, and continue on this destructive path of believing *success* and *perfect* = *happiness*, or I could change direction.

Change begins with learning, and that's exactly where I began. I tracked down every expert I could find in neuroscience, psychology, mindfulness, and ontology (philosophy about the nature of being) to understand why I was so compulsively horrible to myself and how I could cultivate a kinder mind. Turned out, my mind needed some drastic Marie Kondo'ing (I can assure you most of its contents weren't sparking joy).

Spring cleaning your brain is hard work; you have to do the sort of tidying that actually hoovers underneath the carpet, not just around it. But when you do, you finally realize who you are behind all the fear. It is there I found my truest, wildest, most authentic self. The loving, curious, limitless self. She'd been hidden for years, since childhood.

We arrive in this world full of playfulness and wonder, and like a little sponge, we soak up everything. We innocently absorb every comment, feeling, and experience and turn these into a set of beliefs and a rule book for how we understand ourselves and the world around us to ensure we stay safe and survive. The beliefs and rules we create to make sense of the world are not our fault. They are just a by-product of our first environments that none of us chose. But without intervention, we then spend the rest of our lives viewing the world according to these eight-year-old interpretations.

As a little girl, I took on the belief that I wasn't good enough as I was and spent twenty years in search of evidence to confirm my own worthlessness. But I didn't need to do this anymore. I began to see how different life could look with a new lens and how differently it could sound with a dialed-down stream of self-critical thoughts. I no longer needed to be an audience to that. None of us do.

"Everything can be taken from a man but one thing: the last of the human freedoms—to choose one's attitude in any given set of circumstances, to choose one's own way."
—Viktor Frankl

The goal isn't to be perfect, but to be happy from the inside out. Happy is the courage to life live according to what lights me up. For the last few years, I've been practicing stretching my beliefs and thoughts and, in doing so, I've tasted a freedom from anxiety I didn't know possible. When we begin to limber up our minds and rewire the faulty programming that was installed in childhood, our entire experience of life shifts.

As a result of my conscious thought reprogramming, my internal world—once a dark, scary, fearful place—is back to one of curiosity and compassion. I've accepted there will be bumps, highs and lows, twists and turns, but with a new way of thinking, changes aren't jarring or daunting but serve to make us excel.

I only wish I'd found these mind upgrade techniques earlier, as I would have been able to save myself from so many hours and days lost to shame and self-flagellation. This is why I wrote this book: to save you precious time and energy. It's my journey from perpetually thinking I was not good enough to where I am now, accepting that I'm never going to have it all together, but trying is the fun part, and that my destination is forever changing. For so long, I fixated on trying to be perfect, but as this story shows, I found a much more enjoyable path, living a life of flexibility.

Flexibility is the key to being happy (not perfect). I'm learning how to experience my life as a mental, emotional contortionist to adapt and thrive (not just survive) in any situation that comes my way. When you're flexible, there are no blocks, failures, or misfortunes. Pain plus reflection is how we progress and shape-shift forward. Life offers growth nuggets, if we can train ourselves to spot them and use them. There's only possibility, opportunities, and hidden gifts to discover with a flexi-mindset. In a different version of the story, a setback isn't a failure but a step toward a more joy-aligned path. A grievance is a potential gate to growth. And feeling stuck is a chance to connect with our wildest, truest self and unlock the wisdom our emotions are trying to tell us. We are the narrators of our life, so let's practice telling better stories.

The Flex, the method I devised to practice flexible thinking, is a simple four-step framework for daily reflecting that will change your life, just as it changed mine. As a whole, the Flex method is about connecting with your body to upgrade your mind and help you rewire your thought habits so you can untangle from the past, lean into love, and rise above fear. Flexing raises your energy to create a future that chimes with your soul. I'll explain each step—the four Cs of Connection, Curiosity, Choice, and Commitment—in Part Two of this book. In Part Three, I'll show you how the Flex applies in real life. The method is psychologically, spiritually solid. It's the real deal, not a fad, and it does take some time to incorporate. But since I've been living it for a while now, I can guide you to speed up the process.

Life presents us with the same issues over and over again, just looking slightly different. Instead of beating ourselves up or frustratedly saying, "Why does this always happen?!," this framework provides a simple way to navigate through life's hot moments. The quality of our life is based on the quality of our decisions and the Flex is here to keep us on a bendy path to making better and better choices and to managing emotions that get in the way.

The Flex allows you to feel all your feelings without being railroaded by them.

The Flex upgrades your energy frequency and mental outlook.

The Flex is like training your brain to touch its toes.

You might think, "Well, I can't touch my toes, I was born with stiff legs" or "That sounds painful, I'm not going to try." Saying "no" keeps you stuck in Einstein's definition of insanity, doing the same thing over and over again and expecting a different result. Growth only happens when we're skating outside our comfort zone and saying "yes" to discovery.

I invite you to put your mental health cross-trainers on as we get ready to *streeettttcchhhhh* our thinking, thoughts, and actions.

While standing in line for coffee at a tech conference once, I ran into one of the most revered investors in the world, a person who has funded the ideas and technology that have changed our world over the last quarter century. I asked him, "What are the common traits you've found in all the most brilliant geniuses you've met?"

"They're daring enough to think differently, bend their thoughts, and to think outside the box," he said. "They aren't trying to fit into the status quo and they dance to the beat of their own drum."

His words echoed long after this brief encounter. I was in the early days of learning the Flex and was again reminded that growing the confidence to think differently is the path to infinite possibilities and access to the genius we all hold inside.

One could say I have been good at "manifesting," or making a thought become a reality. By the time I was twenty-eight, I'd founded companies, was on *Forbes'* lists, and was attending glamorous parties. But I wasn't any happier having accumulated societal nods of achievement. My Flex journey has been about flipping superficial manifesting on its head, to re-focus on cultivating a safe place to exist inside my head. It's been funny seeing how quickly my outer life has positively changed by concentrating on the internal first! The Happy Not Perfect app was my first foray into the mind and learning how to slow it down and manage it better. It turned daily mindfulness into a game to find inner clarity and calm. This book about the Flex is the next step, a deeper dive into neural reprogramming.

There are no magic spells in this book. Just a scientifically research-backed method to find more magic in our lives. I will be forever grateful for the way the Flex has liberated me. Being free, connected to myself, and open has felt better than any promotion, raise, new pair of shoes, or hot kiss from a cute boy. I am so excited to share a technique that's transformed my life from the inside out and continues to stretch out any thought-traps I fall into.

"I used to think I was the strangest person in the world but then I thought there are so many people in the world, there must be someone just like me who feels bizarre and flawed in the same ways I do. I would imagine her and imagine that she must be out there thinking of me, too. Well, I hope that if you are out there and read this you know that, yes, it's true I'm here, and I'm just as strange as you."

—Frida Kahlo

PART
ONE

FUCK
MY
LIFE

"THE PAST CAN HURT.
BUT THE WAY I SEE IT,
YOU CAN EITHER RUN
FROM IT, OR LEARN
FROM IT."

—RAFIKI, THE LION KING

chapter one

MY TOXIC CORE BELIEFS

At the heart of every human being is a desire to be loved and to love. Love is what protects us from the moment we enter this world. We discover early on that the love we crave is often conditional and in our delicate sponge years, we learn how best to get and give the love we want and need. From these experiences, we form a set of core beliefs for and about ourselves that shape our identity, influence our decisions, and construct the basis of the relationships we have with others.

No one is to blame for the core beliefs we created. They're survival strategies formed in our first environments, and not necessarily all driven by our parents, either. School, siblings, and friends also contributed key plotlines to the internal story we repeat daily, usually without realizing it. And we'll continue to play out the same words again and again until we become aware of the narrative we're stuck in.

Here's my story about my *(faulty)* core beliefs that were installed during childhood, how they turned toxic, and where they left me. As you read, have a think about the three core beliefs that were installed in your head, and how they're still filtering your reality *(not in a pretty Instagram way)*.

As you'll soon see, what protected me at eight didn't continue working as I got older.

Core Belief #1:
NOT GOOD ENOUGH

By eight years old, I learned that if I could just please everyone, I might then be loved, and *nothing would feel better.* But that was a tall order. I was never the smartest, funniest, prettiest, sportiest, had the nicest shoes or most delicious lunchbox. My mediocrity (and soggy cucumber sandwiches) meant I had to try doubly to get approval and win love.

It seemed like I was the only average child in my class growing up. Claire had the voice of an angel. Charlie had the coolest ponytail. Nick was great at swimming. And I had no obvious superpower to attract friends. I had a sense that if I were just *better*, maybe people would like me more.

In school plays, I was relegated to Fairy #6, Orphan #4, or Hysterical Girl #12 in *The Crucible.* I was dumped by nearly all the boys I dated and felt lucky if anyone wanted to go out with me in the first place.

For most of my life I've kept a diary and when I read back old entries from when I was eleven and twelve, I can see my toxic core beliefs starting to show up. At eleven, I was convinced I was not good enough and not worth dating even for a week.

N.B.: Going out with boys at my junior school meant walking around the playground with them for a few minutes at recess (potentially holding hands at most!).

A couple tween agony moments from those pages when I was eleven:

> October 2002 (12 year old Poppy)
>
> I asked out Tom W. he said yes. After the weekend I put hair curlers in. Then he dumped me. I haven't said anything or done anything. I got teased.

> January 2003 (12 year old Poppy)
>
> Going out with David for a week now. He hasn't dumped me yet! I really hope I get the scholarship.
>
>
>
> Lots of Luv
> Poppy
> XXX
>
>

Sports followed the same vein. I sat on the bench more than I played field hockey, much to my embarrassment when my dad came to watch a game. Out of pity, the coach would put me on the field for the last ten minutes and I would then have to act like I wasn't scared of the ball. I was terrified.

My "not good enough…pretty enough…smart enough…thin enough…cool enough" wounds grew deeper, no matter what I did. I was spiraling in self-blame. Even though, objectively, I was doing well in some areas, like academics, it seemed like everywhere I looked, I was inadequate. Not cool enough for the hipsters, and not smart enough for the geeks. I just wanted one person or group to embrace me with open arms. Despite my perma-straightened hair, blue shimmery overloaded eye shadow, and black-mascara-clumped curled lashes, it never happened, and the feeling of being unaccepted was creating a gaping hole inside. The toxic belief that I was not good enough in the way I looked, acted, sounded, and just *was* became as strong of a belief as my knowing the sky was blue. It broke my soul to acknowledge, but as I was wrongly told early on, some things in life were just the way they were, even if we didn't like them. One of those facts was that I wasn't good enough.

Core Belief #2:
MUST TRY HARDER

My quintessentially English childhood *was* loving, but at many times unsettling, with an ominous threat of financial insecurity hanging over our family. Among us—my small-business-owner father, my psychotherapist mother, my two brothers, and me—there were no secrets. Someone's problem was everyone's problem and we could have won an Olympic medal for worrying. My older brother Thomas would stay awake at night, listening to my parents' tense money discussions through the floorboards. He would then repeat what he'd heard to my little brother Edward and me, causing us to think we were days away from homelessness. I grew up with the constant worry that my father's business was going to go under.

July 2002 (11 year old Poppy)

We are going to be bankrupt before we know it. Have to move because the house costs a bomb!!! I am bored fat (because of sweets + T.V. no exercise). I can't look like a fat Baboon in my new Bicini [sic]. I want to look slim jim. So I am on a fittness [sic] programme.

My heart breaks for my younger self. At eleven, I was worried about bankruptcy and looking fat, two fears that stayed with me for twenty years.

Because of our financial insecurity, the idea that fiscal independence was the route to feeling safe and loved became ingrained in me at a very early age. We all became micro-entrepreneurs by ten, washing cars in the neighborhood and setting up illegal sweet shops at school. With my father's entrepreneur mindset, I was taught that anything is possible, you just have to work so hard it hurts.

The route to having my own money one day started with getting good grades, so on our family holidays I began sneaking textbooks into my suitcase, instead of clothes, so I could study more, much to my mother's annoyance. I agonized over my report cards. If I got less than an A, it was a *crisis*, like the dream of a better future was slipping away. If my grades weren't perfect, it meant that I wasn't working as hard as I could.

January 2003

Exams are over and I did really well in maths 82% + 66% but really badly in french 4½ / 25. I started crying. Hopefully I can take a re-test. I am taking a re-test in chemistry. R.S. was difficult. Very difficult. Had netball. I really need this scholarship to not feel bad.

Poppy

XXX

I would cry after bad grades and not stop working until they improved. Better grades meant I could get a scholarship to school and save my parents money.

The drive for perfection, and not being able to obtain it, helped establish my next belief...

Core Belief #3:
HAPPINESS AND SUCCESS WOULD FIX EVERYTHING

This belief was an easy one to develop. Ever since I first switched on the television or attended school, I'd found ample evidence for why "success" and "happiness" was a fail-safe plan and an entry into the world of ZERO WORRIES, where I would never experience anxiety, insecurity, or rejection again:

1. If I am perfect, I will be happy and successful

2. Happy and successful = lots of money and no financial worries

3. Happy and successful = great body and boys fancy you

4. Happy and successful = lots of friends as people will like you

5. Happy and successful people always get married and live happily ever after

6. Everyone wants to be friends with happy and successful people

7. Happy and successful people are *always good enough* and never get rejected

8. Happy and successful people can always prove their haters wrong

9. Anyone can be happy and successful if they try hard enough

I had no doubt about it, this plan was watertight! I wanted to smile all the time, have nice things, get married, and prove my haters wrong! If I could be perfect, just like happy and successful people, then I too would have it all. I just needed to make it happen. My hardworking therapist mother, who kept our family afloat in so many ways, instilled in my brothers and me that self-pity without action was like wanting a car to drive without any gas: It made no sense. We learned the mindset *If you're upset about something, go change it.* So as my sense of unworthiness deepened, my core belief that happiness and success would fix my problems strengthened.

July 2003 (12 year old Poppy)

Ellie is in a completely diferent legue [sic] from me. She is gorgeus [sic] and I'm just plain. Andy just goes up and I probably will just go down.

I had found out the first love of my life was potentially dating someone new, the prettiest girl in school. This confirmed in flashing lights how truly lacking I was in comparison. "I'm not good enough" was quickly becoming tattooed inside of me.

Whenever I felt any insecurity, jab of rejection, or seething inadequacy, I would immediately soothe myself by thinking, *Just wait until*

I'm happy and successful, then it will all go away. My core belief #3 was loud and clear. I believed success would cure emotional pain.

These three core beliefs from childhood— that I wasn't good enough but if I worked harder, I'd be successful and therefore happy—went on to shape my entire life after and became *very toxic*. Had I known what I would eventually learn (in upcoming chapters), I could have prevented my twelve-year-old brain from running the show into destruction.

How My Core Beliefs Affected My Career

My Super Sweet 16 was the antithesis of the MTV show of the same name. On that birthday, instead of riding in a white limo or dabbing on the dance floor, I was waitressing at a diner. It was the first day I could legally work for money, and I could not wait to start my 9:00 a.m. shift. Financial freedom tasted like burgers and fries, smelled like cooking oil, and sounded like a plate breaking on the floor...the chef screaming...and me apologizing profusely.

It was truly joyous! I was enacting my plan, making money, setting myself up for a successful life, fueled by my core beliefs. I kept it going as a teenage entrepreneur, selling "hot pants." I bought plain white and black panties, ironed on the school logo, and hustled them for the whole of my senior year. Boom! My best friend Daisy and I were making £200 profit per week (around $250 at the time) selling wholesale underwear.

Throughout my "try harder/be better" years in high school and into college at the London School of Economics, I fostered the dream that, one day, I would be a TV host. This would mean core belief #3 would be well and truly surpassed. TV hosts were the definition of *happy* and *successful* in my eyes. They all glowed in what appeared to be glorious, delirious happiness. I wanted what they had, too.

My parents thought going into TV was a crazy idea and said, "It's all about contacts and we have none." True. Just like in the US, breaking into TV in the UK was a matter of "who you know," not what you had to offer. I knew no one *and* also had nothing to offer, so I decided to set up my own TV show at university as a creative means to meet real network producers. I began emailing any producer contact I could find on Google to ask if they'd be a special guest on this "prestigious university's TV show." My "official TV show" of the London School of Economics "honoring careers" was anything but. I made it all up to get a foot in the door and, miraculously, I started getting replies.

People at the BBC and ITN (the two biggest news networks in the UK) agreed to be interviewed! I went to the library and convinced some of my fellow students to hold up a camera and pretend to be my crew. With my newly recruited team—paid in chocolate bars—I marched into the first interview at ITV. I asked my questions nervously and so quickly I tripped on every one of them: "How did *ya, ya, you* start? What's, *ummm*, your advice to *um* your younger self?" I sprinted through them to make sure there was time for my big burning question: With wide puppy eyes, I asked, "Can I have a job? I'll honestly do anything!"

The poor producer looked terrified. He knew he'd been set up, but how could he say no with six fresh-faced students staring at him? Mumbling, he said, "Meet me here on Monday."

I was nineteen and had hit the jackpot. Someone in television was willing to give me a chance. But I'd have to "try even harder!!" to pull it off or they'd also discover what I deep down knew, that I was in fact inadequate. I settled into a life of waking up at 5:00 a.m. to do schoolwork, and then rushing to the TV studio by 7:00 a.m., then running back to university for classes. Luckily, the studio and university were within a mile of each other.

For me, college years full of frat parties and tequila in red Solo cups existed only in movies. I worked eighteen hours a day, juggling coursework for a degree in politics and a full-time job at the TV station. For months as Tea Girl, my only responsibility (besides making and serving hot beverages) was logging time stamps on old footage. My first promotion was to Ticker, and this had me writing the news bulletins at the bottom of the screen. I did that for an entire year before I plucked up the courage to politely ask my boss, "I think I am ready to do on-air work. Would that be at all possible?"

"You're too blond and your voice is not right," he said. "People won't like you."

My stomach deflated as if I'd been punched. Growing up, I hadn't been blond *enough*, and now, I was too much? And what was wrong with my voice? Within nanoseconds, my inner bitchy thought monsters—the ones who chanted my faulty core beliefs—came out to play: *See? Evidence! Just like the man said, you aren't likable. You are, and will always be, not enough.*

Through the pain of rejection that surged for days, I reacted by doubling down on numbing and suppressing shame and embarrassment by telling myself that if I just tried harder, I'd prove him wrong. The next day, I bought hair dye and hired a voice coach in an attempt to change myself to his liking, and he'd have to accept me then! I even agreed to start picking up his dry cleaning.

Months later, he finally uttered the words I'd dreamed about: "Poppy, you're going on air."

I hoped it was because he thought I was ready; however, the regular host was off sick and they had literally no other option except me.

But it was still my big shot to make my fantasies come true! I was to host the evening entertainment news segment, and I couldn't wait! I slapped on as much makeup as humanly possible. My caked-on foundation looked like tangerine paint with two red lines of blush for cheekbones. I was *ready*.

At 7:05 p.m., the two-minute spot went live. I delivered the script carefully but clearly, and before I could blink, it was over. I sat back and waited for the deluge of congratulatory texts from my family and friends whom I'd told to watch. But the "well done!" and "I can't believe you were on TV!" messages didn't come. I got just one from my parents.

"Was that you?" they asked.

Was that me? Er, *yeh*!

They were thrown by my new Cockney accent—like someone from *Downton Abbey* was air-dropped into *Peaky Blinders*—and my dyed hair with a bird's nest of clip-on extensions that started to slowly fall sideways during the bulletin.

FINALLY, I'd gotten myself on TV, and it was a nonevent to the people I'd hoped to impress. Even more worryingly, *I* was a nonevent. The reaction from everyone, including the boss, was anticlimactic to say the least. I'd been *sure*, for years, that everything was going to be golden once I appeared on TV. Well, I'd done it, and yet my insecurities were still there—I was now confused. My core belief that once I was successful, I'd be happy, was not playing out like I thought. I quickly overruled any doubt about my master plan to fill the hole of "not good enough" by being on TV and decided that I just needed to *be better* next time around.

That didn't come until MONTHS later when the regular host was out sick again and my boss was left with no other choice but to send me to interview the formidable Keira Knightley (!!) and Jude Law (!!!!!) at the press junket for their movie *Anna Karenina*. I couldn't believe my luck! THIS was the chance I had been waiting for!

I agonized over my outfit and went with a cute white top with an embellished collar and a black short skirt. *Simple but smart*, I thought. *Can't go wrong*. On the day of the interview, the London tube broke down from "signaling problems." *This is not good.* I was going to be late to the biggest opportunity of my career. *Why* would the universe do this to me?

Once out of the tube, I sprinted to the junket, held at a hotel, and dashed up the stairs in a flurry of energy to the suite where the actors were miked up and ready to go. I didn't have a moment to catch my breath or calm the sheer panic slash excitement before I was ushered straight into the room where Jude Law was waiting.

My smile was wide as my face—think Cheshire Cat but with even chubbier cheeks. My forehead was glistening with double the sweat from running up the stairs and beholding this gorgeous actor in front of me. I reached out to shake his hand. My moment was finally happening. *This is going to be the best five-minute interview anyone has ever done*, I thought.

Alas, quite the opposite…I stumbled, missed the interview chair, and landed flat on my face on the floor at Jude's feet. My miniskirt rode up, exposing half my butt cheek to him and every other person in the room.

Fuckity fuck.

I lay there for a second, assuming this was the part of the nightmare when you wake up. But I was reminded of the undeniable reality in front of me—that is to say, Jude's perfectly shiny black shoes.

Everyone in the room desperately tried to control their giggles. The cameramen were practically shaking from the effort. I sprang up, apologizing profusely while yanking down my skirt as I sat in the chair opposite Jude, who couldn't have been more gracious.

Despite how hard I tried to get the interview going, I could not for the life of me contain my nervous laughter. I tried every stop-laughing trick in the book (times tables, pinching myself) but the hysterics continued.

"Would you like some water?" Jude asked. "You came in like a tornado and fell like a stone!" His observation only made me laugh harder and sent my mascara further down my beet-red face. I had royally screwed up. This was going to be the first *and last* time I sat in an interviewing chair.

I'd fantasized that my interview would go viral—and it did, but not in the way I'd hoped. The YouTube video of it was picked up by news stations across the UK. Overnight, it seemed like everyone knew about the interview that went catastrophically wrong.

Back at the office, the reaction was mixed to say the least. On one hand, my bosses were livid, and on the other hand, secretly delighted that I was a mild Internet fad resembling Bridget Jones, as one press article wrote. How I wasn't fired, I have no idea. Bowing to popular demand to see more of the girl who crotch-dived and fell at Jude Law's feet, my bosses allowed me to do more celebrity interviews…until six months later when I actually was given the boot for "being unprofessional around a chocolate fountain" at a film premiere, according to my boss. I'd been accidentally caught on camera dipping my way through a section of marshmallows and brownie bits that I later heard was for decoration purposes only. I did think it was odd at the time that no one else was getting involved in the fountain, but my love affair with melted chocolate drew me in, and before long, my face was covered in it.

By this point, I'd graduated from college, and my career was over before it'd started. I'd never be accepted by the British TV industry. I'd changed my hair, clothes, and accent, and made a hash of my opportunities. I was good at laughing along with my friends who found my endless messes amusing. But in reality, it was all a bit humiliating.

Whispers of not being enough haunted me, but I still held on to beliefs #2 and #3: that if I just tried harder, the sweet promise of success would be mine, and it'd all be worth it. I'd be deliriously happy and problem free *then*.

I couldn't understand why my success + happy master plan was stalled. Despite how hard I tried, nothing seemed to go my way.

At the ripe old age of twenty-four, I feared I had exhausted all my opportunities in London, so I saved up and decided to move to Los Angeles for a few months. Lucky for Angelenos, they were about to meet my insatiable need for approval and my quest for perfection.

For a deeply and secretly insecure person who fought daily internal battles about worthiness, I couldn't have picked a worse place to live. In Hollywood, the only currency people seemed to care about was fame, and I had zero.

I said "yes!" to anyone who would take a meeting with me—like anyone, even people I met in parking lots. I packed my schedule from morning to night and got a lot of feedback that almost always confirmed my #1 core belief. "Not quite right for now" was a common critique and I turned its meaning into "not good or special enough." Because if I were, casting directors and producers would have been jumping to hire me. I felt like Goldilocks's rejected bowls of porridge. I was either too hot, too cold, too nice, too enthusiastic, too English, too fat, too thin, too intellectual, too ditzy, too loud, too intense, too boring, too dramatic, too emotional, too annoying, too blond, and/or too unattractive. I was never "just right." Every criticism knocked my self-esteem lower, but the quest to prove I was enough and to reach the land of success remained present.

The three-month roller coaster of Los Angeles was quickly coming to an end with an empty bank account. I was facing a remorseful move back to England, and no doubt a chorus of "I told you so, you aren't good enough for the US" would be waiting upon my return.

A sprout of hope interrupted my gloom when a woman I'd met on a train the year before (who happened to be an actual producer at MTV) miraculously responded to my email and agreed to meet. She became my first real contact in the States and a fairy godmother who helped me get my first gig as a host for MTV International, covering award shows and red-carpet events. My love for chatting to anyone anywhere had really dealt me a solid because my train friend turned out to be the greatest blessing. I interviewed Tom Cruise, Angelina Jolie, Cameron Diaz, George Clooney, Harry Styles, and whoever else was ruling the pop landscape in 2015.

It was a big break and suddenly, other opportunities started opening up. My endless curiosity to ask questions and my work ethic caught the attention of more people in the industry. After a few months, I landed a job as the host for Snapchat's first-ever talk show, called *Pillow Talk with Poppy*. I interviewed celebrities in my pajamas on a set that looked like a bedroom from the '80s on shrooms.

Overnight, the user figures on Snapchat went from zero to millions. It was great timing for me. I started receiving thousands of messages from viewers in their teens and twenties all around the world and I felt like maybe I had finally found both success and my tribe. At first, fans messaged me about fashion, their friends, and the show. But before long, the notes started to get more personal with many people sharing their struggles and worries about not being enough, longing for happiness, and feeling like they didn't belong.

It was like they were reading my mind. I felt exactly the same insecurities, secret longings, and fears. Did everyone have the same core beliefs as I did? Could the viewers see past my on-camera "happy" persona and tell I felt anxious and overwhelmed, too?

Despite it looking like my career was taking off, I lived in fear that it was going to come crashing down. Money was a constant stressor (TV/Internet hosting wasn't as lucrative as I'd hoped). I took on more work to support myself, including hosting a show back in England at the same time. I had to cover my own expenses, including weekly transatlantic flights, and so with those commuting costs, I barely broke even. But I felt like I had to do it; my core beliefs were driving me. *Work until it hurts, try harder to be less mediocre, and keep going until you're successful…at which point, all your problems will disappear and then you'll have nothing to worry about.*

When I imagined my dream life on TV, I only pictured radiant happiness and universal love. I didn't picture dark circles under my eyes, counting dollars, or getting a crooked neck from so much traveling.

The glitz of being a TV host.

My Core Beliefs Turned into Workaholism

If I wasn't happy yet, then I just had to please people MORE to overcome my insignificance. One core belief amplified and triggered another, and they became a vicious cycle that began to fuel unbridled perfectionism. As upcoming chapters will reveal, had I learned to stay curious and investigate the thoughts I was having, I could have prevented the negative reflex reaction from accelerating into faulty thinking.

Addiction expert and author Mandy Saligari defines addiction as "something outside of yourself to fix how you feel, to the detriment of yourself." My habit of working harder when I felt inadequate and anxious—created to help me cope—had quickly turned into an obsession, now verging on addiction, unbeknownst to me at the time. Others might think they will cope better by numbing toxic thoughts with alcohol or drugs; I had not yet realized that workaholism, perfectionism, and being "busy" were my chosen anesthetic to cover up emotional wounds. It provided me with an illusionary sense of control and distraction. I didn't have time to go inward and ask, "Are my core beliefs actually true or beneficial?" I was just continuing on, as I always did, with the habits and core beliefs I'd learned as a child to best survive.

During this time, I was living with my best friend Suki. We had been introduced through friends a few years earlier and it was love at first sight. She was like the sister I never had. We were two Brits living in a foreign country doing our best, being each other's therapist and cheerleader from day one. I couldn't believe I'd met someone who liked dancing, chatting, adventures, laughing, and dressing up as much as me.

While I was hosting *Pillow Talk*, Suki was shooting her first major movie, crawling into bed after night shoots at 5:00 a.m., covered in fake blood and sand. Our house looked like an explosion had erupted most days, clothes and bits everywhere and both of us too worn out to straighten up, but we giggled our way through the chaos.

Before Suki headed off on night shoots, we would make dinner, rehearsing her lines or dreaming about all our ideas for the future. Both of us loved fashion and would buy countless magazines to flick through to admire new collections and designs. We started brainstorming a project we could work on together, something that could help us get creative in a different way than our day jobs. One evening, the idea popped like a firework. In light of our love for fashion and our joint tendency for enormous disorganization and mess, we decided a practical fashion company for women on the go was needed. We'd make fun accessories that made life easier and could pair with any look at any time. We started pinteresting a mood board, imagining what it could look like. Suki is as impulsive as I am and also shares the same "work harder" belief, so within an hour, we had bought a domain name and were tracking down supply chains.

So, as if two TV shows weren't enough, I decided to jump into an entirely new business. Within three weeks, I met Leo, an Englishman who'd built a tech company at twenty-four and who became our cofounder, as well as another guy in a parking lot who manufactured handbags. The habit of chatting to everyone I meet, whether that be in line at the grocery store, on a train, or at dinner, has come in quite handy over the years, especially when recruiting business partners.

Eight months after our initial idea, we built Pop & Suki in 2016. It was a true labor of love and felt special. For the first time in my life, the "not good enough" core belief that had throbbed continually got a bit lighter. I didn't realize it at the time, but Suki was my first friend who really challenged my core beliefs. Whenever I'd make a self-derogatory comment, she'd immediately respond, "You're not useless. Stop being so mean to yourself." She helped me begin to recognize my strengths for the first time and notice that maybe I *was* quite good at making things happen and maybe I wasn't so unworthy after all.

They were nice thoughts to have temporarily but I was so stuck in the narrative of my core beliefs turned toxic, not even the successful launch of Pop & Suki and a hype bae best friend were able to soften them.

I had gone from grades-obsessed high schooler, to college student working a full-time job, to working two jobs, then three, with a 5,000-mile commute. There was a part of me that felt pleased I was driving myself so hard it hurt, just like I learned when I was little watching my dad do the same.

But I was starting to feel constantly bloated, I wasn't sleeping, I was stress eating. I was becoming very emotionally reactive about things that usually wouldn't bother me, but I couldn't afford to take time off. So I tried to ignore these looming health concerns.

Take a Breather

One Sunday night a friend asked if I wanted to join her at a breathwork class. She said they were excellent in helping reduce stress. That sounded like a perfect thing to try, given how I was feeling. I had no idea what to expect. I entered the room of about thirty people and took a seat on the floor. A man called Jon Paul Crimi, a breathwork practitioner, walked in and started to explain what we were about to do. He asked us to breathe in sharply twice through the mouth, and then exhale. The first sharp inhale was into the belly, the second into my chest. My entire front puffed out, followed by a long exhale, And then we began again. The rhythm was inhale, inhale, exhale. We lay down, the music began, and Crimi guided us in our two-part breathing. I found out later this practice is also called *holotropic*, an open-mouthed pranayama technique. I was also shocked to learn that nine out of ten people breathe using only shallow chest breaths, but it's diaphragmatic breathing that effectively calms our stress response.

Within a few minutes of intense breathing, I could feel my whole body get tired, just like a workout. Crimi acted like a trainer, motivating us to continue this breath pattern even when it felt exhausting to continue. The more I breathed, the more my fingers started tensing up and I felt pins and needles, my head began to feel very light and I began to cry. All the stress I'd pushed down for years seemed to be bubbling up as the breathwork was forcing everything out. Tears streamed down my face as I inhaled, inhaled, exhaled. After about fifteen minutes, we were allowed to just lie there breathing normally before we began again. My entire body felt like it was shedding emotional weight; I had forgotten what it felt like to be relaxed, and allowed tears that I had suppressed for years to gently leave me. It was transformational.

This unique introduction into mindfulness was like opening up a new world. I couldn't believe I could actually do things that created a sense of tranquillity I hadn't felt for a long time, if ever. It was like I had forgotten what it felt like to breathe until now.

A few weeks later, my friend Matt had come to see me, and I excitedly told him about the class and all the breathing exercises I'd started doing to help my anxiety. Matt was the king of sarcasm, so I was waiting for some witty comment about how ridiculous it was to think that mindfulness practices could help with my anxiety. I was practically wincing, waiting for something like "She breathed, and her life changed!"

Instead, he said sincerely, "Can we listen to one of those breathing tapes now?"

"Sure!" Wow, I never thought this was Matt's thing.

We lay there listening to a guided inhale-and-exhale exercise, and out of nowhere, he began to cry.

"Are you okay?" I'd never heard him cry before. He was one of those guys who was always "under control." Even when things blatantly weren't.

"Pop, I'm not quite sure what's happening, I haven't cried in years... I haven't actually told you this, but I've been having panic attacks."

It wasn't just me.

"I know the feeling," I replied softly.

We both lay there in silence that was like a clear night's sky, expansive and reassuring. I began to think how many more people might benefit from this breathing stuff. Everyone who was hustling, partying until broken, avoiding their health (physical and mental), not taking care, using anything, pot, tequila, work, sex, food, and relationships, etc. to avoid dealing with their insides could use these tools to start healing, just like I was.

In that moment, it was like I caught the mindfulness bug. I knew I had to do something to share these things that were helping Matt and me. There was a real need out there and I couldn't go another day without creating some sort of a tool to calm overwhelmed minds like my own. I was privileged: I had access to a breathwork studio, a friend willing to take me, a psychotherapist mum to talk through my issues. There were millions and millions of people who didn't, and that was wrong. Whatever it was to become, I just knew instinctively, it had to be called Happy Not Perfect (HNP).

While I kept up with Pop & Suki and some TV work—workaholism in the name of mindfulness doesn't take a holiday—I started gathering everything I could find about calming the mind and tracking down experts on the subject to educate me further. Number one on my list was of course my mom, who had a practice treating people of all ages, but mainly focused on teenagers. With her experience and having been advocating for more reflection and rest for years, it was a no-brainer; she had to become my partner on the project. Her wisdom and training would ensure HNP could become an effective tool in helping people navigate fluctuating lives and unmanageable emotions.

The more I researched, the more amazed and excited I got. I started meditating daily, journaling, and watching endless mindfulness YouTube channels. My volatile mood started to balance out considerably, and I could feel my energy return to somewhat normal. I kept thinking, *How have I reached twenty-six without being introduced to this stuff?* It was life changing and I knew so many people could be significantly helped, like I was.

Work scaled up even further, but I didn't mind. *The project required this*, I thought.

I began to assemble a team of world-class advisers across many fields of psychology and mindfulness. With their insight and research about neuroscience and brain workings, we sketched out a fun game-like design for an HNP app. Our intention was to simplify the last forty years of work in the field and turn it into a daily ritual that users could practice immediately without having to read ten textbooks. We'd do the work so they could just jump in and have the tools at a moment's notice. I wanted it to be easy to use and delightful, unlike some of the boring meditations I had skipped past.

The main feature would be called The Refresh, a daily practice that included breathing, journaling, a gratitude diary, and a compliments corner (it wound up being called the Happiness Work-Out). I wanted to shape the app into a nurturing virtual space that could teach users in just a few minutes about their anxiety and stress and offer practical ways to manage it. The app was to be a place you could go to feel good rather than comparing likes. It wasn't enough to say, "I know you feel like shit." The app would have to explain WHY users (and I) felt this way. I wanted it to be a marriage of Love + Science.

And it was all coming together, from the research to the design. Everyone was kindly advising me free of charge because they also believed in the mission and saw the need for something like it. The teamwork made me feel great. I was finally a part of something that I felt accepted by. It was soon clear I needed to raise investment in order to properly build and code it out. With no background in anything numerical, it did seem something of a challenge, but I was ready for it. (And yes, if you are counting, this was job #4 I had stacked onto my responsibilities.)

Nervously, I printed my presentation for my first-ever solo investment meeting a friend had helped set up by the pool at the Chateau Marmont, one of the fanciest hotels in LA. I rushed there, parked around the corner to avoid paying the overpriced valet, and then realized I'd spilled coffee all down my lilac polka-dot dress. *Fuckity fuck fuck—are you kidding me? Why now!* I couldn't let this bother me. As I tried to scrub the marks off, I did a quick check on everything else. Phone charged, check; papers printed, check; outfit that makes me look serious, check minus coffee stains. It was like doing live TV. Fuck-ups weren't allowed, otherwise my dream of building a happiness app would be over. I sat down and started talking rapidly about the mental health stats, the idea, the science, the team I'd assembled, the next steps.

The investor paused before responding to my pitch, and I stopped breathing. Finally, she said, "I like it. I'm flying you to New York tomorrow to finalize the deal."

What? I was in shock. (I genuinely don't know what happened that day because my pitches have never been that smooth since.) Within a week, I'd raised just under a million dollars, more than I could ever have imagined.

All I could think was, *OMG, I can't believe someone actually thinks I'm good enough!* I was finally proving my #1 core belief wrong!

I made the decision to stop my TV work to fully dedicate time to Happy Not Perfect. And by this point, Leo was executing the operations on Pop & Suki, so I could go full steam ahead on building my dream app.

Life began to feel really good. Working on creating a tool that could potentially help millions made my soul sing. It had a true aim. Plus, the pressure to look and sound a certain way didn't matter anymore. For the first time in my life, I felt a taste of freedom, belonging, and what it might mean to be just *enough*! Investors believed in me and I was gradually beginning to believe in myself.

This one investor was one of the coolest, smartest people I'd ever met. She seemed to embody my #3 core belief, that success and happiness went together. She was like JESUS had come back to Earth. Over and over again, I had to wonder in amazement why she believed in me.

For her, my core belief #2—please people and work until it hurts—only grew more virulent, which ironically contradicted my desire to calm the mind. I wanted to do anything and everything to please her and repay her for the belief she'd given me. So it began: I said "yes" to every request, revision, and idea, even if her notions moved the app farther from my original concept. It made me feel uncomfortable but if an investor said, "Jump," I thought my job was to reply, "How high? I can go higher!"

If only I knew then how to connect with my body and stay true to my instinct instead of being entirely fear driven, things could have unraveled very differently. Instead I was jumping like an overexcited puppy, desperate for a pat on the head. But it was soon clear: Nothing I did or suggested was ever enough. Two months after taking me under her wing, it was like she'd discovered my real truth, and I was a bitter disappointment. She dropped me as quickly as she'd picked me up. Her passion for Happy Not Perfect didn't fade, but it was clear I was becoming a problem.

Another investor called to check in and I said, "Hey! I am getting the feeling that I've done something wrong."

"Yeah, you're not wrong. I just don't think we feel you're the person to be leading this company…"

"Why?" I asked.

"Umm, well, we don't think people can relate to you. You're not likable. And we really hate the fashion Pop and Whatever thing you do."

My cells and bones shivered, and my stomach dropped. I zoomed right back to age nineteen with that TV producer saying, "No one will like you," and right back to thirteen when I was dumped for a prettier girl at school. I wasn't enough as I am, yet again.

Over the coming weeks, it was clear, my investors believed I would ruin the company I created if I were its spokesperson. I wasn't "cool" enough in their eyes. I spiraled. Were they right? Should I just leave? I didn't want to be the reason HNP failed or the reason millions of others couldn't access these mindfulness tools.

The worst part: I kind of agreed with them. I had not even an ounce of self-compassion and had no idea where to find some (I did learn, and so will you in short order), all I knew was that I wasn't special enough to be a leader. It was a devastating confirmation of my #1 core belief. Unworthiness roiled just under the surface of my thoughts pretty much constantly, and this was just more proof of my not-enoughness.

They say people are sent to challenge, champion, or cherish you. Wow, was I being challenged. They'd unknowingly found my deepest wounds and poured a bucket of acid on them.

My anxiety went through the roof. The irony of being a new mental health entrepreneur who wasn't happy made me feel like such a horrific fraud. My people-pleasing habits went into overdrive, and my toxic survival strategy to emotionally avoid and numb the pain with "busyness" came back in full force.

Core Beliefs and Dating

My core beliefs weren't ideal for romantic success. Believing I wasn't good enough and my fixation on grades and then my career had me avoiding the dating scene as much as I could. I thought my first love was just the greatest human being I'd ever met. Everything he said was *hilarious*, everything he did was *brilliant*, and every text I received made my heart jump. I was head-over-heels infatuated, and definitely thought we'd be together, forever, like in a Disney movie or the romance novels I got lost in growing up. It was a nasty shock when he broke up with me six weeks later and I was left D.E.V.A.S.T.A.T.E.D.

My first love confirmed my core belief that I wasn't special, that prettier girls were. So I made a ground rule with myself not to fall in love with another boy until all my exams were over to ensure I wouldn't lose focus on my studies again.

The promise I made with myself didn't end with my exams, though. Thirteen years later, I still hadn't broken it. I had yet to allow myself to fall in love. I'd been so wrapped up in surviving my work life, my dating life had been as dry as the Sahara for years. But then, while creating HNP, I met Toby.

Toby, 5'10" but when asked said 6', was a lawyer. He had sandy blond hair, blue eyes, a medium build with a pale complexion. He knew what he wanted in life and seemed to like me a lot. I finally broke my promise and practically fell in love overnight. I hadn't let myself be that vulnerable in a very long time. Toby was also a delightful distraction from my work worries and like the dial-down switch on the pressure cooker of my troublesome reality.

It had been all of two months, and I was convinced that any minute, he was about to say those four big words, "Will You Marry Me?" Because, well, why wouldn't he? Couples that liked each other *this much* should be taking logical next steps.

Alas, quite the opposite occurred, and he decided to say nothing. At all. Yep, he *ghosted* me.

WTF! He could have AT LEAST given me the common courtesy of an "It's not you, it's me," or "Work is so busy at the moment, you're great," but no. He offered no alternative story I could cling to to protect myself from my worst fears.

Being ghosted triggered a self-blame so toxic, it seethed inside me. I could feel my organs tying in knots.

For as long as I can remember, my brain has had two people living in it. Me and my bitchy inner critic housemate who likes to constantly remind me of my complete unworthiness. I call her Regina because she is a straight-up Rachel McAdams Mean Girl. Toby's disappearance gave her ammunition for days: "Look at you, you chubby unlovable nonevent! No wonder he ghosted you, you're unspecial, and have to try harder or you'll never be happy!" My own thoughts took the vacuum of nothingness and turned it into evidence to support my core beliefs.

My rational mind said, "He was *clearly* not right. He wore strange shoes and was so arrogant, it never would have worked. What was I thinking?" My emotionally chaotic mind—*so much louder*—shouted me into obsession. I just had to figure out why he'd done it and became fixed in a futile mental rationalizing loop of "It was probably because you were not fun enough...your body isn't good enough...you're not pretty enough...not successful enough...*just not good enough*...no wonder he dumped you."

Just maybe, Toby would want me back if I were better? One of my girlfriends called to help me talk through it for the sixth time.

"Pops, just do the Instagram trick."

"What's that?"

"Just post a really nice bikini pic or something on your Gram. They always come back, it happened to me with Paul."

Bikini pics were not my forte. I didn't even own a bikini, for that matter. I was a repeat buyer of black one-piece shapers that covered everything up poolside, or I avoided any sort of water activity. Had I known about the power of flexible thinking then, I could have avoided an impending car crash. Instead I resorted to my friend's prescribed Instagram trick to feel better about Casper the Ghost. Unsurprisingly, I began to feel even worse.

I was off balance and I wished my app was built already. I really needed it. I had fallen off the bandwagon of doing my breathing and instead turned to excessive exercise to numb my pain. I hit the gym and logged as many high-intensity interval training (HIIT) classes as I could before collapsing in the corner. My new avoid-feelings-of-rejection-with-squats plan was going quite well, I thought (aside from the industrial pots of peanut butter I consumed afterward). Before I had the chance to find any abs, though, the stress I was inflicting on my body and mind, the chronic anxiety, lack of sleep, chaotic life, and endless rejection it seemed was everywhere I looked, took me out.

I broke.

The Crash

The morning I will never forget began at 5:00 a.m., and I felt like a house had fallen on me. I was crumpled in bed, no energy, unable to move, my stomach so bloated, I looked pregnant.

I was about to learn one of the most important lessons in life, that there is no health without mental health. Mental and physical health are without separation, but a manifestation of each other, and neither can operate well alone. My mind and body had given up.

Thinking something was *seriously* wrong with me, I took myself to the hospital because I didn't know what else to do. I was in a foreign country and didn't know where to turn. I lay in the hospital bed sobbing, waiting for the test results. Surely this level of exhaustion, stomach woes, and sadness was going to warrant a diagnosis like meningitis or Ebola.

The doctor returned: "You have burnout."

"What? No! I'm dangerously ill!" I sat on the hospital bed, staring at him blankly. *Don't give me such a pathetic diagnosis. Yeh, buddy. I'm run-down, it's not rocket science. But THIS is something else!*

"Three-quarters of the people I see have stress-related conditions," he said. "You need to rest, eat well, and slow down."

I was almost embarrassed by my diagnosis. I'd gone to the hospital because the pain was so severe, I thought I was at death's door. I wanted a diagnosis that would validate what I was going through. Ignorantly in that moment, I discounted burnout as a fake illness. Later on, I learned that it couldn't be more real. In May 2019, the World Health Organization officially named it an "occupational phenomenon" and included it in the *11th Revision of the International Classification of Diseases*.

The doctor assured me that burnout was not to be taken lightly. Stress releases the hormone cortisol, which causes inflammation, which, if chronic, is an underlying cause for cancer, diabetes, and heart disease. Cortisol makes every physical problem worse because it can compromise the immune system. "People were not built to tolerate the stress levels we're dealing with," he said.

Oh, the irony. I was building a company to manage stress better, and the process was killing me because of my own mind and insecurities.

The shame and guilt rattled through my bones. If only I had stuck with my breathing and journaling, maybe I could have prevented this. My bitchy inner critic Regina had a field day, reminding me of all my core doubts: *How pathetic, you don't deserve to be stressed. You're not good enough.* I clearly still had much to learn about living healthy and shutting up my inner bully.

I went home, googled, and found *Why Zebras Don't Get Ulcers* by Robert M. Sapolsky, PhD, a Stanford University professor of biology and neurology, a book about the impact of stress on humans. Humans, unlike animals, not only stress out about immediate threats, but also psychological threats. We have the dubious ability to feel psychologically stressed *all the time*. Just the thought that bad things COULD happen in the future or thinking back on past trauma triggers a stress response. Zebras, for example, just react to real-time stress (run from lion) and when the danger has passed, they're able to go back to feeling relaxed and safe (eat grass). This is why they don't get ulcers. My mouth was Ulcer City and Dr. Sapolsky had explained why.

I did more digging into the health impact of chronic stress from feeling at war with the demands of modern life, like work, social life, family pressure, emails, traffic, air travel (the stuff I'd been stewing in for a long, long time). Unsurprisingly, I ticked virtually every box: weight gain (check), exhaustion (check), depression (yep), insomnia (what's sleep?), infertility (no? maybe? fuck, cue the hyperventilation and spiraling), and erectile dysfunction (I was spared that one, at least). My brain had gone mushy and I felt extreme anxiety just looking at my inbox (steadily overloading). I had to cancel all meetings since I could barely sit up straight.

I called Heather Lilleston, one of the meditation guides whom I had become friends with, an established yogi and meditation teacher who'd founded Yoga For Bad People. I tearfully told her how I was feeling, and she immediately eased my worry.

"Pops, we all fall down! Don't be embarrassed," she said. "This is normal, you are normal, but this is an important message. I know you're in pain now but listen to your body and don't waste a breakdown. They have been my most transformative moments." Her words stuck with me. *Don't waste a breakdown.* I wasn't quite sure what she meant, but I soon found out.

The only thing that comforted me was searching for answers about why my fatigue felt so heavy and unbearable. This was not only helpful for me but also added to the research for my selfishly much needed app. Every morning felt like I was waking up with a steel vest on. I had also suddenly become hateful of coffee and could hardly take a sip without gagging. Now, this was really odd. Before burnout, I would chug five cups a day without thinking. I consulted Dr. Google and learned I had either pancreatic cancer or abnormally high levels of cortisol (stress hormones), which made my body reject the stimulant caffeine. Made sense.

Burnout took my body, brain, and energy. And then it took my lattes. Rough.

Anxiety to the point of shutting down physically and emotionally wasn't just happening to me. Nationwide studies confirmed that Americans were then (still are) under extreme stress. In 2017, the American Psychological Association's Stress in America survey found that three out of five people described themselves as "very" stressed out. Along with worrying about health care, politics, the environment, money, work, terrorism, taxes, wars, crime, gun violence, we have personal, emotional problems that are inflamed by social media, overwhelming responsibilities, too many choices, too much pressure, perfectionism, FOMO, the list goes on. Younger adults had it the worst. We're called the Anxious Generation for a reason.

The fact that we are swimming in toxic fear, uncertainty, and stress all day, all week, is arguably the biggest problem facing humanity. How can we combat a global pandemic when we're *already dealing with a stress pandemic* that suppresses our immune system and undermines our ability to fight viruses and our confidence in making decisions?

If that doesn't frighten you, I don't know what will. Living with chronic stress is like trying to run a race with an enormous backpack on. It's exhausting and makes normal obstacles that much harder.

For years, I'd tried to be a perfect Wonder Woman to feel accepted and wanted by my friends, family, colleagues, and romantic interests. My core beliefs told me that I'd overcome my unspecialness and inadequacy through diligence, and that happiness and success would be my reward—and my revenge. In moderation, they could have been helpful and at times were a bit like a superpower driving me forward. But as an obsession, they'd turned toxic. Workaholism and perfectionism had done the opposite of their intention. I was oblivious to how destructive my faulty thinking really was. I was highly strung, controlling, reactive, and now physically sick. Here's a picture I didn't dare post on Instagram at the time:

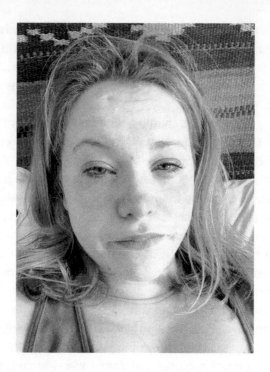

Wonder Woman? That's me, in bed, teary cheeks, body aching, heart heavy, gross sores, stomach bloated, swollen face. The drive to be perfect in search of acceptance left me lost. I didn't have the energy to leave the house. None of my clothes fit. My muscles were so atrophied, when I stood up, my legs wobbled like a newborn pony. I had to lie back down.

I was too embarrassed to share my struggles with most of my friends because others were going through so much worse. I felt such shame complaining about work troubles because deep down I knew how lucky I was to even have a chance to build a dream.

But as I've realized, humans can find destructive meaning in what appears to be the most minor of things. Pain has no hierarchy. Every time life threw a curveball at me, however subtle and seemingly small, my mind turned it into evidence to prove my core beliefs right and fuel destructive survival strategies. It was like my mind wanted to twist whatever situation I was in to show me, yet again, that I was right in thinking I wasn't enough and had to try harder.

As that famous saying goes, we don't know someone's insides by observing their outsides. Plato said it well: "Be kind, for everyone is fighting a hard battle." Even when everything appears "fine," we have no idea how their core beliefs are hurting them by scrolling through their Twitter. There is one certainty in life, that suffering is universal. It's just wrapped up in different packages. We all have a choice, though: Do we hold on tightly or let go lightly?

It took me a while to realize the uncomfortable truth that my breakdown wasn't caused by my investor, the job, the boy. I was lost in my "poor me" victim mentality. I was angry at the world for putting me in this hopeless state. It wasn't about ANYONE or ANYTHING but my broken relationship with myself. My self-rejection and shame lay at the root. The problem existed deep in my psyche.

I was learning the hard way that core beliefs run deep. Emotional wounds do not just clear up like the common cold. If they did, I would have patched myself up with Tylenol and gotten back on the horse ASAP. Self-love isn't as easily achieved as hashtagging it on social media.

Our emotional experiences, beliefs, and behavioral patterns are programmed from a young age and run so deep we have little awareness of them. We will react to old wounds and fears in the same way again and again unless we make a conscious choice to break them and I explore this later on.

But I didn't have that knowledge yet. I wasn't aware at the time that sinking so low would soon force me to have some cold shower reality checks of how toxic my belief system had become and spark a new way of living, loving, and looking at life.

I was not getting back up too soon...physically. But I could do some lifting mentally. I'd gotten myself into this emotional rut, and I knew I was the only one to get myself out of it.

I was soon about to learn what yogi Heather Lilleston meant by "Don't waste a breakdown."

Suffering is the key to growth and adapting, if we allow it to be.

"WHO LOOKS OUTSIDE,
DREAMS; WHO LOOKS
INSIDE, AWAKES."

—CARL JUNG

COLD SHOWER
REALITY CHECKS

I felt truly broken and more fraudulent by the day as my anxiety wouldn't go away. I had nightmares thinking about how ironic the whole situation looked. *Founder of a mental wellness company is actually mentally unwell.* Not only was this the ultimate impostor story, but perhaps a sign that my investors were right all along. Maybe I *wasn't* the right fit for my company. I knew the powerful mindfulness tools I was developing for HNP worked; they were what had helped me manage stress for the last few years. Breathing calmed my night panics, journaling gave me clarity, but my actual state of thinking hadn't changed. The bitchy Regina inside was louder than ever. I needed to find out *why* she was so mean and *why* I kept repeating such self-destructive behavior.

As I began excavating the mental wellness world and all that was on offer, I started to learn there might be a difference between mental health *maintenance* and fundamental mental health *reprogramming*. They support each other, but they're not the same. The Happy Not Perfect app was designed to be used as critical maintenance for supporting mental well-being, like brushing your teeth to keep them clean and healthy. But what happens when you get a serious toothache? Pain is the message that you need to find *the root cause of the problem*. The best brushing ever won't fix a damaged nerve, although it might prevent it from flaring up and protects it from the start. To fix it, however, you need to go straight to the reason why it broke and repair it.

My burnout was like a hefty bulldozer. I was flattened and I needed to go deeper than mental maintenance to make significant change *from the inside*. I'd thought that switching jobs and cities *was* significant change. But in reality, I'd just changed my outside world. What was going on inside my head was exactly the same no matter where I was. *Same shit, different place.*

My brain—where I really lived—was stuck, like that annoying spinning wheel that pops up when your laptop freezes. A quote that I'd heard attributed to Einstein began echoing inside: "We can't solve problems by using the same kind of thinking we used when we created them." If I was serious about not ending up here again, I needed to start thinking differently and changing my core beliefs, or I'd repeat the downward spiral of chronic stress, crash, and then repeat in most likely another two years or sooner. The clock to change was ticking.

Of course, it's one thing to *know* that you have to change. It's another to walk the walk. It was time to get really honest and give myself some cold shower reality checks.

> "We live in a trance of inadequacy, and Western culture is to blame."
>
> —Tara Brach, author
> of RADICAL ACCEPTANCE

Impostor Syndrome

Living on the verge of being discovered as a fraud

I crawled out of bed to attend my first therapy session. Before now my mum had been my only therapist and I felt I needed to speak to someone unrelated to myself or my work. A friend introduced me to a clinical psychologist, Dr. Shona, and before we started the session, I told her that it was important to me to learn the whys and hows. I sat in her LA office with the afternoon sun streaming in through the window, and divulged the last few years, stopping only to sob or munch through the entire plate of cookies in front of me. I ploughed through all the details and was reminded of the great freedom and true value one can find when talking to an unbiased professional.

She didn't say much in this first session but listened and created a safe space for me to unearth my thoughts, good or bad. "I just think that maybe I am not right for any of this," I said. "I'm not fashionable enough for Pop and Suki, I'm not good or happy enough for Happy Not Perfect. Maybe I don't have what it takes because if I do, why am I feeling like this?"

Before I left, Shona gave me some homework. "Your task for this week is to research Impostor Syndrome."

After a drive home, feeling almost like a rug had been pulled from beneath my feet, I opened Google and there it was, a freakily on-point description of someone I knew very well.

The classic hallmarks of people with Impostor Syndrome (IS) are perfectionism, workaholism, and a feeling that everyone else is so much more clever, capable, and cool than you are…fuck. This was me in a nutshell. IS thinking nibbles away at self-esteem until there's nothing left, and I was empty.

I found it fascinating that this syndrome of self-perceived phoniness was originally identified by clinical psychologists Pauline R. Clance and Suzanne A. Imes in 1985 soon after the first millennials were born. It was a phenomenon of and for our age, and I'm sure social media had a lot to do with it. My Insta–double life fed my IS anxiety. I lived in fear that I was only one post away from ridicule when people clued in on the truth, that I was not nearly as polished and happy as I pretended to be.

I often lay awake wondering if my entire TV career was based on a fraud because, as Regina (my bitchy inner critic) liked to remind me, it did kind of begin with my tricking my way into meeting with network execs and practically changing the way I looked and sounded to get on air. I constantly worried my TV shows were about to be canceled and in my mind, I'd remained the "not right" girl. That's the poisonous thing with IS; my brain hadn't caught up to the reality that my show actually did well and that I was maybe good at my job. Mentally, I still saw myself as *all wrong*, even when I was, at last, deemed "just right." I was 100 percent convinced that, when the powers that be realized they'd made a huge mistake, I'd go right back to being on the other side of the door, knocking to get in.

Despite my business successes, I still felt so far away from any success of being a #girlboss or a female leader. My self-care had crumbled. I had completely fallen off the routine of looking after myself, even though I was building a company that encouraged users to do just this. Regina kept saying, *"HOW INAUTHENTIC ARE YOU? Any day now, you're going to be found out, fired and canceled, forever."*

Although my life had changed, I believed wholeheartedly—and Regina reminded me constantly—that I was still the tag-along, the girl whose BFF made the boys go weak at the knees at seventeen while I stood on the sidelines, feeling invisible.

From my burnout bed, I could see how IS had affected my life. But I didn't know how to stop the esteem-nibbling thought process from continuing.

Duck Syndrome

Frantic faking it

My research into Impostor Syndrome led me to realize I was also a participant in Duck Syndrome, aka the desperate need to appear like you have your shit together, but in reality, you're paddling like a maniac under the surface. Going by my old diary entries, you'd think I was leaving a trail of tears wherever I went, drenching airports, cafés, and apartments…meanwhile, my Instagram was full of filtered, curated images of glamorous me, living my #bestlife. Yes, it took 300+ attempts to get the shot using multiple angles and editing tools, but it didn't matter, as long as I nailed it in the end.

The effect of this stark contrast—outward projection vs. inner reality—was an uncomfortable state of being. To feel as though you are endlessly putting on a facade is exhausting.

Duck Syndrome is debilitating because we're not only paddling to prevent drowning, but we also have to put a huge amount of energy into making people *think* we're gliding effortlessly.

So why did I do it? Because I learned at a very young age that you should appear at all times like everything is under control, no vulnerability allowed. To get the promotion or get the boyfriend, I believed you had to look cool, calm, and gracefully collected to get anything. Fake it till you make it. Never let them see you sweat. When I was fired from the television company, my boss had asked me to come into work an hour early so when I started crying, "the office wouldn't see me bleed," in his words. If people had any idea of my failures, and how desperately hard I had to work to stay afloat, they'd be horrified (and I'd be socially rejected along with professionally).

I had been secretly living like a maniac for years, but where had it gotten me? In bed and miserable. Projecting the "I've got this!" life made me feel *more* insecure and incapable. I saw other people effortlessly sailing through life without a problem in sight and couldn't work out why it seemed so much easier for everyone else.

Diary Entry:

I feel anxious but I don't know why. I have a horrible feeling in my chest and stomach and am dreading going to this music festival tomorrow. I have this horrendous fear that I'm going to feel like such a loser and be a bit of a social outcast. It brings up horrible past memories of feeling like a third wheel / 7th Wheel. Urgh it's horrible. I have been hibernating so much lately and forgot I have anything to say to anyone, literally have just work work and more work to speak about which everyone finds really boring! Oh I hooked up with this guy and he never wanted to see me again. Um end of story. No one knows how to respond. Awkward laugh and then quickly ask a question in desperate hope someone will reply and move this conversation on. I was feeling so ok at the beginning of the week but it's just come over me, this feeling of awkwardness and fear I just won't know what to say.

I'm breathing breathing breathing breathing. Remembering it's never as bad as I think. I don't even want to be friends with them anyway.

A diary entry and an Instagram post from the same week. The amount of faking terrified me. I'm an anxious, insecure wreck who's dreading a music festival, and yet things look "perfect."

The reality is, we are *all* struggling and trying to stay afloat.

Intellectually I knew this already, from the Snapchat show viewers and all the research I'd done on the epidemic of stress and anxiety for the HNP app. Hustle Culture was everywhere; social media magnified the expectation that success was effortless, and I assumed it was because I'm just not very talented or qualified enough. I would read countless "How I Make It Work" articles by inspirational glorious specimens who were organic farming and/or producing chemical-free skin care lines while raising three perfect children with their just-as-awesome partner. I didn't even have children and could barely make it work!

When I finally was forced to slow down—nowhere to rush to when you can't get out of bed (except to a therapy or doctor appointment)—I began to question the authenticity of these supermoms and organic farmers and wondered if they were Duck Syndrome–ing, too. How energetically sustainable really are these "a day in the life of" articles about running a 10K and then whipping up a batch of homemade gluten-free pancakes for breakfast? What if the glowing articles are really just another thing fueling our toxic belief that success is effortless and, if it's not, there's something wrong with us?

I decided to pick up the phone and call one of these glorious specimens, my incredibly impressive friend Amy (an entrepreneur I had always idolized) to discuss #thehustle. To my shock, she said, "I agree!! It's really *really* hard. I struggle so much with all this pretense." I set off like a volcano as my perfect friend spilled on how crushed she felt by trying to keep up with it all, too. *Wow, she does? But she's perfect!* I was more grateful for her honesty in that moment than she would ever know. The reassurance that I wasn't alone felt like a warm hug. After that chat, which felt like the first honest one we'd ever had, our friendship changed to something more real and meaningful. The vulnerable acknowledgment that we both shared the same feeling of trying to keep up with the never-ending game was a huge step forward for us both, and healing for my process.

Duck Syndrome is a terrible coping strategy, but my brain clung to it. I thought projecting a problem-free life would make me likable but in actual fact it caused me to lose sight of my true self. I was so busy performing and acting outside of my integrity, I'd lost the ability to know how I was really feeling or what I really wanted. Duck Syndrome was sabotaging the things I was actually craving for, connection and acceptance.

Speaking with Amy helped me see I wasn't the only one who found this existence exhausting, and that lightened the load. I was able to normalize the uncomfortableness rather than be shocked into shame every time I felt like I was drowning. Perhaps paddling just a little slower didn't have to mean rejection was inevitable either?

The Need for Validation

*Relying on others to make us
feel good about ourselves*

What became abundantly clear when chatting to Dr. Shona was my insatiable need for others' approval. Nothing tasted or sounded sweeter than a gentle tap of "you're killing it," and this was a dangerous addiction. For as long as I can remember, I have craved external validation as if it were oxygen because it was the only thing that would shut up my inner Regina for a second. If people were happy with me, I felt safe. When a teacher complimented my work or gave me a gold star, I basked in the wonderful reassurance. Someone saying "you're okay" eased my fear of being less-than and, for a glimmering second, made me feel like I belonged but left me wanting more.

My childhood hunger for gold stars turned into "the disease to please" in adulthood. The only way I could feel confident in myself was if I was receiving validation from others. In dating, this was a nightmare. If men gave me just enough to make me think they were interested, I'd be hooked and obsessed. I later found out drip-fed approval is a manipulation tactic called "bread-crumbing." You're never given the whole loaf to feel safe, but just enough to keep you "there." My need for reassurance had turned me into a professional Gretel. *Argh, the horror! Just throw me a slice.*

The validation thirst sabotaged my career, too. I worked myself into the ground just to get a "great job!" which rarely came from my impossible-to-please bosses and partners. The disease to please eradicates good judgment because you end up just doing whatever it takes to get that figurative pat on the back even if it goes completely against what you actually think.

The fear of upsetting or disappointing others comes hand in hand with the desire for approval. I would say "yes" to parties and dinners even though I could barely lift my head off the pillow after a full day working. For me, FOMO was a function of people pleasing. In every aspect of my work, social, and love life, I put everyone on a pedestal of hero status and made their feedback mean even more. A dangerous habit.

Instagram is a hardcore drug for anyone who craves gratification. On social media, validation is quantifiable. Those double taps turn into sugar. I'd post a photograph and literally hold my breath until someone, anyone, liked it.

In September 2016, my Snapchat show was gaining popularity and I was asked to write a TEDxHollywood talk. I decided to explore my—and my generation's—thirst for approval. The talk was called "Addicted to Likes." I connected the rise of social media and the dramatic uptick in anxiety, pointed out the suffocating pressure we put on ourselves to project a perfect life online, and explained the addicting dopamine (a "reward" feel-good hormone) hit associated with getting likes. I told the gathering, "Social media has the ability to magnify human emotions and then slap you with them on a daily basis," and that certainly hasn't changed.

The irony: I had JUST delivered a talk on why we shouldn't be addicted to Instagram or care about our online numbers, and afterward, I was counting the video's views and obsessively reading the comments. The harsh reality of feedback is that it takes A LOT of inner work to be indifferent to it. I was NOT THERE YET and will probably always have to work extra hard to release the importance I place on external opinions, no matter how psychologically flexible I become.

As I was learning and Dr. Shona was teaching, everyone enjoys positive feedback. "The human condition causes us to always be yearning for more and poking holes in what we have. We fall prey to the illusion that validation from others will heal an emotional wound."

I was beginning to see how tricky external validation was: Like Doritos, it always leaves you wanting more. Dr. Shona ended our session by saying, "We are all leaking buckets, Poppy. Some faster than others. I have yet to meet someone who doesn't enjoy praise and approval, but the trick is to train yourself not to *need it.*"

Later that day, I read Jack Kornfield's book *A Path with Heart*. He described our leaking buckets as a "Hungry Ghost with an enormous belly and tiny pinhole mouth, who can never eat enough to satisfy his endless need." I reflected on how we have all been sadly reminded that external validation by no means assures long-lasting happiness. The tragic suicides of many famous, successful, beautiful souls are cold proof that attention, money, and public love do nothing to cure inner, personal feelings of pain and unworthiness. I was chasing an illusion, thinking that when I finally found that pot of gold at the end of the perfection rainbow, I would never feel inadequate again. But I was beginning to discover that there was no evidence to support this fairy tale.

> *"The deepest principle in human nature is the craving to be appreciated."*
> —William James

The Terror of Rejection

The feeling of being left out, unwanted, or not belonging

Since I was so sensitive to rejection, why did I keep choosing career paths that guaranteed a high rate of it? It was another of my nonsensical decisions, but I did learn to handle professional rejection for the most part. Having experienced it so often, I got used to turning it into more of a challenge.

Romantic rejection, on the other hand, didn't get any easier. Not feeling pretty, smart, or successful enough to attract a guy seemed like the darkest shadow of them all, the one I feared more than anything. It felt personal. Despite how hard I tried to not let it affect me, those rejections pierced my insecurities like a can opener.

I had read that hypnotherapy could help pinpoint where some of these feelings started so I tracked down Chris, a hypnotist in LA who specialized in anxiety. I'd tried it before and knew what to expect. Hypnosis is like entering a deep relaxation; it feels quite lovely, actually. You are fully aware of what's happening and there is no "act like a chicken" BS as you see in movies.

During the first session, Chris asked, "Poppy, when did you first feel a sense of rejection?"

I was silent, eyes closed, and it felt like my brain was ransacking dusty old filing cabinets trying to find some very old information. I suddenly spoke up: "It was with Arthur, I was six." Arthur, a family friend, then five, had rejected my attempt to kiss him on the cheek. He pushed my cheek peck away and screamed, "I hate girls."

More than twenty years later, that memory of rejection was still influencing me. Not in a "like it was yesterday" way, but the idea that romantic pursuits were doomed from the get-go was clearly something I still believed.

I'd met and started working with life and performance mindset coach Polly Bateman after a friend recommended her to me as the queen of helping you change your mindset. I told her about the Arthur experience. She explained to me how all our unwanted thoughts were just a product of what we innocently learned in childhood, and we then liked to find evidence to support whatever initial beliefs were instilled. I always left Bateman's sessions feeling a million times better after she would roar with laughter when explaining to me how normal it all was and tell me hilarious stories of all the rejection she'd overcome.

"We *all* find rejection terrifying. But I'll help you rethink it," she said. I couldn't wait.

Later that night, I started researching "rejection" and found a study by researchers at the University of California, Los Angeles, who'd hooked participants to fMRI brain imaging machines and asked them to play a virtual ball-tossing game.[1] The researchers started to exclude some of the players to see how their brains reacted to being left out. On the scans, the same part of the brain—the anterior cingulate cortex—that is activated during physical pain lit up when subjects felt the emotional pain of exclusion. How crazy is that? Social ostracizing or romantic rejection feels like a gut punch because your brain reacts the same way to both. *Any* kind of rejection, in person or online, from a friend or stranger[2] or even by a computer game,[3] decreases our self-esteem and sense of belonging. No wonder social media can be so toxic to our confidence. Our brains stick to mean comments like glue.

I began to see, without my consciously realizing, I'd developed the coping strategy of workaholism, aka avoidance, to manage my deep fear of rejection. I thought that success could shield me from ever being pushed away again, that if I became successful and care-free my fears and insecurities would magically disappear forever. The fantasy of acceptance and safety from rejection was so seductive, I let it blindly drive me into the ground.

Perfectionism

Refusing to accept any standard but perfection and believing that we will never measure up

After a teary session with Dr. Shona, she handed me a glass of water and said, "I want you to research perfectionism."

Back on Google, my trusty friend, I had another cold shower when reading the risk factors of perfectionism: obsessive-compulsive dis-order, obsessive-compulsive personality disorder, eating disorders, social anxiety, social phobia, body dysmorphic disorder, workaholism, self-harm, substance abuse, and clinical depression as well as physi-cal problems like chronic stress and heart disease.

Well, I related to five of those symptoms and that was a hard pill to swallow.

I don't blame my eleven-year-old self for latching on to the idea that no boy would turn me down again when I reached peak per-fection. Or that no friend or even employer would turn me down if I were perfect. I mean, who *didn't* see perfect as a safety cloak? I became a tweenage workaholic and piled on unbearable pressure to meet my own impossibly high standards. As an adult, my search for perfection manifested in workaholism and massive amounts of social anxiety.

I realized how loopy "hooked on work" sounded, but as Dr. Shona explained, in the brain, the mechanism is no different from a gambling addiction or eating disorder. The number of hours I worked in a day was something I could control. If I was going to be addicted to any-thing, hard work I guess was more helpful than some other addictions.

But any behavior taken to extremes to distract from emotional wounds is a ticking time bomb.

The problem with unmanaged perfectionism, I was learning, is that it leaves you with NO tolerance for error.

If something interrupts the perfect little plan, we move from hero to zero and sheer panic rushes in at the speed of light. Cue industrial levels of cortisol pumped through our system, anxiety, stress, and irrational behavior (family and friends stay clear), an immune system shot to hell. Perfectionism can make you sick (I knew),[4] has been linked to suicide,[5] and drives procrastination.[6] It's more and more common in younger people who are spurred on by the great expectations placed on them by themselves or others.[7]

As I reflected on my list of cascading cold shower reality checks, I saw a common theme. They all spoke to a **deep yearning for acceptance** that I was clearly missing. The lack of self-appreciation and toxic shame Regina spouted forth daily meant I relied on the external world to feel better. Knowing I wasn't the only one fighting an internal battle was helpful.

One cloudy afternoon, Dr. Shona said, "You have nothing to be ashamed of. All humans desire to be loved, heard, and seen and we just choose different journeys to find it."

I'd been looking everywhere for that soul-nurturing reassurance and coming up empty. I had to wonder if I'd been looking in the wrong places. I'd scoured the Internet to find it. I'd worked myself sick in the media, fashion, and tech. I'd searched high and low at Hollywood and London parties and nightclubs. I certainly didn't find it diving into chocolate fountains or at the bottom of peanut butter containers.

But now I could feel I was finally heading in the right direction, thanks to my work on the HNP app and with Dr. Shona, by looking for acceptance inside my own brain. And that bit of insight caused a five-story drop of insight in my stomach.

In order to accept myself and find soul-nourishing fulfillment, I needed to apply my superpowers of focus and drive (#makeshithappen) to a new mission to learn about the mechanics of my own mind and why it made me—and so many other anxious, stressed-out people—susceptible to perfectionism, Impostor Syndrome, Duck Syndrome, and the thirst for validation.

Assessing my cold shower reality checks with the help of experts helped me start to understand my triggers and the bad coping strategies I'd put into place. But to rebuild my emotional heath permanently, and not slip right back into old bad patterns, I had to learn how to stop them from ruling my life. It wasn't enough to know that I had all these self-negating habits. I needed to know *why* I had them and how I could get rid of them.

Why did my brain make me feel so unworthy?

Why did it tell me that the only path to happiness came from pleasing other people and perfectionism?

Why, exactly, was my brain insisting that if I didn't work myself sick, I'd never feel loved and accepted?

In short, why was my brain such a bitch?

"WHO IN THE WORLD AM I? AH, THAT'S THE GREAT PUZZLE."

—LEWIS CARROLL,
ALICE'S ADVENTURES IN WONDERLAND

chapter three

WHY YOUR BRAIN IS SO BITCHY

I'd watched so many *Friends* reruns while stuck in bed, I could recite the punch lines before the characters. It was time for me to go back into research mode, and I knew right where to start. I had a stack of wellness books my mom and others on the HNP team had recommended over the years that I hadn't had time to read. The book on top of the pile was *Sort Your Brain Out* by neuroscientist Jack Lewis and motivational speaker Adrian Webster. The back cover asked, "Ever feel like your head is in a scramble?"

Why, yes. Yes, I did.

I started reading and didn't stop until I consumed that book, and every other book on the pile. One rabbit hole led to another, a new Cheshire Cat smiled broadly at the entrance of each. I met many Mad Hatters as I explored brain research, and odd as it might sound, they all gave me hope. The more I read, the more I understood why I'd been stuck in destructive habits for so long. I finally began to see some light at the end of the tunnel.

One of the rather shocking discoveries: Our human brains are surprisingly simple to decode.

If you were trying to manage your life right now using one of those early computers from the 1950s that took up an entire room and needed an hour to calculate 2 + 2, you'd be frustrated and in a constant state of ARGH. That's pretty much what's going on for all of us right now. Our brains were developed to run 2 miles per hour, but we push them to go 200 while balancing on a pineapple. It's NO WONDER modern life makes us feel on edge and overwhelmed. We need to upgrade our minds urgently. But you can't upgrade anything until you know how it was constructed in the first place.

> "You can't fix what you don't understand."
> —Marisa Peer

Our Internal Radio Stations

One of my favorite books, *Hardwiring Happiness* by psychologist Rick Hanson, taught me that the brain has only two settings.

Just two! When I found this out, I was deeply disappointed. Despite the wondrous things we have created, humans are actually incredibly simplistic. Dr. Hanson calls the two settings the Green Zone and the Red Zone. I prefer the metaphor of our brain playing only two radio stations:

Station WCHL's slogan is "I am safe." It plays lullabies and whale songs, soothing sounds to our parasympathetic nervous system, aka "rest and digest" mode. Our body loves this station! Our digestion runs smoothly, absorbing antioxidants like a sponge, and our heart rate stays normal. Our immune system fights off bacteria and viruses and our higher-functioning brain regions are full of oxygenated blood, so we can make smart decisions. When our brain is playing the chill station, we are more compassionate, make thoughtful decisions, able to access gratitude, and everything has a 1,000 times greater chance of going our way.

Station WFML's slogan is "I'm in danger!" It plays loud static that sets off our sympathetic nervous system, aka "fight, flight, or freeze" mode. This "fuck my life" station is pure panic. It turns on whenever we are threatened—whether we can see the threat or not, whether the threat is real or not. Just the *thought* of attack flips the WFML switch, and the brain screams, "RELEASE THE CORTISOL!" to our adrenal glands. Immediately, our heart rate goes up, the immune system shuts down, and our digestive system grinds to a halt. That weird stomach sensation we get when we're anxious? That's blood rushing out of our GI tract and into our limbs so we can RUN AWAY. Blood rushes out of the brain, too, and when it's oxygen-deprived, it doesn't make smart decisions. It doesn't think. It just reacts.

We are programmed with two brain stations in order to survive. When we're chill and safe, we can rest, restore, and turn nutrients from food into energy. When we're freaked out and in danger, those systems are put on hold so we can respond *automatically*, without thought. Our brains evolved to be supersonic danger dodgers, and we are here today because of it. When the threat is gone, we're wired to switch back to the "I'm safe" station. Cortisol dissipates. We return to digesting, a relaxed state, and using our intellect to invent the wheel.

Your brain plays only one station at a time, but the radio is always on. You are either in chill mode or freaking out in fight-or-flight, perpetually.

According to Dr. Hanson, the human brain is wired for survival, not happiness. Our ancestors had to develop a sensitive danger detection system to prevent them from dying brutally. Arguably, nowadays life is a lot easier! We're not running from tigers and have relatively safe lives in comparison. But, on the other hand, we are bombarded by psychological threats that our ancestors didn't have so much of. Whenever we have to deal with an unexpected bill, a social rejection, traffic, a job interview, a hot date, a weird look from a colleague, a loud talker on the subway, *a pandemic*, we get a toxic cortisol dump similar to the one we'd have if an actual lion were chasing us. These days, our WFML station is blaring more than it's not, and the heavy metal scream of our nervous system is not keeping us safe like it used to. It's actually *causing* health issues—adrenal fatigue, chronic inflammation, high blood pressure.

Psychiatrist and neuroscientist Daniel Amen, founder of the Amen Clinics, once wrote, "Most people don't realize that your body responds to every single thought you have. If you have negative thoughts, your hands get colder and wetter, your muscles tense, your heart rate [is affected]." If we swim in anxious thoughts all day, it's no wonder our back hurts. For optimal physical and mental health, WCHL is the place to be but increasingly hard to stay in.

Since Regina, my bitchy inner critic, was constantly firing stressful and anxiety-triggering thoughts, my brain played "I'm in danger" 24/7. Before my burnout, my digestion practically stopped (hello, serious bloating). Every email, text, or voicemail from my scary business partner triggered a cortisol flood. Just reading the words "Can we have a chat?" set off overwhelming, chest-tightening anxious dread. I'd been under psychological threat for so long, I began to accept daily panic attacks as a way of life. But it's not normal to run from an imaginary tiger for ten years straight. No wonder I was in bed, feeling battered and bruised.

My friend Gala recommended the writings of Elisabeth Kübler-Ross, a twentieth-century Swiss-American psychiatrist most famous for identifying the five stages of grief, and I was inspired by this passage about the dichotomy of our thoughts. "There are only two emotions: love and fear," she wrote. "All positive emotions come from love, all negative emotions from fear. From love flows happiness, contentment, peace, and joy. From fear comes anger, hate, anxiety, and guilt." She explained that people can't feel these two emotions together, at exactly the same time. "They're opposites. If we're in fear, we are not in a place of love. When we're in a place of love, we cannot be in a place of fear....We must continually choose love in order to nourish our souls and drive away fear, just as we eat to nourish our bodies and drive away hunger."[8]

Wow. I read this passage again and again. You could say the stressful WFML radio station played fear, and the WCHL chilled mode played love. I'd been stuck listening to Bitchy Regina and living in fear as she bombarded me with worries about the future and regrets from the past. Obviously, I needed to switch stations and lean into love by making WCHL my default instead. WFML static was destroying me from the inside out, and despite the mindfulness breaks that were preventing me from spiraling further, I was still disproportionately living in a state of anxiety. I just needed a better manual to do this.

Our Brains Are Negativity Magnets

No matter how hard I tried, my brain couldn't seem to escape the negative thoughts and anxiety that flooded in daily. Regina liked to give me a destructive running commentary on everything; as soon as one negative thought left, another would appear almost instantaneously. Catherine M. Pittman, PhD, wrote in her book *Rewire Your Anxious Brain: How to Use the Neuroscience of Fear to End Anxiety, Panic and Worry* that we are descendants of "the worry people." For example, our great-great-great-times-a-thousand grandmother noticed that her cave by a lake flooded after a storm. Worrying about that happening again led her to seek out and find a new cave farther back from the lake. Excellent! Because of worry, her family survived the next flood, and we are all here today because of it. Worrying was the key to our evolution. Modern humans are just as skilled at worrying as our ancestors were. Our desire to survive causes us, as Dr. Hanson explained, to be completely obsessed with looking out for what could go wrong. There's a scientific term for this: negative bias.

As I've said, my family and I have always been Olympic worriers. I'd find twenty things to fret about before breakfast by comparing myself to others on Instagram, scrolling through a news app to be reminded that the world is in trouble, taking a shower and fretting about my wobbly parts. Then I would dive into emails, tweets, messages, Snaps, and as a result of the overwhelming messages I'd freak out about my work demands. My life was negativity overload from the moment I opened my eyes, and I'd find a way to be "wrong" every twenty seconds for the whole day.

James R. Doty, MD, professor, neurosurgeon, and author of *Into The Magic Shop: A Neurosurgeon's Quest to Discover the Mysteries of the Brain and the Secrets of the Heart,* explained how our DNA hasn't changed for thousands of years (since cavemen times), but our environment has changed beyond anything we could have planned for. Our worry skill, once a strength that ensured our survival, is now so overwhelmed and has no time to process incoming information in the modern world. It's turned toxic and is hindering our state of living.

The Power of Thought

We have around 6,000 thoughts per day,[9] and the vast majority are the same as yesterday. We spend most of our waking life on autopilot— and the autopilot isn't flying the friendly skies. Raj Raghunathan, PhD, author of *If You're So Smart, Why Aren't You Happy?*, told *Psychology Today*, "Even though people claim to hold themselves in high regard, the thoughts that spontaneously occur to them—their 'mental chatter,' so to speak—are up to 70 percent negative." In our conscious minds, we *want* to feel good about ourselves and optimistic about our future. But our unconscious, made up of faulty beliefs learned in our early years, pulls us back to negativity nearly three-quarters of the time! It's that bitchy voice like Regina in our head. Our brains find and stick to negativity like dog's hair on our favorite jacket. We are our own worst enemy because we are hardwired to spot and cling on to the negative in *everything*—first and foremost, in ourselves.

Even if good things are happening, we tend to still focus on that one bad part, believing it's helpful. Whenever people said complimentary things about my TV interviews, for example, I'd forget the praise instantly. But if one person made a single nasty comment, I'd focus on that and beat myself up about it for days. We all do this! I'm sure you can remember the criticism you've received in your life with far more clarity than the nice things.

Most of us aren't fully aware that this mean "mental chatter" is happening automatically. When I first read about "automatic negative thoughts" (ANTs), I was horrified, instantly picturing those annoying little insects streaming up my leg, just like when you accidentally sit on a nest and get a line of bites on your skin. Brain ANTs do similar damage by nibbling at our psyches.

My educator about ANTs was primarily Mike Dow, PsyD, coauthor of *Healing the Broken Brain*. According to his research, they usually play out in eight distinct patterns:

1. **Dramatic all-or-nothing-ism.** Guilty! Things are either TERRIBLE or the BEST. A boss is AWFUL or GREAT! You HATE this or LOVE that. When I was on live TV, if my performance wasn't perfect, it was a TRAIN WRECK. This thought pattern turns us into cruel, merciless bitches that amp up our fears by 1,000 percent.

2. **Overgeneralization.** Guilty again! After I'd been on a bad date, I would bounce right into, "There are just *no* good men *in the entire city of New York.*" When a friend was cheated on just once, she declared, "All men are lying cheating scumbags!" This thought pattern turns us into pantomime dramatists.

3. **Spiraling down.** A classic downward spiral sounds like, "I didn't get the job. I won't get *any* job. Ever. I'm useless. I won't be able to pay my rent. I'll be evicted. I'm a hopeless case. I'll become a homeless person and die alone on the street." (This is actually taken from my own past spirals; yours may look different.)

4. **Paralysis by analysis.** I think of it as spiraling in place. "Why didn't Emily text back? Is she upset with me? What did I do wrong? Was my email annoying? Too eager? Too boring? She DID give me that look the other day…what did it *mean*?"

Overanalyzing is my naughtiest ANT. My brain writhes with these thoughts!

5. **Fortune-telling.** So guilty! These ANTs assume that whatever shit we're in now is going to be the same place we'll be stuck in *forever*. If someone is single and unemployed now, then they'll NEVER have a partner, get a job, or be successful. **We predict gloomy futures sometimes without realizing we are doing it.** I would write in my grateful diary daily, and then my fortune-telling ANTs would swarm in with "But what if the thing I'm grateful for today goes away tomorrow?" These ANTs drive anxiety like a speeding bus that's late for school.

6. **Rejecting the positive.** Compliments "don't count" for some reason or another. We shrug off anything that goes right as a lucky fluke. Anyone who seems to like us must have deep emotional problems, as in, "He must still be single for a reason!" These keep us locked in "not good enough" and "will never be good enough" territory.

7. **Personalizing.** The blame-taker ANTs that say, "It's all my fault," and "If only I hadn't done this, then that would have worked out." I've even blamed myself for rain on vacation by thinking, "I cursed us by wishing for sunshine!" These ANTs burrow a lovely deep hole of self-blame and self-hate that's hard to get out of.

8. **Should-ing.** Every time we say, "I *should* have gone for a run" or "I *shouldn't* have eaten that cake" or "I *should* be married with kids by now," these ANTs team up with self-hating thoughts, and we have a mega infestation. This pattern leads to shame, guilt, resentment, and regret and pulls us into some really low-vibrational states (more to come on that).

My negative bias and ANTs created mental and physical havoc for years. Just learning about them gave me a rush of reassurance that I wasn't the only one with these infestations. *I inherited these worries.*

They are normal, *even a sign my mind is functional.* (I guess that was a positive thought? One down, 5,999 to go?) Surely, we can reprogram our protective mechanism, and let our minds have more options than just focusing on the wrong?

Our Brains Are Conditioned

You've probably heard that the brain is like an iceberg. Our *conscious mind* is only the small fraction—most experts say 10 percent—that's visible above the surface of the water. It's responsible for whatever we're thinking in the moment and what we're aware of—like if we're cold or hot, what we'd like for lunch, the words in front of us right now. The rest of our mind, the 90 percent of the iceberg below the surface, is our *unconscious mind.*

An iceberg sank the *Titanic,* and the bulk of our iceberg brain, the negative unconscious, might sink us, too.

What lies below is a giant block of ice that freezes and stores every nasty comment that we've been told, every trauma (micro and macro), every belief we've formed from our culture and childhood conditioning—all the emotions we're afraid to deal with. Oh, and it doesn't have a delete button. Ugh.

My intro to conditioning started with Psych 101 figure Ivan Petrovich Pavlov, the famous Nobel Prize–winning Russian physiologist. When feeding his dogs, he would ring a bell, conditioning them to know the bell meant food. Even when it wasn't dinnertime, the dogs would drool whenever they heard that sound.

Humans are no different; we have conditioned reflexes that are particularly intense when they're associated with fear.[10] American psychologists John Watson and Rosalie Rayner proved that with a (slightly sadistic) experiment on "Little Albert." Before the experiment, Albert, a baby, was shown a rat, and wasn't afraid of it at all. Then Watson and Rayner blared a loud horn when they showed him the rat, and the shock of the noise taught poor Little Albert to be terrified of it.

People can learn to fear or dislike anything if they associate an object or experience with danger. We can be conditioned to fear the smell of cigarettes if we grew up disliking the babysitter who smoked. Associative conditioning can even create fear for a day of the week. My older brother fears Sundays because he used to dread going back to school, and still now, decades later, he can't shake off his dislike of the day.

Conditioning explains why our unconscious mind "pattern matches" emotional triggers with behaviors. American psychiatrist, neuroscientist, and author Judson Brewer, MD, PhD, has talked about how people who eat junk food for comfort might be pattern matching that behavior to the joy and celebration of childhood birthday parties. For many of us, those parties gave us free rein to eat as much pizza, chips, and cake as we wanted. The brain learns to crave birthday party foods because it historically associated those times with freedom, fun, and friends. Breaking the habit of emotional eating is really hard because it might also feel like we're sacrificing childhood joy whether we consciously realize it or not.

Everything we believe to be true has been taught to us, and those lessons began in the sponge years, before age six, when we absorb, absorb, absorb and don't squeeze anything out. The critical part of our brain hasn't formed yet, so we take in everything and accept it all as 100 percent fact. We're quite vulnerable when we're first learning about the world. That's why our parents and teachers were so influential in our development for good or bad.

We may have had wonderful parents who programmed us only in the best way, or we may have had parents struggling with their own battles who unintentionally compromised our initial programming. Regardless of our individual situation, none of us are immune to the imprint culture has made on our unconscious minds. For example, many of us have been conditioned to believe that more is better, money leads to happiness, and buying things helps us belong.

Anything—be it a small moment or major trauma—can cause bugs in our programming.

While looking at YouTube videos, I found one of Eckhart Tolle, bestselling author of *The Power of Now*, explaining how learned beliefs get stuck in our minds as kids and affect us as adults. He told the story of a boy who would throw a tantrum until his parents would give in to his demands to make him stop. In these moments, the child learned that acting unhappy was the route to get what he wanted. So, as an adult, he continued. He would rage and complain, thinking that that was the route to happiness. But that kind of behavior (as we know) had quite the opposite effect: Being an asshole was the cause of his *unhappiness*.

Naturally, this education on conditioning made me start to challenge every single belief I had. Were my political beliefs mine, or my parents'? What about my religious beliefs? My preference for city or country? Even the food I liked! Wow, when we break it down, we begin to see that everything we think or believe was most likely influenced by what our parents, communities, or culture taught us. Major revelation for me: I've walked around carrying a garbage bag of insecurities because somewhere along the line, I've believed other people's negative comments were true and as a result they became my own.

The Stories We Write

Marisa Peer, a British hypnotherapist, made a point that really stuck with me. No baby comes into the world with fear or beliefs like "I'm shy." They smile and gurgle away at everyone. The innocence and love we see in babies is evidence that we are all, deep down, just a bundle of love, curiosity, compassion, and innocence. We learn to be anxious. We learn our insecurities. We learn our prejudices. We learn our fear. Generations pass down toxic beliefs and habits as easily as the common cold.

Some of our most formative, damaging beliefs don't seem bad at all until you take a closer look at them. Growing up, my mom trained my brothers and me to be "good kids" and I learned that "likable" was essential. As an adult, I took that to an extreme, and that conditioning often prevented me from standing up for myself out of the fear of not being likable.

What we "know" to be true about ourselves, all of those labels we absorb as our "identity"—that we're "a good kid," "lazy," "bad at math," "a troublemaker," or "not good enough"—came from somewhere outside of ourselves. And yet, we tell ourselves that story over and over again. I started to ask my friends about who they thought they were down deep, and I began to see they also had just as bitchy inner critics like my own Regina inside. One thought she was a loser, even though she's very clever and successful. Another thought she was stupid, although she was a publicly acclaimed speaker.

The golden nugget was there: If something can be learned, it has the possibility to be unlearned. Conditionings shows us that our "identity" is just a construct of what we have been told about ourselves and it's basically made up from a bunch of opinions (we probably didn't ask for). The human brain's love for spinning stories means it's possible to rewrite them into new, nicer, happier (but not perfect) ones, and to reform the perception we have about ourselves.

The human ability to evolve constantly means no one needs to be trapped in the stories others have given them.

This thought alone was so liberating and I began to taste what a different future could look like, one that wasn't bound by my past. I didn't need to be imprisoned by my demeaning ideas. I could take charge and be free of them.

I was talking to my mom about all of my exciting findings when she told me a story I never knew. When I was twelve, I was told by a teacher that I was bad at English, and as a consequence I started hating and failing the class. I had accepted the bad grades and the criticism as pure fact and I would have gone on believing it for my entire life had my mom not stepped in. She secretly went to speak to my English teacher and said, "How will Poppy know what she's doing right if you only tell her what she's doing wrong?"

A week later, this teacher started to give me gold stars for everything. I remember thinking it odd how in a matter of days I'd suddenly woken up some English genius. But I enjoyed racking up the stars for putting punctuation in the right place. Within six months, powered by positive feedback, my confidence had skyrocketed, which led to enormous improvement. I became one of the best in the class, and English turned into my favorite subject.

I was astounded on hearing this story decades later. I couldn't believe that just a mild change in belief could impact the course of my life in such a dramatic way. I wouldn't be writing this book now had it not been for my changing the narrative "I'm useless at English" into "I must be quite good if I'm getting this many stars." The power our beliefs have over what we think and do is as terrifying as it is empowering. Theodore Roosevelt's line "Believe you can and you're halfway there" was beginning to make a lot of sense.

Author Tara Brach wrote in *Radical Acceptance: Embracing Your Life with the Heart of a Buddha*, "Perhaps the biggest tragedy of our lives is that freedom is possible, yet we can pass our years trapped in the same old patterns…We may want to love other people without holding back, to feel authentic, to breathe in the beauty around us, to dance and sing. Yet each day we listen to inner voices that keep our life small."

The process of conditioning is partly the reason so many of us have these bitchy inner voices that spout forth lies! We absorb the critical comments and play them on repeat, keeping us locked in "small world syndrome." I wasn't bad at English. I was just criticized by a teacher, and as a sensitive child, I accepted her word as fact. I wasn't fat, either, I was just teased by an insecure boy in the playground and took it on as gospel. A tiny vote of confidence at the right moment can change a person's entire life but the opposite can also occur.

We can supply that voice for ourselves and break our conditioning by challenging every belief we have. But most of us, in the course of our lives, we just get on with it and don't give ourselves the time or energy to question our thoughts.

I had been existing on the thoughts equivalent to bad hamburgers for breakfast, lunch, and dinner. My thought diet was awful, but I was too conditioned by the idea that perfection equaled happiness to slow down and contemplate my own unhealthy patterns. I had to unlearn what I was CERTAIN was true and question what I really wanted. I was beginning to stretch my thoughts for the first time by looking at whether my "factual" beliefs about life and myself might very well be lies. I had to screen the fake news in my head just like I'd begun to on Facebook. Our bitchy inner critic might be an echo from a mean English teacher, and why should we be carrying around that any longer? It was then that my deconditioning process started.

If Our Basic Needs Aren't Met, Expect Trouble

I had not had a regular bedtime in over seven years. My normal was working or partying into the early hours of the morning, sleeping for five hours, and waking up at the crack of dawn to start all over again. The doctor had made it *very* clear that sleep was going to be critical in my recovery. According to a recent UCLA study, sleep deprivation is as bad for the brain as being intoxicatedly drunk.[11] "We discovered that starving the body of sleep also robs neurons of the ability to function properly," said Itzhak Fried, PhD, the study's senior author.[12] Sleeplessness is linked with depression and anxiety, as it slows down the ability for conscious thought. I had basically been trying to manage life as if I'd guzzled two bottles of rosé and a vodka shot by 8:00 a.m. No wonder my emotional compass had lost direction.

While recovering, a friend sent me the link to clinical psychologist Julia Rucklidge's TEDx Talk called "The Surprisingly Dramatic Role of Nutrition in Mental Health," and I began to see why my diet was another need I'd neglected. Food affecting mood is such an obvious thing. Being "hangry" is very real. I'd almost forgotten how critical it is to meet this basic human need to make our biological hardware work. No wonder I was on anxiety overload when I relied on such a nutrition-devoid diet.

We humans are incredibly sensitive to our physical needs. However, our emotional needs are equally impactful on our overall health. When we feel unsafe, for example, it's practically impossible to perform at our best. The most famous model exploring this comes from Abraham Maslow, PhD, an American psychologist. In his groundbreaking 1943 paper called "The Theory of Human Motivation," he wrote about human needs as a hierarchy. We have to satisfy the bottom tier of the pyramid before we can move up to the next tier. It's like striving to level up on a videogame. Maslow said, "Man is a perpetually wanting animal."[13] Yup! So as soon as one need is fulfilled, we look up to the next one. He believed the feeling of wanting/needing never really goes away.

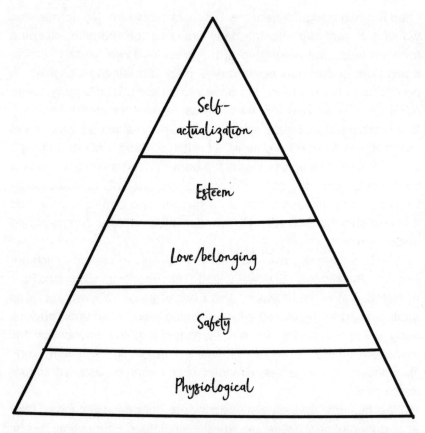

It's a long way up from food and water to self-actualization. #goals

At the bottom of Maslow's pyramid are our physiological needs, like food, water, clean air, and sleep. When that's taken care of, we start worrying about safety, like a stable environment, a place to live, a job that covers expenses, a feeling of security that we will have the resources we need to survive.

After that comes love and belonging needs, like romantic intimacy, the sense that you feel accepted in a community. Maslow argued that it is critical for humans to love and be loved by others. Without love, we're at risk of emotional dangers like loneliness, anxiety, and depression. But only when our lower basic human needs have been met (shelter and safety) can we fully begin sharing love with others.

My love and belonging tier was in shambles. BELONGING was the feeling I was chasing, and what it would give me: feeling safe, loved, and enough. This human desire to belong created and drove my need for perfection.

To fit in and feel part of the group, I felt I had to change myself.

I thought I wasn't enough as I was and, unconsciously and consciously, hid parts of myself that I believed prevented me from belonging. Gradually, I lost connection with my true self and, without even realizing, was pretending to be someone I thought would be more impressive. Since I wasn't living truthfully, I struggled with decision making. *What does the manufactured version of me really want?* How should I know? We'd been divorced for so long.

The irony is, the more we accept our true selves and find belonging from within, the less we need to feel outside belonging. However, I didn't know that yet. I was just learning all this like a newborn baby opening their eyes for the first time.

Back to Maslow's pyramid: Once we feel loved and accepted, we can proceed to self-esteem, comfort in our own skin, feeling worthy enough to have the respect of others, a sense of achievement, and confidence in our own ability. At the top of the pyramid is self-actualization, the optimal state of reaching our highest potential as human beings, striving to perform our personal best, and seeking fulfillment. Maslow describes this level as "What a man can be, he must be." Dr. James Doty describes this level of new self-awareness, "transcendence." The nature of transcendence occurs when we "recognize that we are not separate individuals but part of a whole, and that whole is humanity," he once told the website Excellent Reporter.

Another human needs model showed me again how crucial it was for human beings to have a variety of needs met in order to stand a chance at feeling happy. Created by neuroscientist David Rock in 2008, it's called the SCARF model.[14] SCARF is an acronym for:

Status, a sense of importance compared to others

Certainty, confidence about predicting the future

Autonomy, a sense of having control over our lives

Relatedness, feelings of safety around other people

Fairness, a perception of social justice

Looking at which needs are not being met helps us to see why we might be struggling. Dr. Rock believes all five are necessary to thrive. If a SCARF need is met, we get a "reward," a dopamine hit of satisfaction. If a need is unmet, we feel a "threat," which triggers a cortisol cascade. For example, a woman goes to a party. If her best friends who love and adore her are there, her Status and Relatedness are high, and she feels safe because she knows she's appreciated! But if the party was hosted by someone who has never liked her, it would be stressful because her Status and Relatedness would be low. The brain cranks WFML.

Again, no wonder I crashed and burned out. I'd stumbled along with no Certainty, fearing my work was on the brink of collapse; no Relatedness because I thought my coworkers hated me; no Autonomy or Status with investors in charge. According to this model, I was emotionally bankrupt. It was an accurate reflection, and I was finally beginning to understand maybe why I'd broken. I had been trying to survive (let alone thrive) in the desert without water.

Even though I had too many threadbare SCARFs and was stalled at the bottom of Maslow's pyramid, I still felt a rush of reassurance just by learning about all this and seeing plainly that a lot of my issues were caused by my environment, like not having a sense of routine, bad sleep, poor diet, and having no certainty or autonomy over anything. My unhelpful thoughts, behaviors, and habits were partly a product of my unattended needs. The hard pill to swallow was that I'd created this situation for myself. I'd set myself up for a fall, but if I had led me into this, I was beginning to see, I could also lead me out.

Thoughts Are Energy

A colleague on the HNP app turned me on to the teachings of David R. Hawkins, MD, PhD, author of *Power vs. Force*, a psychiatrist known for his research about levels of consciousness. He created a Scale of Consciousness, which ranks emotions and energy.

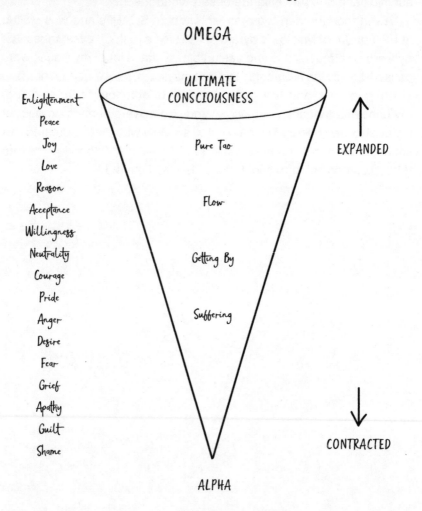

OMEGA

ULTIMATE CONSCIOUSNESS

Enlightenment
Peace
Joy
Love
Reason
Acceptance
Willingness
Neutrality
Courage
Pride
Anger
Desire
Fear
Grief
Apathy
Guilt
Shame

Pure Tao

Flow

Getting By

Suffering

EXPANDED

CONTRACTED

ALPHA

The lowest emotions? Shame and guilt. Ugh, no shocker there! The highest? Enlightenment and peace, what I sought and had no idea how to get.

Hawkins proposes that low alpha emotions like humiliation, blame, desire, regret, anxiety, craving, hate, scorn, guilt, and shame are "force" energies and make us weak. High omega emotions like trust, understanding, optimism, forgiveness, serenity, and bliss are "power" energies that make us strong. When I saw this chart, something clicked for me. Learning that various emotions can cause us to vibrate at a different frequency helped me understand why emotions are so contagious.

Our thoughts and feelings are made up of energy.

The idea that we are magnetic beings who experience energetic waves (emotions) and connect with other energetic vibrations fits so well with my own view of how the mind and body work together. Of course, my mental health was affecting my immune system. I had been stuck in very low-vibrational emotions, downgrading my whole system, making me weak. Learning about the Scale of Consciousness helped me understand that I needed to up my vibe ASAP and start experiencing higher-energy emotions rather than being stuck on the low levels, getting sick and draining my reserve tank.

The Greatest Discovery of All: Reeducation

The book that convinced me that change *is* possible and really turned my life around was *The Upward Spiral: Using Neuroscience to Reverse the Course of Depression One Step at a Time*, by Alex Korb, PhD. I loved the book so much, I became a full-on neuroscientist stalker and tracked the author down on Twitter! After a few tweets, he kindly agreed to meet up and we became friends. Inside Starbucks on the UCLA campus, Alex explained the science of the brain to me in language I could finally understand, including a crash course in brain architecture. Simply put, different regions control different functions:

The prefrontal cortex is like the CEO badass of the brain, the rational "executive functioning" decision maker. This region says, "Maybe it's *not* a good idea to call my boss a narcissistic asshole."

The amygdala is the emotional monkey mind, always ready to react to any sense of a threat and start screeching.

The basal ganglia is the "lizard brain," the lazy crocodile inside that tells you when to eat, sleep, flee, or fuck. It controls habit-based learned actions for the things we don't consciously think about.

I pictured the CEO badass, monkey mind, and lazy croc in a room together. Wouldn't it be nice if the CEO badass could get the monkey and croc under control and harness their powers *for good*? We shouldn't aspire to get rid of our emotions, because that just isn't possible. But if we could harness them, ride them, and access their power, we'd be thriving and enjoying life so much more! As it was, my emo monkey and reactive croc had been overpowering my rational mind for years, making me feel like I was being constantly railroaded.

Something else that I first read in Alex Korb's work really gave me some peace: that the CEO badass region (the prefrontal cortex) isn't fully developed until age twenty-five! So in my early twenties when my emotions had been haywire, I'd been missing a vital piece of hardware to make sense of everything. No wonder my emo amygdala had been doing whatever it wanted. It had free rein! My clear-thinking CEO brain hadn't been fully functional! I'd been controlled by a monkey and I'd had no idea.

The true revelatory nugget Alex shared that changed my understanding of mental health forever: **I didn't have to keep feeling this way.** And it was all because of *neuroplasticity*, the science that has proven our brains are not made of stone. Far from it. Our brain is "plastic," putty, malleable, rewireable, FLEXIBLE. This research confirmed **I wasn't stuck.** I didn't have to live the rest of my life feeling stressed and out of control. I had biology that could change. I screamed, "Hallelujah!"

Despite all the factors that perpetuate negative thinking, we humans *do have the ability to reshape our minds* and reprogram patterns that we've been repeating forever.

Just like snakes can shed their skins, we can shed our old thinking and patterns.

It was there in black and white, science vetted and approved. I didn't have to be locked into my current, destructive miserable mindset. I had the ability, like all humans do, to take advantage of our malleable biology and break out of conditioned thought patterns and behaviors that weren't helping me. It was 100 percent possible to reprogram, and all I had to do was find the best way to bend my brain around to a new way of thinking. But as Alex explained, if I was serious about change, it would require daily nurture and repetition.

I fixed on the idea of nurturing my thoughts, like one would nurture a child. I had been so verbally abusive to myself over the years. I'd never treat a kid or a friend the way I'd consciously and unconsciously shouted at myself for mild fuckups like misreading a situation— "Poppy, I can't BELIEVE you said that, how embarrassing"—or reacting destructively when something went wrong. My poor friend Jules had to witness a tearful meltdown when my flight was canceled and I was about to miss an investor meeting; I was blaming myself for the storm that grounded the plane. It was ludicrous and unnecessarily bitchy. It wasn't surprising my body and mind broke down after how cruel I'd been.

Just like a child becomes startled and afraid by constant screams and critique, my brain had done the same. It was crying out for something so simple: patience and kindness. I needed to learn to treat my inner self with as much compassion as I would treat a kid who was feeling equally lost. As Mexican shaman and author Don Miguel Ruiz said, "The real you is still a little child who never grew up." German philosopher Friedrich Nietzsche believed "in every real man a child is hidden that wants to play." No child blossoms in an unstable abusive environment, and our inner children do not, either.

This quarter-life crisis was causing me to discover things about my biological hardware that were changing my thinking forever. A silver lining was quickly emerging from my fall to rock bottom.

Unless we take a nurturing, caring EMOTIONAL approach to reprogramming our minds, we will continue to play the WFML radio station and react in extremes to rejection, anxiety, and stress, in all situations. I was yelling at my brain, rather than negotiating with it, and I was finally getting the fact that I needed more than a glue stick and some social media "likes" to hold myself together.

There was only one way forward: I had to ask my ANTs to find a new nest, teach Regina to be less mean, switch radio stations to WCHL, upgrade to smarter software, and put myself back together with the Gorilla Glue of self-acceptance, awareness, challenging beliefs, and having faith that I could break the habit of toxic thoughts. If I was ever going to live a life of fullness, I needed to learn to loosen up and become a more nurturing and flexible thinker. Science showed me this was possible after all. My brain was plastic; I needed to bend and stretch it into a shape it hadn't been before.

The Three Golden Mantras to Put on Your Mirror

Through the power of education and openness, I learned that my faulty core beliefs were causing the vast majority of the problems in my life. I hadn't even realized I was so prone to get stuck in negativity until I'd dug into the science. All I knew was that I was unhappy and overwhelmed. Now that I understood how brain biases, ANTs conditioning, and faulty coping strategies triggered my emotional chaos, I could get to work on healing my wounds and working on health (in mind and body) in a meaningful way.

As bizarre as it sounds, I am grateful for the many days I spent in bed feeling broken with a tear-stained pillowcase. But I don't believe that I, or any of us, should dwell at rock bottom for one second longer than we need to. Learning brought me back. My education about the brain was the light that entered my life and took away the dark. During my period of intense self-teaching, I kept going back to three liberating, simple ideas that would, in the coming years, flip my life, career, and mindset upside down.

I've stuck these golden reminders on my mirror and fridge to ensure I'm reminded the moment I wake up, go to sleep, and every time I fetch the milk. Just by glancing at them, spirals are stopped in their tracks.

1. **Thoughts are not facts, be kind.**
   Our brains lie to us constantly. My bitchy Regina had whispered "wrongs" and made me look and create problems where none existed.

2. **Mental flexibility eases fears.**
   We're all dealing with constant anxiety and negativity, the biases that we were born to think and feel, and the faulty beliefs we learned along the way. The one strategy that eases deeply rooted thought patterns that trigger anxiety is *flexibility*, being able to bend, reframe, and challenge, and to see oneself and the world with a new perspective.

3. **Our brains need updating.**
   You know how Apple often sends those reminders to "update your software" that we ignore forever and then suddenly our laptop or phone starts to slow down? When it basically stops working, we THEN realize, *Oh, it's because I haven't installed that latest update.* We finally update and, as if by magic, our devices get back up to running at full speed.

Our brains are crying out for us to update the systems that were installed by evolution and our individual childhoods. I learned workaholism, emotional avoidance, and a habit of overreacting in childhood as a way to survive. I learned the belief that perfection equaled love and safety without rejection and built my work-addicted life around it. The notification that I was desperately in need of an update came from my body in the form of chronic exhaustion and burnout. I received this notification and swiped it away. I was the champion of ignoring notifications. Finding out my brain was to blame for my health crash was the rocket I needed to figure out how to reprogram my brain biases and conditioning.

My post-burnout research was just the beginning of my education. I swapped talking to cute boys for sliding into the DMs of neuroscientists. I created the *Not Perfect* podcast so I could interview and learn from experts further and share these conversations with anyone else who might want to cultivate a kinder mind. Over the past few years, I've now met an incredibly wonderful, weird, brilliant tea party of Mad Hatters whose work has reformed my entire way of living. With the help of many of these great thinkers and researchers, I've been able to more than just recover, but actually upgrade my mind and replace stuck-in-a-rut thinking with flexible approaches. In Parts Two and Three, we'll get deeper into how you can, too.

Being flexible is about allowing yourself to be human.

Fundamentally, we're all the same. We're trying to satisfy the same need for love and belonging, and we're all vulnerable to the same fear of rejection and loneliness. As much as we learn how to find love and soothe fear, we will still have to learn more, and more. Fortunately, as T. H. White once wrote, "Learn why the world wags, and what wags it. That is the only thing which the mind can never exhaust, never alienate, never be tortured by, never fear or distrust, and never dream of regretting."

In this lifelong learning process of being alive, every human is going to get bruised along the way. How flexible we are about navigating unexpected blows determines how badly we hurt and how quickly we heal. Ironically, what we often do to protect ourselves from getting hurt—being rigid, robotic, and avoiding—can cause the most pain.

I started my journey as an unforgiving workaholic desperately trying to be perfect and craving acceptance to feel like I mattered or had any significance.

Now I'm a woman who can finally appreciate herself, embrace a full emotional life without feeling controlled by it, and have the confidence to be proud of who she is. A video call with my investors used to throw me into spirals or a guy not texting me back would trigger hateful thoughts, but this doesn't happen anymore. When anxiety starts to rise, I've learned to pause and connect with myself. Choosing to stay connected to my authentic unconditioned wild side means I stay in tune with my truth. I can now challenge any mean thoughts and bat them away, allowing me to hold my ground without needing to shrink into a corner or beat myself up in the shadows.

This major upgrade didn't happen overnight. But it continues to happen, and my life has opened up in ways I never thought possible before I learned to be emotionally flexible. The whole process started with a desire to learn and a commitment to change, once I believed change was possible. And I learned the only person who could transform my life was me. Just like someone couldn't go to the gym and do my sit-ups for me, alas, I had to work out my mind myself.

The only thing anyone can do for you is open you up to new perspectives and understandings. By sharing my story and introducing you to the plethora of experts who inspired me, I hope you'll feel less alone. I hope you'll see you're not crazy and that you don't have to feel you're "not enough" anymore. Trust me, you're more than enough.

PART TWO

FLEX YOUR LIFE

"THE MEASURE OF
INTELLIGENCE IS THE
ABILITY TO CHANGE."

—ALBERT EINSTEIN

chapter four

WHAT IS FLEXIBLE THINKING?

At the start of my recovery, one of my mentors sat me down to share a life metaphor that I think about often. "Life is like a tower bell, always swinging left and right with the inevitable ups and downs that happen. Most people spend their life clinging on in fear as they are thrown from one side to another." *Well, at least I have company in this,* I thought. "But there is another way to move through life," she continued. "You can learn to climb the ropes and sit on top of the bell. The bell still swings. The ups and downs still happen but you don't need to move with them, you can remain centered."

Not being whacked daily seemed like a fantasy to me. I had no idea how I would ever *not* be affected by emotional swings.

For me to find wholeness, I needed an approach that was easily adaptable and could work across all my issues *and* be accommodating enough to help me no matter what the situation. Something flexible.

No question, I had a serious problem: chronic stress, an overabundance of negative thoughts, a miserable outlook, and the resulting health crisis. This problem is not just mine, of course. It's epidemic among the people of the Anxious Generation, and so many others. We're all awash in anxiety, with good reason, internally and externally. I'd been trapped by mine for too long and was on a determined mission to reprogram this toxic mindset.

Through my research, I came to learn that THERE IS A SOLUTION. We can liberate ourselves using biohacks and proven techniques to get out of the mental cage of dread, doubt, and insecurities.

If we want to wake up every day full of fear, covered in ANTs, and thirsting for a sense of belonging that always feels out of reach, we can just keep existing as we have.

But if we want freedom from fear, the confidence to challenge negativity and turn it into positivity, and to finally feel loved and accepted from within (the only place it really matters), we need to stretch our minds and exist in a brighter world, lit up from within.

I've named this approach to stretching our mind—the Flex. It grew from the things that tangibly aided my recovery as well as insights from coaches, mentors, and the hundreds of people I've since work-shopped it with.

The Flex is about turning stiff thoughts into flexible ones. It's essentially a system upgrade that fixes the bugs of self-blame, anxiety, perfectionism, the disease to please, and avoidance. It helped me find wholeness, peace, and freedom from my past—and now, by sharing it, it's yours.

It's a model designed to help you become your best self by allowing emotions to flow but not being bowled over by them.

Flexing takes mindfulness to the next step. I agree with Dr. Rick Hanson, who said, "Mindfulness is the training you do off the field that makes you perform well during the game." No question, nonnegotiable "off field" meditation, tapping, yoga, breathwork, and sound baths will keep us in WCHL with our parasympathetic nervous system activated, making the game of life A LOT easier. BUT. How can we raise our game and change the way we play, forever? Neural rewiring.

Um, what? Neural rewiring means turning down the volume on old shitty thoughts that keep us stuck in holes. It does NOT mean that we become a completely different person with a whole new personality. The Flex is not a brain transplant! It's a technique that helps upgrade our individual thinking so we can enjoy stronger mental, emotional, and physical health.

I'm very much in the ongoing process of challenging my negative thoughts and resisting the lie that perfection equals happiness, but Flexing has made everything in my life feel a bit easier. It's been strange, but good strange. I feel more in control of my emotions minute-to-minute and day-by-day than ever before. My thoughts feel constructive, instead of destructive. Tense conversations don't trigger panic and doubt. My relationships feel more relaxed. My mind has become a nicer place to be.

My personality hasn't changed; I still love pushing myself to operate at my best, taking on challenges and making stuff happen. I'm still me, only bendier and with A LOT kinder voice inside. Had I not started Flexing, I *definitely* wouldn't have had the confidence or strength to return to the corporate hustle and bustle, try dating again, launch my podcast, or write this book. It's been my rescue plane and has had me flying ever since.

Don't get me wrong: The Flex is not a one-and-done. It's not like you can do it for a day and all your problems will disappear. I still have unhealthy thoughts and notice the occasional backslide into old habits. But fear doesn't rule my life anymore because I know a method to overcome it.

The Flex mind upgrade is available right now, right here. This is your notification. The only person who can hit download for you is you. Just like you can't hire someone else to do squats for you, that peachy bottom is created by you only, and so are your brand-new thoughts!

Bend Your Mind

The Flex is based on the concept of psychological flexibility, defined as "the ability to stay in contact with the present moment regardless of unpleasant thoughts, feelings, and bodily sensations, while choosing one's behaviors based on the situation and personal values."[15] I first heard about psychological flexibility from the work of clinical psychologist Steven C. Hayes, PhD, the codeveloper of Acceptance and Commitment Therapy (ACT), a highly effective psychotherapy for anxiety and depression.[16]

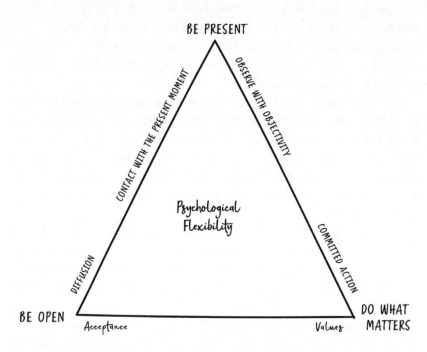

BE PRESENT

OBSERVE WITH OBJECTIVITY

CONTACT WITH THE PRESENT MOMENT

Psychological
Flexibility

COMMITTED ACTION

DIFFUSION

BE OPEN

Acceptance

Values

DO WHAT
MATTERS

Be present, be open, and do what matters. #flexinspo #nothingfancy

Dr. Hayes's teachings have us *bend* with our negative emotions, not deny them. I *loved* this idea of bending thoughts like "not good enough," "people hate me," or "I'm a fat, ugly loser" rather than forcing myself to push through them with "grit."

I was getting tired (and sick) from trying to be gritty all the time. I pressured myself to bounce back when I was still walking wounded. Resilience training gives me horrible flashbacks to Barry's Bootcamp classes, being completely out of breath, hair frizzing, face beet red, muscles burning, and the instructor screaming, "Keep running!" You are so wary of being the only one in the class wanting to stop and crawl, that despite feeling like you're about to collapse, you carry on. Urgh, my worst.

Pre-Flex, my whole life was like bootcamp; my brain screamed, "Ignore the pain! Don't give up!" And I didn't. But ignoring pain does not make it go away. It only makes it worse. I'll repeat that for my stiff-upper-lip readers:

Ignoring pain does not make it go away. It makes it worse.

We need a new strategy and an exit from bootcamp life. The mentality of pushing ourselves to the breaking point *because that's just how it's done*, is making us chronically sick and miserable. There's a better alternative: living life flexibly! Going through life knowing how to bend is not about seeing things as black or white but exploring gray areas. It's about listening to our bodies, making mini pivots to enable us to shimmy out of tight spots, and consciously choosing to step away from fear. Of course, hardships happen, and we all have to keep moving when we'd rather curl into the fetal position on our beds. But rather than gritting through it with *Terminator*-style determination, or feeling frozen like a bunny in headlights, being flexible is about acknowledging difficulty, and then allowing ourselves to think differently. It's about becoming a thought gymnast where an obstacle is never a block but an opportunity to leap-frog over.

Our culture tells us to be driven and relentless. Psychological flexibility, on the other hand, gives us the permission to slow down, be kind and compassionate to ourselves, knowing that by doing so, we'll always find a better way forward. Just because we can eke out the energy to "KEEP RUNNING!!" doesn't mean we always should. Squeezing today's energy is just stealing tomorrow's, after all.

Flexi-thoughts are considerate, challenging, accepting, curious, and motivating, like, "How do I feel right now?" "It's fine to feel that way." "Why do I feel like this?" "What can I learn here?" Bendiness of mind begins the moment we become aware of the chatter going on inside and remember that thoughts are transient. They come and go and can be stretched in a million directions. A key aspect of bending the mind is what's called "critical thinking." Critical thinking is how scientists approach a problem, by trying to see it from every angle and imagining multiple possibilities.

Rigid thoughts on the other hand are critical in the worst way — stuck with one point of view that's usually belittling, demanding, and energy sucking. They lay down the law, as in, "This is how I've always done it, so I'm going to keep doing it the same way, even if it hurts and

I'm struggling." Stiffness of mind is having a fixed outlook—"I *knew* it was going to be like this"—that doesn't grow and change, and never asks, "Why?" or "What's this based on?" As Karen R. Hurd, nutritionist and author of *And They Said It Wasn't Possible: True Stories of People Who Were Healed from the Impossible* writes, "When a battle plan is failing, we shouldn't say, 'I'll try again, but I'll try harder this time' but instead 'Go back to the drawing board and formulate a new battle plan. And if that one fails, formulate yet another battle plan.'"

Stiff Thoughts	Flexi-Thoughts
Ignore the pain and it'll go away.	I'm hurting today. Where is the pain and what is it trying to tell me?
I can't do it.	I'm frustrated, which happens in life. Before I jump to conclusions, I am going to gather more information and change my energy.
Everyone hates me.	I'm feeling a bit insecure right now, which seems to happen at parties. What about this situation makes me doubt myself? Has anyone done anything to prove my doubts are real?
It's always going to be like this.	I'm feeling defeated about the future, which is normal and okay. What can I do in this moment that will make me feel more optimistic about what's to come?

One of my bendy inspirational heroes (totally intellectually crushed on this one) is theoretical physicist Leonard Mlodinow, PhD, author of *Elastic: Flexible Thinking in a Time of Change* (he's written books with Deepak Chopra and Stephen Hawking…#idols!). He was the one who introduced me to the term "elastic mind." In an interview in *Scientific American*, he summed up what it means to have Flexi-thoughts perfectly: "We *have* to be willing to rise above conventional mindsets, to reframe the questions we ask, to be open to new paradigms. We have to rely as much on our imagination as on logic, and have the ability to generate and integrate a wide variety of ideas, to welcome experiment, and be tolerant of failure. I call that manner of thought elastic thinking, in contrast to rational or logical thought."[17]

HELL-YEH! I wanted ELASTIC to be my default way of thinking, a way that sits in the intersection of curiosity, openness, imagination, and the desire to rise above the conventional. The best part about mental elasticity is that we ALL possess the squishy neuroplastic biology to unleash this human superpower of being better narrators to our lives. So, how can we all unlock this inner superpower? "Recognize the needed skills, and nurture them," Dr. Mlodinow wrote.

I made a quick list of Flexi-skills: learning, dreaming, adapting, seeking outside-the-box solutions to conventional problems, challenging old ways of thinking. It is only when we make thinking differently our focus that we can move forward in technology, architecture, business, and the arts. We'd have no lightbulb if Edison wasn't willing to stretch his imagination and consider an entirely new way of creating light.

It makes perfect sense: The most successful individuals are those who continuously bend their minds to meet new problems. The pandemic was a great example of how inventive, flexible people, almost instantly pivoted to make face masks fashionable and figured out how to social distance date. They found lockdown easier than those who got stuck mourning the old world. Mlodinow uses the example of Blockbuster vs. Netflix. Blockbuster remained stuck in its ways and didn't bend with the moving trends, and look what happened. Netflix, on the other hand, was as flexible as a splitting gymnast, harnessed the rapidly moving tech developments, introduced us to streaming and bingeing, and changed the way we consume content forever. Elasticity of thought helped us survive in caveman times and it's at the heart of entrepreneurship; flex or die.

The route to a happier, healthier, enjoyable life is to remain elastic.

Most of us spend our days locked in default autopilot mode, repeating the same battle plans. We barely think which roads we are taking when we're driving because we've become so comfortable in the "way we do things." It takes effort to think, and our lazy minds prefer to replay historical action patterns, even if it does lead to old circular arguments in relationships, the same mistakes at work, and the same reactions to triggers. When we don't take time to *stretch*, we stay stuck recycling and repeating. *Atomic Habits* author James Clear wrote, "The first mistake is never the one that ruins you. It is the spiral of repeated mistakes that follows. Missing once is an accident. Missing twice is the start of a new habit." The Flex helps prevent this from happening.

Reset the Mind

It's one thing to *know about* Flexi-thoughts, it's another to *have* Flexi-thoughts. To make the shift, I needed to understand how our brains learn habits. I turned to one of my other flexible mind #inspos, Judson Brewer, MD, PhD, author of *The Craving Mind*. On my podcast, he described the process of new habit formation with the words "set and forget." "We like to learn skills and then push them into our unconscious minds to free up space in our conscious mind," he said. For example, we learn how to walk, it becomes a habit, and then we forget it consciously to free us up to ponder other things. Our clever brains are very efficient like this. They want us to be able to do two things at once, like solve the world's problems (consciously) while washing our hair (unconsciously).

"Set and forget" is not always so fabulous. I have many friends who react to any stress by lighting a cigarette and chain smoking five without thinking. When I'm stressed, I devour everything and anything in my fridge without even realizing until it's all gone. This is an example of unhealthy autohabit mode and the reason why nutritionists advise not eating in front of the TV to prevent unconsciously consuming double what we need.

Fortunately, we can override these habits by using the same brain chemistry to set and forget new, more *beneficial* ones. As psychologist and creator of Emotional Mastery Joan Rosenberg, PhD, said, "Live a life by design, not default." Rather than sleepwalking (and eating) through life, when we consciously decide to wake up to our autopilot patterns, we can choose to bend and shift them. All the process requires is a lot of repetition.

As we reset our brains with new healthier thought habits via the Flex, expect some internal conflict. Our emotional monkey mind won't want to give up the run of the place so easily. But as we learn to silence our internal alarm system, the monkey will simmer down. After learning the basics of neural rewiring, I knew I needed a method I could repeat endlessly to help me "set and forget" this new flexible style of thinking.

Flexercise: Reset the Mind

Awareness is everything, truly. As you learn about flexible thinking, it's crucial to clue into all the ways you've been stuck. So, below, list three habits you've set-and-forgotten that you would like to reset into better ones. (Mine are looking at Instagram first thing in the morning and when I'm bored, saying "I'm sorry" when I have nothing to apologize for, and eating when I'm stressed.)

1. _____

2. _____

3. _____

Unlock the Mind

Brilliant thought leader and psychologist Tara Brach, PhD, wrote[18] a story about an endangered tiger that was rescued from a tiny cage and moved into a great big park with endless places for him to wander and explore. But when the tiger arrived, despite the vast open land in front of him, he continued to pace a patch of grass the size of his cage until that stretch of grass wore down to dirt. Dr. Brach compares our minds to this tiger. Despite the freedom awaiting all of us, we pace in cages formed by our default settings and conditioning.

The greatest skill we can all learn is how to control the part of our minds that will *never* make good decisions or have the courage to unlock the cage—the part that is terrified of pain and suffering. Living in fear is a cage. We are so scared of what's out there or if it will make us feel bad that we learn to avoid anything that doesn't feel good. We make ourselves believe we don't want things, when actually, all we really want is what we're denying.

I've heard myself say, "I don't want a relationship" when I *very much* wanted one.

When participants in workshops have told me, "I don't like people, I prefer being by myself," I didn't believe they were speaking truthfully because they'd come to a group session that advertised itself as a way to have fun and meet new people. Now, there are certainly those in the world who really don't want a relationship. I only said that in the past because I was terrified of rejection and this was a preemptive way to protect myself. We make outlandish statements to avoid feeling vulnerable about having very normal, natural human desires to be accepted and embraced by a group.

Avoidance doesn't get rid of bad feelings, however. It just delays the inevitable. Sooner or later, the fear catches up.

Fear is a nonnegotiable in this life, as is joy. Every one of us has wounds, fears, troubles, things that keep us locked in a protective cage. How wounds affect our behavior defines our humanity. We are so much better at compassionately understanding other people's battles, but forget to be kind about our own. The bitchy inner voice would much rather keep us locked up in fear than risking love and connection. When we flex by exploring our feelings instead of avoiding them, the cage door has a chance to open.

We will continue to live in fear until we do something about it. It's our job to uncage our own minds.

Living life open to peace, harmony, love, and great surprises doesn't just happen. No one just magically wakes up without insecurities and shame. But when we consciously and repeatedly override the bitchy negative voice in our heads by the power of flexible thinking—connecting to ourselves, challenging negative thoughts, making the choice to be compassionate, and committing to actions aligned with our values—freedom awaits.

Waiting for these negative thought loops to disappear is wishful thinking, not flexible thinking.

Annoyingly, our parents were right when they said, "Working for something is so much more satisfying than it just being handed to you." Science has proven that actually not getting what we want straightaway has a greater impact on our long-lasting happiness levels. It's an odd paradox: Life's challenges have the capability to actually make us *happier* in the end.

When we start to broaden our perspective beyond the confines of our conditioning and fears, we realize the endless possibilities that await. The fact that you're reading this book shows that you're curious and courageous and ready to open your own cage of habitual thoughts and behaviors so you can explore the luscious great, green world.

Flexercise: Unlock the Mind

I lived in a cage of perfectionism, workaholism, and anxiety that I refused to leave because I thought that I would find happiness in there. But once I left that mind prison by Flexing my thoughts and changing my behavior, I have been able to escape into a much kinder, happier world.

How have you imprisoned yourself? What faulty thinking habits have you been stuck in? List three ways you'd like to unlock your mind. For example, I wanted to feel more relaxed and in control of my emotions, value myself, and raise my confidence.

1. _____

2. _____

3. _____

Okay, so we've warmed up with larger concepts around having an elastic mind. Next up, a step-by-step breakdown of putting flexible psychology into practice.

The Flex has four steps: **Connection, Curiosity, Choice,** and **Commitment**.

Each of the four C's (they're easier to remember that way) will stretch the mind. In combination, they become a beautiful thought dance of life. The more you do the steps, the more limber and flexible you'll become.

My mum and I talked about the most impactful way to learn the Flex, and we agreed that each step really needs several days of focused mindful attention and repetition on its own, and then, once we're really good at each one individually, we can combine them for exponential impact.

This approach makes intuitive and practical sense to me. It's been my experience as a dancer—amateur but enthusiastic!—that I learn a routine better when I do one step over and over again until I've got it down cold. And then the next step, and so on. Once each step has been practiced enough that I can do it from muscle memory, I can combine them. Any combination, in any order. The point is, we need to learn each step very well first. And then we can build on those basics to choreograph a Flexi-dance that our minds can enjoy moving to. The hope is, we learn these techniques so well, our mind can then start flipping negative thoughts and behaviors on their head automatically without effort. ANTs (automatic negative thoughts) turn into AFTs (automatic flexible thoughts).

So, for the first few days of learning to stretch your mind, you'll focus on **Connection**. During that time, whenever the bitchy inner voice says something that triggers anxiety, practice the step of linking the body and mind (much more detail coming up in the next chapter).

Once you've practiced Step #1 until you "get" it, you can move on to focus on **Curiosity**. Challenge any negative thought that comes up by asking, "Is this even true?" and identify the naughty ANT at play. Overgeneralizing? Fortune-telling? Black and white thinking?

When you're solid at that, move on to **Choice**. When those mean thoughts and derailing emotions happen, continually ask, "What's the flexible choice here?" and train yourself to see all the options, and to most fundamentally pick love over fear, every time.

Finally, focus on the step of **Commitment** to practice compassion and search for the hidden gifts in all experiences (even the seemingly bad ones).

Just by doing the individual steps, one by one, your mind will start to limber up and stretch away from the anxiety that's trapped you. Once you've developed these new skills enough to start combining them…you'll be dancing through life to a much better soundtrack.

With the Flex Upgrade, You Can…

Build confidence

Stop anxiety

Call BS on bogus thoughts

Break old, destructive patterns

Respond rather than react

Gain wisdom about yourself and others

Tap into your inner guidance system

Support your immune system

Change brain chemistry

Create new neural pathways

Change how you think of yourself

Make smart decisions

Move toward wholeness

Get that "hug in a mug" feeling of being at peace with yourself

Reframe thoughts with compassion

Shift toward value-based action away from fear-based action

Handle uncomfortable situations with clarity

Energize positivity to raise your vibe

Forgive to release the grip of old hurts

Broaden your perspective on your past

Improve relationships

Be nicer to yourself

Drop the victim act

Live life with an open heart

"THE ONLY WAY TO MAKE SENSE OUT OF CHANGE IS TO PLUNGE INTO IT, MOVE WITH IT, AND JOIN THE DANCE."

—ALAN WATTS

chapter five

CONNECTION

Step #1 of the Flex is Connection. For the next three days, whenever a triggering thought or feeling pops up, practice:

Connecting with the brain and body.

Connecting to yourself via movement.

Connecting with a higher vibrational energy.

If there is nothing else you take away from this book aside from this step I'll be over the moon. This step changed my life. I found it near to impossible just to "think" my way out of a problem, or "think" my way into a new mindset or healthier thought pattern. What changed everything for me was welcoming back my body to the conversation. The Flex technique starts by connecting to your body and harnessing the power of movement to instantly upgrade your energy. It is truly the best thing I've ever started doing.

I'd been chronically disconnected from my body and real feelings in my pre-Flex life. I lived a highly stiff life of GO GO GO as a means to distract myself from what was really going on inside. When I felt triggered by a casual criticism or feeling of unworthiness, my brain sounded the alarms, my bitchy inner critic started getting louder, and I began spiraling. Right on cue, cortisol released, my breath got shorter, and my mind was like a fireworks display of potential threats I tried to manage, badly. I'd panic, or snap, or freeze up completely.

In this moment, it doesn't matter what I did or said to myself or what someone else tried to tell me. I'd gone to war with my thoughts and feelings and would fly blindly into overreaction. My monkey mind tricked me into believing that doing something was better than nothing.

P.S.: I've learned this is completely normal. When the monkey mind is in charge, our badass CEO goes offline. Only when we switch back to WCHL can our rational mind come back online and create new solutions.

Between any trigger and reaction, I never took a pause but instead let my monkey mind respond frantically.

I'm not alone in this. Many of us ignore scary, upsetting feelings and "power on through" using avoidance and suppression to do it. Many of us can't sit with our feelings or connect with ourselves for fear of what we'll find. Connection might require us to feel vulnerable, and that is terrifying. Culturally, we've been conditioned to believe that emotionality and vulnerability are not welcome in the workplace. I for one have been terrified of displaying emotions at work and in relationships for fear of being labeled as "that emotional woman."

But we've understood them so wrong! Emotions are not a nuisance but a sign that we're alive! They exist for a reason, to send us messages about what we need to pay attention to. Feeling and expressing ALL emotions needs a rebrand. Why should it be so horrifying or annoying to feel? Attempting to control our mad-sad-scared emotions has them controlling us. The bendy approach is to *surrender* to an emotion as it comes, to give in to it and accept its presence. When we're not fighting a feeling, we ironically allow it to pass quicker and, in the process, create the silence and space to hear its message.

Having feelings is not the problem. The problem is that we just haven't been taught how to welcome, process, or communicate—to connect with—our emotions effectively. Without that mastery, they run rampant and can get us into trouble.

Sync Our Brains

Nothing can change unless our body and mind are playing on the same team. For most of us, our body goes left and our mind goes right because, instead of listening to our body, we try to detach from it. This tug-of-war isn't *just* due to having a rigid mind about the way things are. There have been many times I've found myself upset, and did everything I could to not open the tear gates. I might have been temporarily successful but in actuality, I'd locked the emotion inside to fester.

Stiff thinking says, "I'm in control!" setting off a mind-body battle. The resulting chronic anxiety, insomnia, weight gain, bloat, and other stress-related conditions and diseases prove that, in fact, we are not in control at all. The mind doesn't "win." The surest way to "lose" is to foster disconnect between our minds and bodies.

Flexible thinking requires our mind and body to work together toward wholeness. It begins with becoming aware of what our clever bodies are saying first, so we can self-diagnose. It might be something as simple as acknowledging that our body is exhausted and needs to turn in early, instead of pushing ourselves to stay up working or partying. Imagine what life would be like if we trusted what our body was trying to tell us. The first step of the Flex connects physical sensations with emotions, accepting what is happening in the moment and giving ourselves permission to feel.

Healing doesn't happen when our head goes in one direction and our body goes in another.

To make the mind-body connection, we have to sync up the body's four emotional centers, the "four brains." The brain in our head is just our First Brain. What are the others?

The Second Brain is our gut. The gut and brain are linked via thirty neurotransmitters, including serotonin, the happy hormone. Ninety-five percent of the body's serotonin is produced in our bowels. Five hundred million neurons connect the brain and the gut, including the truly amazing vagus nerve, which runs from one to the other, and sends feedback back and forth. Our immune system and physical wellness are gut-reliant for absorbing antioxidants and fighting bacteria. Studies have found that GI problems like irritable bowel syndrome can be improved by psychotherapy. We know intuitively, and research shows, that the gut affects emotion, and vice versa. When we feel nervous, we get butter-flies in our stomach. Our guts sink when we have a hit of sudden insight. The gut send us messages all the time, **and we need to start listening to them.**

The Third Brain is our heart. Don't roll your eyes when someone says, "What does your heart say?" I used to think that was another #selfhelp mumbo jumbo question, too. Aristotle believed the heart was the center of reason, thought, and emotion, and even more important than the brain. We can all hear it beating out signals at least sixty or seventy times every minute of every day. It races when we're afraid or in love. It aches when we're suffering and in pain. Dr. Frankenstein gloried in the fact that the heart continues beating after it's removed from the body due to its own electrical pulses. It produces oxytocin, the love and bonding hormone, even more than the brain.[19] When we feel joy, contentment, and other positive emotions, our heart rhythms get stronger. But when we're chronically angry, we're at greater risk for coronary heart disease.[20] The brain and heart are in constant communication energetically and through nerves and chemicals, and when we start tuning into our life beat, we're further reminded how important it is for us to proactively create higher vibrational emotions to keep this brain healthy. When we hold on to resentment and regret, our heart suffers.

The Fourth Brain is our musculature. When our shoulder muscles clamp down, that is another message of stress and anxiety that needs to be heard. Our body keeps the score in our tight trapezius. Stiff thinking contributes to our stiff necks.

We need to connect our four brains so they can function like teammates. Teams are stronger than individuals. If one is having an off day, the others will step up. By allowing our four brains to work together, we are open to receiving critical intel about our emotional reactions (the opposite of avoidance and suppressing). The body doesn't lie, the mind does. When we use our body's wisdom and regularly tap into our inner guidance system, suddenly answers to questions:

Should I take this job?

Is this the way forward?

Why do I feel anxious?

Am I doing it right?

What next?

How should I feel about this?

Become a great deal clearer.

Most of us have stopped listening to anything other than our bitchy inner voice, and through our mind-body disconnection, we're denying ourselves access to wisdom from multiple sources of excellent intel.

Flexercise: Sync Our Brains

Linking our four brains is like syncing your phone, laptop, tablet, and desktop. We function better when we can access all our info from various devices. To sync your four brains, listen to what they're saying and reach a consensus.

Practice this for the next three days whenever you have to make a decision or feel unsettled by asking, "What are my four brains telling me *right now*?"

Close your eyes and tune in. Picture your brain, gut, heart, and muscles and search each for sensations and clues. Describe whatever you can pick up.

I recently started dating this guy and left confused. Here's how I practiced connecting with my four brains to find clarity in the confusion.

First Brain (head) signal: *He is great on paper. He's nice-looking, he is intelligent, he has a job, and he's sweet.*
Second Brain (gut) signal: *Not into this. Stomach is flat.*

Third Brain (heart) signal: *Yearning for love and romantic attention.*
Fourth Brain (muscles) signal: *Shoulders and back stiff.*

I had the mind-body feeling that it wasn't right, and thank God I didn't just listen to my first brain. My Second Brain and Fourth Brain KNEW he was not my one. Prior to Flex life, I would have shut off the signals to the other brains and now, I trust them more. Time saved, feelings saved, and greater clarity about what I really want gained.

....

Pump up the volume of your body's messaging by relaxing. *Elastic* author Dr. Mlodinow said, "When your mind is relaxed, you can play with the idea of a new paradigm. You're not worried about why your ideas might be wrong. You're not worried about failure. You can experiment. Your mind can wander to new territory, and stumble upon novel ideas, and new ways of looking at a thing." He recommends physical activity that's mild enough to let your mind wander as it can bring on inventive, stretchy thoughts that might not otherwise bubble into consciousness. When we're relaxed, we're in "I'm safe" mode, and our brain's antennae are open to tap into our internal guidance system and receive wisdom from our multiple body brains. But when we're in "Fuck, I'm in danger!" mode, the lines are cut. No wisdom or useful idea has space to enter.

In child psychology, behavioral experts use the phrase "connection before correction." Before they can give a child feedback on how to change a behavior, they have to get down on the child's level and connect with them through eye contact or a soft voice first. Screaming at a child after they've done something wrong does not work, for reasons we all know by now. It triggers their fight-or-flight reflex, and they kick into defensive protective mode, effectively shutting down and unable to learn. If you notice a child's pupils widen during a telling-off, that's a sign they're cut off and not receiving anything you are saying. Jane Nelsen, EdD, author of *Positive Discipline*, wrote, "Research shows that we cannot influence children in a positive way until we create a connection with them. It is a brain (and heart) thing. Sometimes we have to stop dealing with the misbehavior and first heal the relationship."[21]

We are no different from children. To be open to listening and learning from ourselves (or anyone else), *we have to feel safe first.* **We can't scream criticism at ourselves and expect that to be positively absorbed; instead the opposite occurs and we trigger more stress and undesirable reactive behavior.** I found safety in the idea that any message from my four brains is only information. It's not a judgment of my character or self-esteem. When my stomach roils with doubts after a podcast interview, rather than fire an insult like "I suck," causing WFML to blare loudly, I practice connecting with myself to calm my stress response first. With a deregulated nervous system and WCHL playing, I am able to explore where there is "opportunity for improvements" in a constructive way. Connection is creating a state of safety for learning, growth, and flexibility to occur, allowing positive behavior to happen.

I'm gradually getting better at finding four-brain consensus instead of just zooming straight into fear-based WFML reactiveness, sparking self-blame, self-punishment, or self-criticism, where nothing good happens.

Accept and Connect

The very idea of acceptance used to make me feel deeply uncomfortable. I was horrible at accepting anything and excellent at shoving my feelings into the cupboard. At the smallest glimpse of emotional pain, I'd kick into busy mode. Busy *working, doing things, catching up with Margaret, Jenny, and Sammy, checking Instagram, writing DMs. God forbid I missed Cherry's latest #OOTD post, or she would think I hated her.* Shudder.

I believe we are a nation of professional-level emotional suppressors, and that avoidance is as epidemic as anxiety and stress. As soon as we feel anything other than *good*, we do anything/everything to lower the volume on the fire alarm inside and push down uncomfortable feels. The Internet is an all-too-accessible distraction from unpleasant emotions.

If suppression worked long term, I'd be fine with it. But emotions don't just disappear because we refuse to accept them. HNP adviser and life coach Angelika Alana once said, "Most people try to squeeze their uncomfortable thoughts into a wardrobe for so long, thinking they are keeping that room tidy, but when it's one rubber ducky too much, the entire wardrobe explodes."

My one-rubber-ducky-over-the-line emotional outbursts have left me in unnecessarily sticky situations.

There was this coworker.

He haunted my dreams at night and made my days a living nightmare. I felt undermined by him constantly. He'd try to turn colleagues against me and made hostile, gendered comments about how "irrational" and "unprofessional" I was behind my back. I had no choice but to suppress my anger and irritation because he had more power than I did, so "Just live with it" seemed like the easiest option.

With so many big feelings pushed down, I turned into a steaming jack-in-the-box, ready at any moment to *pop*. He sent me a humiliating email and cc'ed all the higher-ups. I read it and flipped without drawing a breath. *HOW FUCKING DARE HE SAY THAT! HE'S LYING!* In a hot blind rage, I furiously typed a high-octane reply. Like a child, if anyone had tried to talk to me in that moment, I wouldn't have heard one word. All I could think was, *I have to clear my name!* It felt like my identity, my integrity, years of work, were being threatened. Without even reading over my email, I smashed the send button.

Approximately two minutes later, the inevitable happened.

Yep, I got called into the boss's office and was given a talking-to about my attitude. My rage shifted to regret, and I realized that I'd fallen right into the little weasel's trap. I'd proven him right that I really was an "unhinged woman" when my goal was to prove him wrong. I was *mortified*.

Without connecting to my inner guidance system, my response to uncomfortable feelings was often bigger than the circumstances called for, but I was too busy to notice. According to my friend, human connection specialist and Create the Love podcaster Mark Groves, if something *really* sets us off, it's probably not about what's happening in the moment. But rather it's tweaking an unhealed, throbbing old wound from the past. The stronger the (over)reaction, the bigger the clue that it goes DEEP.

It's as true as day. How could one email make me react so extremely? Because it wasn't *really* about the email. It wasn't even about the weasel's bullying. His email triggered my oldest, deepest wound, the feeling of not being good enough. Public criticism prodded my buried, unaddressed pain.

If I'd just taken a second to *connect* with my feelings, they wouldn't have needed to explode out of me. I did not want to embarrass myself to everyone I cc'ed on that email. But in the moment, I wasn't thinking tactically. I was only seeing red. I was playing the WFML station and the "heavy metal" was deafening me to any sense.

To avoid suffering, I suppressed.

Because I suppressed, I disconnected.

Because I disconnected, I was without wisdom.

Without wisdom, I exploded.

By exploding, I suffered.

Repeat. Repeat. Repeat.

Quickie Flexercise: Acceptance

Have you ever gone ballistic, and realized in hindsight that you might've blown things out of proportion? If so, what experience, feeling, or old wound were you trying really hard to ignore? Write it down:

_____

_____

If I'd accepted my fear of not being enough instead of suppressing it with a rage email, the whole cycle wouldn't have rolled over me.

So how to accept instead of suppress? Cracking good question.

Psychologist Joan Rosenberg, PhD, author of *90 Seconds to a Life You Love*, explained the "emotional math" of emotional acceptance to me. We all have eight unpleasant emotions that we try to avoid: **sadness, shame, helplessness, anger, embarrassment, disappointment, frustration,** and **vulnerability**. Those feelings usually start in the Second Brain (the gut) before we perceive them in the First Brain (the mind). Our physical reactions, caused by a surge of hormones, are set off by our monkey mind alarm system. It happens so quickly, we don't even know what we're thinking.

In Dr. Rosenberg's research, she discovered that the physical symptoms of the eight unpleasant emotions only last for ninety seconds. I was shocked to learn this. "I swear I've had emotional thunderstorms that lasted years, not just seconds!" I said to her.

"You were surfing the same ninety-second wave over and over again," she replied. "Every time you replayed the memory of what happened, it triggered the emotional cascade to begin again."

To move *through* a wave rather than get battered by wave-after-wave, Dr. Rosenberg has a reset technique called the Rosenberg Reset. It starts with the key word, **acceptance,** as in, "I accept I am having a wave right now, but it's only going to last ninety seconds. If I can just stay here present with the discomfort for just a short period of time, there will be no tsunami."

The Flexible thought here is to say, "I'm feeling pissed and embarrassed, but it'll only last a minute and a half. I'm just going to ride this out."

To know when the wave has passed, do a brains-system check. Are my cheeks still red? Does my stomach still hurt? Is my heart still beating like crazy? That analytical curiosity isn't a distraction, it's a super tactical and brilliant way to ensure we are connecting with our body and gifting ourselves the pause to stop the knee-jerk react-and-regret response. Dr. Rosenberg kind of changed my life teaching me this ninety-seconds-to-inner-guidance trick.

One of the reasons I fought my feelings for so long was because I feared that if I DIDN'T react right away, I would lose my big chance to be heard and tell my truth, as in "speak now or forever hold your peace." But by jumping in, I attracted my greatest fear. No one listened to my monkeyish responses, even if they made sense, because all they registered was my overreaction and blaring WFML mode. By connecting for a minute and a half to my emotions until they passed, I got insight into what the feeling was really about, and I was able to stop myself from doing further damage.

Emotional arousal is a beautiful part of being human. We'd be robots without it. But flexible thinking allows us to enjoy the benefits of intense feelings, without being their prisoner.

Flexercise: Acceptance Reset

1. When you feel the emotional intensity, locate it in the body.

2. Ask yourself to get specific: Which of the eight painful core emotions was triggered? Sadness, shame, helplessness, anger, embarrassment, disappointment, frustration, and/or vulnerability?

3. Ride the wave for ninety seconds by doing nothing and curtailing any reactions.

4. Try the mantra "I surrender, I surrender, I surrender" while waiting for the wave to recede.

5. When it's passed, ask yourself: What primal fear was pinged? Not enough? Unloved? Unsafe? You're looking for insight, not necessarily an action plan. We don't have to act on every passing feeling. It's enough to let it happen, look at it, listen to it, and let it pass by like a light breeze.

Describe and Connect

In 2007, UCLA researchers[22] used an MRI machine to study the brain activity of participants while showing them pictures of angry, scared, and sad faces. When subjects saw the emotion in the photos, their amygdala region—the monkey—lit up. But when the subjects described the feelings they saw in the pictures, the amygdala activity decreased. Just saying "angry" or "scared" made their brains calm down.

Dr. Rosenberg cited this study to me and explained, "The research shows that putting feelings into words changes how the brain responds. By labeling emotion, this shifts the emotional state into a thinking state. Less activity was found in the amygdala and more activity was found in the thinking part of the brain."

Describing unpleasant emotions actually helps us slow down, process, decrease the cortisol flooding, and prevent impulsivity. The words can be spoken or written. So if we are under a deadline and feeling overwhelmed, screaming or scribbling, "I'm frustrated and upset!" will instantly make us feel less of those things. Identifying and labeling emotion with words dissipates it. I just LOVE when science shows us how the simplest of things can be excellently effective!

The opposite effect is also proven. If we try saying, "I'm not annoyed at all, I don't care about the fact Tom didn't call me back..." or "I'm not angry, I'm totally fine Suzy took the credit from me..." it'll backfire. Denying the pink elephant in the room only makes it bigger and the monkey mind more activated.

On the HNP app, we ask users to do a daily Emotional Check-In and write down how they feel each day to recognize patterns that they need to pay attention to. Why so grumpy in the morning? Why so sad in the evening? It is only when you start the habit of connecting to yourself that you can begin to figure out the *why*.

What we feel is not who we are.

Labeling *ourselves*, instead of our emotion, can be an excuse for bad behavior, or yet another way to practice avoidance. Furthermore, we can fall into a lazy labeling habit. For example, when people say, "I'm an anxious person," Dr. Rosenberg calls it a cover-up for what they are really feeling. A more accurate and useful label is to identify the underlying emotion, like sadness, shame, helplessness, anger, embarrassment, disappointment, frustration, or vulnerability. By saying statements like "I am just an anxious person," we fail to receive the wisdom that the root feeling is trying to give us. Lazy labels like this can become self-fulfilling prophesies that lock us into further negative patterns; our brain is unconsciously being told to search for evidence to confirm our self-labeling statements. It's as if we're giving our brain a shovel to dig an even bigger hole we can't crawl out of.

Having an emotional identity is a hallmark of stiff thinking. Here are some identities you may have adopted that aren't helping:

- **The Martyr** is always suffering for others and getting little in return. "I have done so much for her and she gives me nothing back. I'm done," she said. *Goes to drop off cookies the next day.*

- **The Victim** is always being hurt by others and the world. "I just got so fucked over, this always happens," she says. I clung to the identity that I was a "victim" for a few years and blamed everyone else for my lack of self-esteem. It was true some characters were tough, but by not recognizing my own agency to change, I was stuck in a narrative I had no control over. Emotional identities serve no purpose but make us stuck. As soon as I learned to step away, I could start embracing flexibility.

- **The Blamer** is always in the right and ready to point a finger at everyone else. P.S.: Blamers are usually narcissists who lack self-awareness, so you won't recognize yourself.

- **The Shamer** always takes the blame, judges and criticizes herself to feel better about things. "The relationship ended because I was too needy," she says. P.S.: You weren't needy, you were dating a narcissist.

- **The Pessimist** always thinks things are going wrong and has zero trust that the world will bring him joy. "I don't think it's going to work," he says. "The world is fucked and we're all fucked."

- **The Worrier** always frets to protect himself from further sadness. "I'm just worrying that in ten years, I'll wake up wondering if I made the wrong decision," he says.

I am often happy, but I'm not a "happy person." I'm sad some-times, but I'm not a sad person, either. I'm anxious, but I'm not an anxious person. *I'm just me.* I am a mix-match of chaos, calm, happy, sad, and everything in between.

Since I've started labeling my emotion without the burden of iden-tification, I've noticed how transient emotions are. Without the need to attach myself to one, I feel this uplifting freedom and it's taken away my fear of ever being stuck in a nasty one.

One last brilliant tool to use verbally or in writing that allows us to connect and feel with confidence and control is called "defusing." It comes from Dr. Steven C. Hayes's Acceptance and Commitment Therapy (ACT). It's a super-simple trick I use constantly to cut the fuse on an emo bomb.

Rather than saying "I'm feeling so anxious," defuse with "*Today*, I am feeling anxious." The word "today" further modifies the anxiety or frustra-tion or anger as temporary. We subtly reassure the mind that feeling some-thing *now* doesn't mean *forever.* A time-specific "today" or "right now" qualifier helps lower the volume of our inner critical voice and soothes any hot moment with the reminder that now doesn't mean always.

We can also defuse by depersonalizing the emotion, as in, "Today, *my mind* is feeling anxious." This is another fantastic trick I use all the time. It sounds counterintuitive, but to connect with our feelings, it's critical that we *separate* from them a bit. Some distance allows us to see them better. Dr. Hayes has said, "We cannot prevent the bad or distressing things from happening. We don't need to be a prisoner of these experiences. Keep a healthy distance, not a disassociated dif-ference. You can't appreciate a picture with your nose touching the canvas. By stepping back, you can appreciate and describe it, but not practice avoidance or disassociating."

Putting this in action, recently, I was thinking about texting a boy I fancy and, like clockwork, I felt this whirl of sensation in my belly. It's only natural that I would feel vulnerable about putting out my intention that I liked him, as it hadn't yet been affirmed that he liked me back. But instead of reaching for peanut butter, calling a friend, or stalking his Instagram, I jotted down, "This minute, my mind feels vulnerable." Just by writing it, a weight lifted from my Third Brain (the heart).

Flexercise: Description

Language, spoken or written, is a superpower for connecting with ourselves. With self-expression, we are much more able to manage our emotions. By using mere words, we can mitigate our pain and connect with our inner guidance system. It'd be magic, if it weren't *science*. To dig into how language affects feelings, WRITE DOWN the answers to these questions:

1. What are you feeling right now? _____

2. Do you identify yourself with an emotion? If so, which one? Are you committed to writing off that wisdom-crushing habit? _____

_____

3. What's the defused version of experiencing a negative emotion that you will commit to remembering and using? *(i.e., "Today, my mind is feeling x.")* _____

Energize and Connect

You know how, when the Wi-Fi is bad and your battery is dying, the line cracks and drops in and out? But when you plug in your phone and get a better signal, you say, "Oh, that's MUCH better, I can now hear you perfectly. Go on, what were you saying?"

Now imagine that weak connection is with ourselves. We can't hear the messages clearly if we're energetically low. What I mean by this is when we're surfing those low vibrational waves (shame, fear, or regret as defined on Dr. Hawkins's Scale of Consciousness), we've sometimes barely got energy to get out of bed, let alone force ourselves to think differently. If we energize, however, we have a much better chance at *really* hearing what our internal wisdom is saying and have the *energy* to Flex!

Upgrading your energy is a very important final part of the mind-body connection step. It's the seal on the deal. Without a higher vibration, it's that much harder to make the mental effort to sync up with your body and flex change.

Sometimes, even now, I get knocked off my feet by life, and before I can even say, "Flex, Poppy!" I'm full of ANTs and stuffing emotions in the cupboard because I don't have the energy to deal with them. This usually happens when I'm low on overall energy reserves. A few bad nights' sleep and/or being hangry is a recipe for emotional outbursts. Flexing takes concentration! You can't train for a marathon or reprogram your brain with zero energy.

Thought work requires so much energy because we're creating new neural pathways and often going against what feels normal.

We've developed stuck patterns and dominant neural circuits for reacting to stress. Even if our patterns are unhealthy, they feel safe and comforting because we've been down these circuits so many times before. In a way, our brain likes anxiety, because it's so familiar. New, unfamiliar pathways might be much better for us and bring peace, but our familiar loving human brains will always opt for the known over the unknown. We're creatures of habit, and new habits require energy and repetition to override the old ones.

So. To succeed and make *unfamiliar* neural pathways feel more normal, we need energy! The quickest way to generate fuel to blaze new pathways and overrun default negative caveman brain settings is to move our body! When we activate *our mind and body*, it is 1,000 percent easier to shimmy into healthier thought habits.

Just like Einstein put forth, if we want to *think* differently, we need a different energy creating the thoughts, otherwise we're back to the same patterns. Switching energy states is like throwing a breaker switch on spiraling thoughts. Suddenly, we can stop them in their tracks.

During one raw period of relapse into bad thought habits, I was walking home in New York City, freezing, fingers too cold to type on my phone. I felt like the city was sucking the life out of me. My company was in a financial crisis, and I was terrified we wouldn't be able to pay salaries that month.

Crippled by the thought *I'm letting down my amazing team*, I was hit by wave after wave of physical sensations, chest tightening, sick stomach, muscles tense. As chance would have it, I passed a dance studio called Forward Space. Curious, I peeked inside and discovered they taught hip-hop, pop, styles everyone can do. A class was just starting, so I stripped down to my leggings and a T-shirt and walked into the studio, hiding at the back. Kaiser Chiefs' "I Predict a Riot" started playing, and we began jumping.

It felt like I was dancing for my life. The room was dark so no one could judge my out-of-sync moves, not even myself. I was only able to feel my way through this class and with every jump and kick, tension began to release. Tears started running down my cheeks. The music and the movement seemed to help me shake off the weight of the world I'd been carrying. I felt lighter by the second. By the time "Crazy in Love" came on, my brain wasn't screaming at me anymore and a dose of serotonin and dopamine (happiness hormones) flooded my brain. The class stepped left; I stepped right and crashed into the person next to me. I said, "Sorry!" and carried on dancing, a smile on my face that had been missing for weeks.

When I left, my brain felt miraculously cleansed. Solutions to the problems I'd been mulling became clearer and more manageable. That night I slept properly for the first time in weeks. I couldn't believe that amid the internal and external chaos I'd forgotten the power of exercise as a tool to reset my mind and allow me to literally dance out of a locked thought-cage. I haven't stopped moving since. Running got me through COVID-19. Music and movement are my foundational building blocks of change.

If you are rolling your eyes about my "a dance class changed my life!" story, consider the science. Exercise lowers cortisol and adrenaline, the two main stress hormones, and increases production of endorphins, the body's painkiller and mood booster. Psychologist Julia Samuel told me on my podcast that twenty minutes of exercise five times per week has been proven to be as effective as a low-grade antidepressant medication.*

Obviously, it might be tricky to hotfoot it to a dance class every time we get a funky energy. Fortunately, we don't need to. Just a short burst of activity has the same effect.

Let's dive into the PURE MIRACLE of how breathing can be used as the ultimate energy changer. My mentor, clinical psychologist Belisa Vranich, PhD, founder of the Breathing Class, trained me to be a breathing instructor and taught me how to harness the power of breathing to help surf a stress wave with the most epic surfboard imaginable.

Belly breathing stimulates the vagus nerve (which has nothing to do with the VAGINA, so get your mind out of there). It is the longest, farthest-reaching nerve in the body, starting in the brain, branching and twisting down on the left side and on the right, entwining every vital organ, to the Second Brain, the gut. It controls the parasympathetic nervous system (aka "rest and digest," "the brakes," or "the monkey sedater"), and relays messages between the gut and the brain, and regulates heart rate and mood. Researchers in Switzerland have found that a well-toned and -stimulated vagus nerve can reduce inflammation, treat depression and PTSD, and tamp down stress and anxiety.[23]

All of these benefits can be accessed, just through breathing! How brilliant is that?

---

* If you are taking medication for depression, consult your doctor about the effects of exercise in conjunction with it, but don't take yourself off medication on your own! And if you believe that exercise alone isn't effective for your symptoms, go to a doctor to discuss medical options.

Flexercise: Tone That Vagus!

Deep breathing counteracts the *get out of the burning building* feeling and allows your rational mind to reboot. Oh, and on top of that, it stimulates nitric oxide, which calms your nervous system down even more. One of the main reasons for creating the HNP app was to make breathing easier to fit in daily. By just consciously inhaling and exhaling for several minutes, you'll notice the extraordinary change in your entire energy. How epic is that? I love shortcuts. After me: I say "Bio," you say "Hack." "Biohack!"

Sit in a chair with your feet on the floor or sit cross-legged on the floor

Put your hands on your knees

Inhale through the nose into the belly for a count of four. (Sometimes while I inhale, I say a silent "surrender" to myself. "Surrender" is another word for "accept.")

Hold for six

Exhale low and slow by tightening the belly for a count of seven

Repeat five times

Bonus: Hum or OM while exhaling to stimulate the vagus branch in the neck

---

Don't underestimate the power of a posture change either to instantly energize. The phrase "embodied cognition" means that our thinking is influenced by our physical bodies—*and vice versa*. So if we are slumped down in the chair, head forward, in a posture of misery, we are going to feel miserable; and if we feel miserable, we're going to slump down in the chair. Thinking into a happier headspace while slumping is nearly impossible. Our body is sending *stronnnggg* signals that we're tired, weak and should go lie down now. But by sitting up tall, shoulders relaxed, head high, jaw unclenched, it's phenomenal the surge of good feelings we get almost instantly, which translates into actual confidence. Harvard Business School social psychologist Amy Cuddy's research on "power poses" showed that when we stretch out our arms with our chests open, we will feel like Wonder Woman. So uncross those arms and legs and spread out.

Psychologist and biofeedback expert Erik Peper, PhD, a professor of health education at San Francisco State University, studied[24] the link between posture and mood on 110 college students by asking them to first walk down a hallway in a slouch for a couple of minutes, and then do it again, skipping. After each lap, the subjects rated their energy level. Universally, the students reported increased energy after skipping compared to slouched walking. "If you start integrating more body movements into your daily life, your energy level stays higher and your quality of life is better," Dr. Peper told *SF State News*. "You can convince your body to have more energy" in only two minutes.[25]

Dr. Peper and his team have proven[26] that simply changing your posture reduces the negative effects of bad memories. In a different study, when his 145 subjects were in an upright posture, they were better able to get a new perspective on past experiences. In another study,[27] he found that when anxious students did mental math equations, they performed worse and reported more difficulty when they were in a slouch position vs. seated upright. We become emotionally and intellectually impaired when we're in a cowering posture. On the other hand, sitting up straight signals "I'm safe" to the brain, creating a domino effect of slower breathing and relaxed muscles that allows your mind to stretch to solve problems.

Flexercise: Micro-Energizers

Right now, are you slumped over, head down, staring at your phone/book? If so, you're more likely to be self-critical, to be reactive to a threat, and to stress out over past and present experiences. Your body is **not** in a position to help you **energize** healthier thought habits. So change the flow. Small energizers can be just as impactful as a sweaty hot yoga class.

Stand up

Do ten jumping jacks

Whack on your favorite song and dance for a track

Pace the room

Stretch your arms over your head and gently lean back

In order to connect with ourselves authentically, we have to be honest, and get really real. We can't truly have an honest relationship with anyone else if we aren't willing to be honest with ourselves first. Anne Lamott wrote in *Help, Thanks, Wow*, "It would almost bring tears to my eyes, tears of pride in you, for the courage it takes to get real— really real. It would make me want to sit next to you at the dinner table." I loved reading this because it reminded me how deadly dull it is talking to someone who doesn't want to get real and insists on skating on the surface. It's no one's fault for fearing real. We have been conditioned to think "happy" is the only thing we should be projecting. Meaningful relationships with others and ourselves begin at the gates of honesty. Living an emotionally authentic life is what makes each and every one of us interesting and it is only then that healing can take place.

So, for the next three days—or however long it takes to get these techniques down cold—practice connecting deeply with your emotions every time they come up and get REALLY REAL. As soon as the bitchy inner Mean Girl like Regina pipes up or you have any unpleasant emotion or physical sensation . . . welcome it all in.

Sync the four brains. As soon as the emotion comes, before you react, pause for a sec and go in to listen out for what your four brains are saying. They're a winning team if they work together. These four guardians make up your internal guidance system and are full of endless wisdom if you take the time to hear.

Accept emotions and ride the wave for ninety seconds. It doesn't take long to allow a bad feeling to flow and recede. The Rosenberg Reset gives us the chance to decide how to act, or even whether action is really needed.

Mitigate negative emotions with language. Label them, define your emo zone, and defuse them with words that code them as temporary and separate. This is the moment you get very real and honest.

Energize out of a bad mood or any tricky emotion you are managing. Before you try to think your way out, move. Thought work requires energy to upgrade our frequency and move into higher emotional states as per Hawkins's Scale of Consciousness. Get into the habit of walking, jumping, consciously breathing, or just sitting up straight before you begin challenging your thoughts.

My greatest transformation happened when I began integrating Step #1 into my life daily, not just reactively. I no longer wanted to only Connect when I was feeling off kilter, but I wanted to live a connected life, mind, body, heart, and soul. I recommend practicing these techniques in the first thirty minutes of your day, every day. Check in: "How am I feeling today?" And most important, upgrade your energy and thoughts with a brisk twenty-minute walk or dance to your favorite song. Sometimes my connection ritual only lasts a few minutes, but it means that when curveballs are thrown throughout the day, I can return to my connected state because it's become familiar. Once you have this step down—and practice creates habit—you can move on to the next step: **Curiosity**.

> "As I reinvent myself and I'm constantly curious about everything, I can't wait to see what's around the corner."
> —Pam Grier

"EVERYTHING WE HEAR IS AN OPINION, NOT A FACT. EVERYTHING WE SEE IS A PERSPECTIVE, NOT THE TRUTH."

—MARCUS AURELIUS

chapter six

CURIOSITY

Step #2 of the Flex is Curiosity. For the next few days or a week, whenever you notice an unpleasant emotion or the thought that you're stuck spiraling, focus on being:

Curious about your thoughts.

Curious about your current reality and memories.

Curious about who you are behind your social masks.

Living curiously is a way of life as well as a key step to the Flex. It is the opposite of being a sponge. Instead of believing everything your bitchy inner critic or anyone else lampoons you with, question everything and be shrewd with the information you let in long term. Curiosity is just common sense. When fear speaks, it speaks lies that are disguised as truth and it can be very convincing. Curiosity is the language of self-love because you're protecting your delicate mind from believing BS.

To be more flexible, we have to become explorers and detectives, to question everything before we form opinions or draw conclusions. Flexible thoughts challenge convention to widen our perspective. Flexibility is having a mindset of openness and a childlike hunger for knowledge and discovery.

Inflexible thinking relies on conventional set-in-stone beliefs about everything. Stiff thinkers find comfort in the familiar and are too afraid to think differently, face their fears, and actually learn something new or of value about the world and themselves.

Curiosity pushes us out of unconscious autopilot mode. Dr. Mlodinow explained, in *Subliminal: How Your Unconscious Mind Rules Your Behavior*, how our iceberg brain effortlessly, rapidly assesses all incoming information without us having any conscious awareness of it. It searches our memory banks to check whether we've experienced anything like it before and then it puts events in a context and alerts us to the incoming information if our subconscious decides it's useful. This process is why, when people eat rabbit for the first time, they say, "It tastes like chicken!" Context becomes reality, which would be okay if our data storage were perfect. But it's not. It's full of holes, and our brain fills in those spaces with the cement of faulty beliefs and negativity. We don't realize when contextualization is happening, or how limiting it is. After all, rabbit doesn't really taste like chicken. It tastes like rabbit. Flexibility lies in challenging the mind not to overly contextualize and compare but to experience fresh experiences for what they are: new and exciting.

A friend called me to complain about her boyfriend. She started listing all the things he'd said and done to upset her, and then announced, "We're done."

"What makes you so sure?"

"Well, in my last relationship, the same shit happened, and we broke up."

"Are the guys very similar?" I asked. "Is the relationship the same?"

She thought about it for a moment and said, "No, not at all."

"So why would you expect the same result if you're dealing with a completely different person?"

A side effect of contextualization—and stiff thinking—is jumping to conclusions, usually dire ones. We all do this because our caveman brains love to pattern match and go neg in their constant search for threats. It made sense for our survival. Our instinctual lizard brain sees a stick on the ground and just to cover the bases, might think, "Snake." Then our monkey mind reacts with fear and screams, "Danger! Rattler!" at top volume. By having this super speedy survival instinct and reactional WFLM "unsafe" mode we've been saved from many a snake bite, but it also makes us jump to the worst scenario possible, even if we don't have enough information to know for sure that the oblong thing in the grass is really something to fear.

This is what was happening to my friend. Her last breakup was so painful, the faintest sign of conflict in her current one triggered a cortisol gusher. She got really anxious, the internal alarms went off, and her monkey mind leapt to the worst-case scenario.

If she'd been able to connect with herself, she could have arrived at a calmer place (the Flex Step #1). Then moved on to Step #2: Curiosity to assess the situation and explore what *really* triggered her anxiety about her BF. What bedrock fears and faulty beliefs was she running from or projecting onto the current situation as she leapt to her conclusion? Was there *evidence* that he wanted to end it?

Reminder: The human brain has up to 6,000 thoughts per day, and 70 percent of them are negative. Those rigid, unforgiving thoughts are: (1) automatic negative thoughts, aka ANTs, (2) the squeak of our monkey mind, (3) the grunts of our inner caveman, and (4) fuzzy echoes from the past. The Curiosity step challenges our thoughts and assumptions about what is true. Not saying that *all* 6,000 thoughts are lies. But *some* of them are, and it's up to us, for our mental health, to question what we believe is true, especially the negative stuff.

Another reminder: Our brains are simple. As it turns out, there are only two ways humans react to what we experience: (1) we attach meaning/put in context or (2) we remain wide-eyed and curious. Ninety-nine point nine nine percent of the time, we attach meaning before we even know we have. Our brains are SO FAST at doing it. For example, I was getting feedback on a project just last week and my colleague hadn't responded yet. I immediately jumped to the conclusion that she must be HATING it and was afraid to tell me because there had been a delay. I had to remember to withdraw from assuming anything. As it turned out, she'd been on a holiday and hadn't had Wi-Fi! We need to build the curiosity habit of saying, "Wait a sec. Before I attach meaning to this, I'm going to look at it with fresh eyes and maybe I'll see something new, wild, different, surprising."

Terence Watts, PhD, founder of BrainWorking Recursive Therapy, has spoken of the dichotomy as being someone who says, "Interesting!" to new info vs. someone who says, "Yeah, right" with dismissive cynicism. "Interesting, tell me more!" opens us up to a multitude of possibilities and learnings. It's always searching for new insight, new knowledge. "Yeah, right" is stiff because it closes off further exploration and thoughts. No new ideas can be found when we're stuck in the same old, same old.

Events in themselves are neutral, just things that happen. We get to decide whether they are positive or negative, fact or fiction, useful or not worth it, by examining them. In so-called bad experiences, with curiosity, we can still turn shit into golden nuggets of wisdom. I think back to the thousands of times I reacted to experiences—meetings at work, conversations with friends—as if they were replays of previous experiences, projecting all my emotional baggage onto them. Back then, I didn't question my self-blame. I just used my observations as factual evidence to prove again that I was not likeable, lovable, or enough.

For a couple years now, I've been challenging *everything*, and starting with the premise that my brain might very well be lying to me. I've stopped taking my thoughts at face value, and it's widened my perspective and changed my life. Being an emotional detective will do the same thing for anyone, deerstalker hats optional.

Investigate Thoughts

THOUGHTS ARE NOT FACTS (I put it in all caps to remind myself, too). It is critical to free ourselves from our outdated biases and liberate ourselves from the suffering we have been enduring. Questioning our thoughts and our interpretation of events is the key to breaking away from the loops of faulty thinking. If we don't, we'll just be stuck reliving the (usually mean and degrading) stories we've told ourselves about who we are.

Since I became curious, I have realized that most of my old stories about who I am are cruel fictions, not facts.

Humans are terrible culprits of creating in their minds a perpetual newsfeed of lies. And the worst thing about it: We believe our own BS, day in, day out.

To rewrite the bitchy voice's cruel fiction in our heads, we have to start by investigating our thoughts. Spiritual innovator and life coach Byron Katie, one of my rays of light during my burnout recovery, provided us a road map for this process in her book *A Mind at Home with Itself: How Asking Four Questions Can Free Your Mind, Open Your Heart, and Turn Your World Around*.

The four questions to ask ourselves at any moment:

1. Is it true?

2. Can you absolutely know that it's true?

3. How do you react, what happens, when you believe that thought?

4. Who would you be without the thought?

The basicness of asking, "Is it true?" is genius. There might not be a shred of evidence in the thought that's circulating, yet we attach so much power and meaning to it. "We don't hear what someone said," wrote Katie. "We imagine what they meant."

Identify and Label Naughty ANTs

Most of our BS thoughts are automatic negative thoughts (ANTs). Getting into the habit of labeling what kind of ANT we're experiencing keeps us curious and crushes those little fuckers.

Quick reminder of the eight types of ANTs:

1. **All-or-nothing-ism,** aka "Everything is GREAT!" or "Everything SUCKS!"

2. **Overgeneralization**, aka "All men are cheaters" or "All women are crazy."

3. **Spiraling down**, aka "I didn't get the job. I won't get any job. I'm going to be evicted, go broke, become homeless..." and so on to the very bottom of the bucket.

4. **Paralysis by analysis**, aka "What does it mean? I'm going to turn this over in my head until I'm spinning."

5. **Fortune-telling**, aka "I know what's going to happen, and it's going to be ugly."

6. **Rejecting the positive**, aka "Thanks for the compliment, but I look like shit" and "It worked out, but I just got lucky this time."

7. **Personalizing**, aka "It's all my fault!"

8. **Should-ing, aka** "I *should* be married by now."

It's an extremely therapeutic Curiosity exercise to work out which types are nibbling at your mind and then stamp them out.

I find myself constantly crushing the fortune-telling and paralysis-by-analysis ANTs. Admittedly, I have a wild imagination and love to create stories about why people say and do things. Humans are expert players in the "filling in the blanks" game. If a work contact doesn't email or text back, my mind quickly writes a short story about her reasons. "She's pissed at me...she hates me...she thinks I killed her cat...she doesn't think I'm talented enough." The story never has a happy ending! (Hello, negative bias.) It's never "She's probably just waiting to tell me face-to-face how great my last piece of work was!"

Our brain loves to be proved right about everything, even about the most self-critical thoughts we have. It turns our experiences into proof that we're correct in our worst fears/beliefs. This is called "confirmation bias" and it rears its ugly head for me when something cuts close to my "not good enough" wound, like getting dumped.

Even now, as soon as I sense the horrible feeling of rejection coming on, I have to catch myself and consciously ask Katie's four questions to battle back those ANTs:

Is it true, that I got dumped because I wasn't wanted or good enough? Well, I guess I had no proof that the guy who loved Hawaiian shirts and smelled of patchouli didn't want me or that I wasn't good enough for him...but it felt that way, because if I was worthy, why would he want to break up?

Could I know absolutely that it was true? Nope. I wasn't inside the guy's head.

How did I react when I believed the thought? I reacted with self-blame, thinking I deserved to be dumped and listing the reasons why, like I should have worn Hawaiian shirts, too, and wasn't pretty enough for him. I showered myself with hateful body- and personality-shaming thoughts that made me feel starved for approval. Then I downloaded every photo editing app, called up blogger friends and asked how they filtered, then took a million pics, chose one, posted like a maniac to social media, hashtagged the world for likes, and sat there waiting for external approval to feel like I belonged. #trainwreck

Who would I be without the thought? I'd still be single, but I wouldn't be terrorizing myself. I would have experienced far less suffering over the relationship's end and parted ways without driving my self-esteem into a hole. I would have been able to move on more quickly, with more confidence, and I probably wouldn't have sought to validate my existence with Instagram likes.

Our brain doesn't want to be bitchy, it just finds safety in certainty, in what it thinks is "right." Curiosity has us exploring uncertainty and asks us to prove ourselves wrong about what we think is correct (but isn't).

Flexercise: Sherlocking

The critical "how to" is to find brain BS at every opportunity. Then you will stop buying it. Think of a recent or past event that triggered insecurity, anxiety, or uncomfortable vulnerability. Then run through Byron Katie's four questions:

1. **Is it true?** Dig around a bit by looking for EVIDENCE. An actual email or text, a photo, or some proof that what you believe is true *is* factually true.

2. **Can you absolutely know that it's true?** If a journalist can't confirm a fact, it doesn't go in the article. If a cop can't confirm a fact, she can't make an arrest. If, after a thorough investigation, no evidence exists that your thought is true, you have no reason to believe it.

3. **How do you react, what happens, when you believe that thought?** Connect to your feelings and objectively consider the impact of them. Use curiosity to explore where shame, for example, might have come from in your past.

4. **Who would you be without the thought?** Imagine how thinking differently can give you many things, including an instant mood shift. This question helps us see how heavy our thoughts can be, how they weigh us down. By reexamining and exploring new meanings, we can feel calmer, happier, more balanced, instantly. With a new perspective, a new person awaits! As baker and writer Ruby Tandoh once said, "The only thing more thrilling than quitting something is starting something new. In the vacuum that quitting creates, countless new maybes rush in."[28]

Just by saying, "This thing I've always believed is not necessarily true," you will create space for new neural pathways to start etching a path. Do it whenever the bitchy mean storyteller voice pops into your head. This step is really where the work starts, and change begins!

Don't take my word for it. For a recent UK study, researchers looked at the effectiveness of "cognitive defusion"—learning to separate from your thoughts instead of getting caught up in them.[29] Half the subjects were trained to ask, "Is this thought true, important, or worth holding on to?" and to examine how the thought's negativity affected them. Compared to the incurious control group, the first group reported that they were significantly *less* likely to believe the negative thought, were more comfortable in their minds and bodies, were happier in general, and had fewer negative thoughts afterward. In just five days, curiosity Flexed their thoughts. Boom, how simple and brilliant is that?

Brain BS Warnings

Sherlocking the brain's lies does have some potential pitfalls.

- **Don't beat yourself up about it**. As mindfulness expert and professor at the University of Massachusetts Medical School Jon Kabat-Zinn said, "Most of our thoughts are mundane or imprisoning. How do we have more of the healthy thoughts and less of the ones that hold us back?"

- **Ask "Is it true?" only about *thoughts*, not feelings**. The thought that triggered the emotion might be false, but the emotion itself is real.

- **The caveman brain is NOT okay with this**. It would *much* rather stay stuck on its familiar pathways. But, as Deepak Chopra wrote, "[h]olding on to anything is like holding on to your breath. You will suffocate. The only way to get anything in the physical universe is by letting go of it." Let's start with loosening the grip on faulty fake thoughts.

Remove the Mask

Curious people love to explore new places and learn new things. That includes adventuring inside and discovering ourselves. To do so, we have to take off the edited, face-tuned, and filtered social masks we wear to hide our insecurities. It's about stepping away from projecting who we want to be and getting honest with who we actually are.

If there is a gap between the projected self and the real self, all kinds of crap falls into it. Shame. Self-hatred. Doubt. Self-criticism. We wind up in a state of constant self-flagellation about how we fall short of being the person we pretend to be. Social media has widened the gap SO MUCH. I'm perpetually surprised when I mention how great someone's vacation looked on the Gram, and then they tearfully tell me they fought with their BF the entire time and were miserable. So even though their holiday was awful, they commit to making everyone believe the opposite. Is creating envy rather than honesty the whole point? Perhaps. Billions of users around the globe not only compare their lives to others' but compare their own reality to their 'Grammed life. They feel jarred when the disparity of this double life is as bright as the Amaro filter.

For a life of wholeness and fullness, we have to meet ourselves in the zone of truth. The only way forward is to lose the social mask and close the gap between the 2D public face and the true 3D self. For many of us who have been hiding for so long, it feels vulnerable and scary. But wholeness is just on the other side of learning to like every part of ourselves, even the parts we want to keep in the shadows.

Swiss psychiatrist Carl Jung said, "The Shadow is the person you'd rather not be." He theorized that emotional suffering stems from suppression of that person, and ONLY when we decide to accept and love our Shadow can we heal.

I had no idea what it would feel like to learn to love the parts of myself that I intentionally suppressed—or the parts I unconsciously hid and/or denied because I deemed them unlikable. And then I read the groundbreaking book *The Dark Side of the Light Chasers* by Debbie Ford. It's about how we humans hate and suppress sides of our per-

sonalities because of social conditioning and childhood identity formation, and how devastating it is to our well-being to force them into the
shadows.

Per Ford, messages like "you're unworthy," "you're not good
enough," or "you're unlovable" come from the "darkness." We avoid
really going there and confronting these painful beliefs because we're
scared to explore the dark side of ourselves. It'd be like entering a
cauldron of insecurities.

Out of fear of going there, we work double time to project the
"lightness" side of our personalities, the agreeable, socially acceptable
one—as Jung might say, *the person you'd rather be.*

We are all professional suppressors of our own darkness.

I know that sounds bleak. But if that point touched you, it's only
proof of our fears. Of course, it's frightening to dive into the darkness
like it's a shark-infested pool. We've been told since we were little to
avoid dim alleys, to be wary of what you can't see, that curiosity kills
the cat. Simba explored the shadow lands and nearly got eaten by
hyenas. Eve was arguably kicked out of the Garden of Eden because
of her hunger to learn! Very few cultures, if any, support and encourage
curiosity.

We have to be able to talk about what scares us if we're ever going to
break out of the rigid thinking that imprisons us. The shadow we refuse
to acknowledge casts its darkness over our thoughts nonetheless.

Modern-day life is like pumping air into a furnace, making our fear
rage brighter and larger. Everything from the media to caffeine to technology squeezes every second of the day from us, and we can easily
distract ourselves from doing shadow work, to run from fears. But not
even Usain Bolt can run that fast. Our fears will catch up eventually.

For starters, our brains are programmed to search for danger
(negative bias) pretty much all the time. So that's the baseline. Next,
our faulty memories are dominated by childhood experiences of feeling unloved, unwanted, and/or unsafe, in one way or another. Those

fears are alive in us right now and our confirmation bias unconsciously affirms them at every opportunity. On top of all that, trying to suppress our fears only makes them more powerful.

By facing our fears, we can reduce their power. If we really want to free our minds, we have to shine light into the shadows and accept what frightens us about ourselves!

Our dark sides are actually a lot more interesting than our bright sides. If we were nothing but sparkles and light, we'd be *sooooo* boring. Realizing this made me laugh. All I'd ever wanted was to be accepted and welcomed and I thought I'd have to be a perfect Suzy Sunshine. Quite the opposite is true. I'm more likable and interesting when I embrace my whole personality, the dark thoughts and so-called unattractive qualities we all have. Every one of us. What led to greater happiness than I ever thought possible was getting curious, meeting and befriending my shadow selves—my egotistical, jealous, controlling, drama queen–y, difficult, uptight, martyr-y, vain, competitive, simpering (I could go on…) sides—and welcoming them into my conscious life.

We *need* to befriend them. Our shadows are like naughty children. They aren't just going to sit in a corner because we tell them to. They'll start causing trouble EXACTLY when we try to ignore them. Our inner monsters are not going to let us have a moment's peace until we pay attention to them.

To set out on an exploration of the shadow lands, start by looking at really annoying people, the ones that really grate and cause an instant bad reaction. Can you think of someone who triggers those feelings for you? What we hate in others is usually something we haven't addressed or accepted about ourselves.

When the COVID-19 crisis began in the spring of 2020, a friend of mine called to rant for ten minutes about how disgusted she was with her neighbors. They came home one day with a car trunk full of toilet paper. Honestly, I'd never heard her go off like that on anyone before.

I asked, "What pisses you off so much about it?"

"Hoarding is greedy!" she said.

"You're never greedy? Isn't hoarding a response to fear? You're never fearful?"

I happened to know this friend was a hoarder in her own way, an obsessive saver, a bit of a Scrooge. She'd rarely splurge on herself. I suggested gently that maybe what triggered her anger about her neighbor's hoarding was that deep down she could relate to the fear. In fact, she could. Work had declined during the crisis and her anxiety had risen as her savings diminished. Fear is contagious: Was her own fear about money and the uncertain world situation being triggered from seeing other people's fearful reactions like hoarding?

Our fears require delicate conversations but to her credit, my friend admitted that deep down she was feeling triggered by her own fear and self-denial. Acknowledging her fearful shadows made her feel less annoyed with others and more motivated to change her own thinking.

> "It is in acknowledging the pain of others
> that we achieve fully our humanity."
> —Hamza Yusuf

Doing shadow work and diving into our deepest, darkest fears promotes a curious, questioning mindset. What shadow self is pinging now? What am I keeping hidden about myself and projecting onto others? It also prevents us from jumping to conclusions about our feelings toward others and about ourselves. Everyone and everything is a reflection of our internal world. By getting to know our internal world extremely well from the outside in, we can roam freely in it. If we don't get curious, though, our shadows stay locked inside, where they can torture us forever.

Flexercise: Discover Your Shadows

Mindset and performance coach Polly Bateman asked me to do this Flexercise, and I found it fascinating. I hope you will, too!

Write down three people you admire: _____

What do you admire about them? What are their strengths? _____

_____

What do you think their possible weaknesses are? _____

_____

Analyze your answers. Do they sound familiar? It will come as no surprise that you are describing someone very similar to yourself. We can only recognize the dark and light in others if we hold it ourselves. What we admire and disapprove of in them reflects the best and most feared aspects of our own personalities. When we love *all* of ourselves, our strengths grow, and our weaknesses shrink. By being at home in ourselves, we create the feelings of safety, love, and enoughness, and feel at home in our skin like never before.

Whether we're naturally curious or not, we can adopt a mindset of questioning and challenging what we know is "right" or true, and in the process, learn, change, and grow. I think of this step as like going on a trip to a place I've never been and feeling excited about what I might discover around every corner. And then, when I get "home," I bring that shiny new perspective with me, and it changes how I view everything.

To get that "eyes of a child" sense of wonder, a hallmark of creativity and flexibility, we need to do a few things:

Think before attaching meaning to anything. Before the mind jumps headfirst into a pool of biases and contextualization, blow a whistle and say, "Just one minute! Is there even any water in there?" Break out of autopilot mode by challenging assumptions, certainties, and the known.

Find the brain BS and identify the naughty ANTs at play. Our conclusions, associations, and formative memories? They might all be complete BS. The only way to find out is to run through Byron Katie's four questions and look for evidence that what you think is true, actually is or isn't. In the absence of evidence, news is then fake, so how does this change your thoughts and feelings? Identify the naughty automatic thought at play for extra detection points.

Face fears. We do this by being radically honest with ourselves and getting really real about what's triggering us. When you finally allow light to shine into the shadows via gentle curiosity, you begin to see, like I did, that the warts we're trying to hide behind social masks or the parts we deem conventionally distasteful aren't so bad, but have their own merits, and are *very normal*. Whether we like it or not, they are us, a less socially curated version but a refreshingly full one. When we accept our shadows along with our light, we edge toward reuniting our unique 3D being.

Spend three days or more practicing curiosity, asking the four questions, identifying and labeling any mischievous ANTs when they appear and Sherlocking for true truths about who you are and where your brain BS comes from. After a good portion of a week challenging all thoughts by saying, "Interesting. Let me look for more evidence before I confirm this," and "Is this true?" until it's second nature, then you are ready to move on to Step #3: **Choice**.

"The big secret in life is that there is no big secret. There are no back doors, no free rides. There's just you, this moment and a choice."
—Oprah Winfrey

"TO PERCEIVE THE WORLD DIFFERENTLY, WE MUST BE WILLING TO CHANGE OUR BELIEF SYSTEM, LET THE PAST SLIP AWAY, EXPAND OUR SENSE OF NOW, AND DISSOLVE THE FEAR IN OUR MINDS."

—WILLIAM JAMES

CHOICE

Step #3 of the Flex is Choice. Once you're sufficiently skilled at the previous two steps, it's time to devote your focus to a new lesson. Whenever faced with a difficult feeling, thought, or situation, make a conscious...

Choice about which inner voice you listen to.

Choice about how you treat yourself and others.

Choice about what you ask for in life.

So far, in the Flex, you've trained yourself to make a Connection to accept your feelings as they happen and take that necessary pause to energize the body and access your internal guidance system. Then you concentrated on Curiosity, exploring new perspectives and establishing an "Interesting!" mindset. And now, the week's objective is to make Choices about how to think and what to do next by leaning into love and away from fear.

Flexibility is understanding that, no matter what we're going through, we always have multiple choices going forward.

What could be stiffer than believing we have NO CHOICE? Whenever I hear someone say, "Well, I have no choice but to..." I can't help myself from thinking, "NOT TRUE, you're stuck in Stiffland!!"

It's no one's fault for feeling trapped there. Very few of us are taught to think bendy. I used to think I had no choice but to achieve perfection, because I believed with every fiber of my being that it was the ONLY way I'd feel accepted and loved and would finally belong. Realizing that there are in fact unlimited paths toward love and acceptance, and that perfectionism might be one of the rockiest, meanest ones to take, has been one of the greatest gifts of this process.

Automatic negativity—the bitchy inner voice—will always prevail unless we make a conscious Choice to change the direction of our focus and let go of stiff thinking. I had spent years living in fear, obsession, anxiety, and stress. But this wasn't my fault, and neither is it yours if you feel the same. Our biology encourages this if we don't intervene. Stiff thoughts grow in a fear-based life. Flexible thoughts grow in a love-based life. Or, as we say around the garden shed, "If you plant weeds, you get weeds. If you plant flowers, you get flowers." I wanted full-on blooming love-filled flowers.

The crazy thing about all of this mind stuff is that when we slow down, we have *so much* more control than we think we have, over what we choose to think and how we react and behave. This Flexi-step is perhaps the most liberating because it gives us the power to steer our lives. Consciously reminding ourselves that we are in the driver's seat and *we can choose* to either put a mental muzzle on our chattering monkey minds or give in to it. We can choose to embrace wholeness, accepting our brilliant mix of beauty and flaws, or continue to feel fraudulent. We can choose to forgive ourselves and anyone else for mistakes and transgressions instead of beating ourselves up or holding toxic grudges. It's like taking a second when arriving at a fork in the road to decide whether to drive north into love or south into fear. Choose true north.

The mental and emotional choices that lie before us might not always be painless. But choices always exist, and how we experience life within our heads is *completely up to us*. Once we call BS on our brain's lies, we're no longer guided by our innate biases, and we create space to independently decide how we view our lives. Acknowledging the power we have to make different choices and thus new thoughts is the greatest freedom offered to us. This is empowered flexible thinking.

Which Wolf Do We Want to Feed?

During an interview with Dr. Rick Hanson, he brought up the beautiful parable that inside our minds, there are only two wolves.

One is the Wolf of Fear, which feeds on anxiety, darkness, despair, all the horrible awfuls.

The other is the Wolf of Love, which feeds on hope, light, love, all the beautiful wonders.

Our thoughts become food and the two wolves are always fighting over who eats because we can only feed one at a time. Every choice we make gives sustenance to either fear/darkness or love/light. When we flood ourselves with mean, worrisome, regretful thoughts, the Wolf of Fear gets fatter and stronger, demanding more tasty morsels. Meanwhile, the Wolf of Love, deprived of food, will get smaller and weaker.

Our negative and confirmation biases automatically offer heaping platters to the Wolf of Fear, so he'll always have the advantage. Therefore it is not possible to strengthen and grow the Wolf of Love without making **a conscious effort**. So we need to focus hard on serving up a banquet to the Wolf of Love—with heaping portions of forgiveness and compassion to ourselves and others—if we want to create a new, happier future.

Deepak Chopra similarly talks about how the brain can't experience gratitude and fear at the same time because it's the same part of the brain that feels both. So the emotional center is in a state of either gratitude or fear, just like we can't be playing WFML and WCHL at the same time; we have to choose one.

Flexercise: Love Feeding Mantra

When I first heard the two wolves parable, I thought, "Well, yeah, of course I want to feed the Wolf of Love." But in a blink, the Wolf of Fear has snatched the T-bone.

Performance coach Polly Bateman said to me, "The universe doesn't give a fuck about the decision you make, it gives you what you ask for. So if you want to stay stuck in fear, it gives you more of it! And if you want to flex with love, it'll give you more of that."

As the Wolf of Fear has very fast jaws, Bateman suggests having a couple of mantras up your sleeve to help slow that hungry wolf down. Whenever we are listening to our negative mental chatter or making a decision, she recommends (along with breathing) a mantra like "I am ready for change" and/or "I expect the unexpected." Openness is flexibility. If we choose to challenge fear with openness, we create space to bend toward gratitude and love.

The health industry has spent decades teaching us about the benefits of having a healthy food diet and exercise plan. Eat your five veggies a day, walk ten thousand steps, minimize sugar intake, etc., etc. All good. But we can't continue leaving out this one critical Choice when designing a healthy life: choosing high-quality thoughts. Studies prove physical health is integrally linked to what's going on mentally and any physical health plan benefits from loving, positive thoughts. A hating mind can rarely create a healthy body. The brain is so powerful, it can create brilliant medicine for us, or it can pump toxins into our bodies. Loving, hopeful, optimistic thoughts are the finest anti-inflammatory and antioxidant pills in the universe. Hateful, fearful thoughts are like swallowing poison.

The Mind Is Medicine for the Body

The Body on Love	The Body on Fear
Awash in dopamine, oxytocin, endorphins	Awash in cortisol
Low inflammation	High inflammation
Healthy digestion	Sluggish digestion
Stronger immunity	Compromised immunity
Regular heart rate	High blood pressure
Better sleep	Insomnia
High electromagnetic field vibrations, which are contagious and enjoyed by one and all	Low electromagnetic field vibrations, also contagious and a bummer for one and all

Cruel or Kind?

Compassion is often looked at as a soft, fluffy thing, but its benefits to the mind and body are beyond what any pill or purchase promises to give you. By actively rising above our bitchy brain thoughts, accepting others vulnerabilities, and having the desire to alleviate the suffering of others as well as our own, we can reduce stress[30] (and all of the inflammation-related diseases associated with that), depression, ruminating (obsessively thinking about the same thing), and anxiety.[31] Compassion increases positivity and social connection—*and prevents burnout!*[32]

> ## What will change our perception of the world—and the world itself, if we can all get on board—is *choosing compassion.*

I know we can all feel a bit eye-roll-y about the word "compassion." It's become an overused word in some contexts but until we can think of something better, let's get on board. We all have kindness needs! Being compassionate does mean we have to choose letting our guard down. But if we don't give ourselves permission to be fragile at times, we'll cut ourselves off from truth, and most importantly prevent growth and spend longer grappling with anxiety and stress in epidemic numbers. As I've said before, if we're afraid to be vulnerable, we avoid relationships. If we're afraid to fail, we are paralyzed by perfectionism and procrastination. If growing pains become too painful, we avoid learning. Flexibility is about opening the mind and the heart to embrace a bit of vulnerability and upgrade.

Research proves compassion can actually make us mentally stronger. Dr. James Doty, professor for neurosurgery at Stanford School of Medicine and founder and director of the Center for Compassion and Altruism Research and Education at Stanford University (His Holiness the Dalai Lama is the founding benefactor), has been one of my heroes for years. He studies the impact of compassion on depression, anxiety, and chronic stress. "Compassion can change the world," he once wrote. "While survival of the fittest may lead to short-term gain, research clearly shows it is survival of the kindest that leads to the long-term survival of a species. It is our ability to stand together as a group, to support each other, to help each other, to communicate for mutual understanding, and to cooperate, that has taken our species this far."

Self-compassion is the practice of understanding and accepting our own faults, as well as acknowledging that other people go through the same crap that we do. According to the queen of compassion research, Kristin Neff, PhD, University of Texas at Austin psychologist and author of *Self-Compassion: The Proven Power of Being Kind to Yourself*, self-compassion involves three key choices:

Self-kindness vs. self-judgment. When our inner critic says, "You screwed up royally!" counter it with kindness by saying, "Hey, we all make mistakes." Choosing kindness doesn't mean we have self-pity or are denying responsibility for errors. It bends the bars of the prison of judgment. Treat yourself as you would a child, by being honest about mistakes but delivering feedback with kindness and taking into account how scared your core is deep down.

Common humanity vs. isolation. No one is alone in their struggle. We can be reassured that we're not the only ones who've felt the sting of rejection. The positive side of that is that, in our pain, we are connected to the whole world. That phrase "we're all in this together" might make us think of Zac Efron in *High School Musical* or the pandemic or climate change (or all three). As cloying as it sounds, we really are all in it together, and that knowledge can make us feel less isolated, alone, and different. (N.B.: The data shows that we *are* all suffering. According to the 2019 Gallup Global Emotions Report,[33] a "snapshot of people's positive and negative experiences" based on 151,000 interviews with adults from 140 countries, 55 percent of Americans reported feeling stress "a lot of the day"; 45 percent worry "a lot.")

Mindfulness vs. overidentification. Mindfulness is living and thinking in the present moment and learning to sit with a thought without having judgment. Overidentification is what happens when our emotion response is *too* intense, and we go from having a feeling to being consumed with it. I used to be so guilty of being engulfed by my emotional waves, and, naturally, overidentified feelings aren't usually positive. Cue spirals of anger, shame, frustration, regret, and anxiety. If we practice self-compassion by guiding ourselves toward kind, forgiving thoughts, we lessen the chance for negative ones to take over.

> "The greatest weapon against stress is our ability
> to choose one thought over another."
> —William James

"Self-compassion provides an island of calm, a refuge from the stormy seas of endless positive and negative self-judgment, so that we can finally stop asking, 'Am I as good as they are? Am I good enough?'" said Dr. Neff. "By tapping into our inner wellsprings of kindness, acknowledging the shared nature of our imperfect human condition, we can start to feel more secure, accepted, and alive."

On reading Dr. Neff's work, I only had one mission: Find the map to this island of calming compassion she speaks of. To fight off the darkness, I didn't need Harry Potter's spells or Hermione Granger's intelligence, I needed my own pot of glorious self-compassion that would allow me to treat myself with as much respect as I would a friend.

To add to the list, compassion also helps alleviate the burden of self-centered thoughts, which is something I (me, myself) deal with a lot. Psychologist and author of *The Happiness Track*, Emma Seppälä, PhD, of Stanford's Center for Compassion and Altruism Research and Education and Yale's Center for Emotional Intelligence, wrote, "Research shows that depression and anxiety are linked to a state of self-focus, a preoccupation with 'me, myself, and I.' When you do something for someone else, however, that state of self-focus shifts to a state of other-focus." She went on to describe an experience I can absolutely relate to, when you're feeling bad about yourself, and then a friend calls with a problem. Suddenly, just by helping someone else with their troubles, you feel better and kind of forget about your own for a second. Ever happened to you? The science shows that being kind to a friend releases oxytocin (the feel-good love hormone), and gives us a nice, cuddly feeling in the reward center of the brain.

This dovetails into an essential self-compassion tool that is as simple as it is genius and life changing:

Just ask, "What would I advise a friend experiencing what I am now?"

Humans are so odd. We always know how a friend should handle their situation, but we're stumped when it comes to our own. The reason for this is because when we are talking to ourselves, our emotional brain is activated. The monkey, ego inner chatter. But when we're advising a friend, we use the analytical brain, our badass CEO prefrontal cortex. So when we remember to give ourselves that third-party mental shift with that simple question, "How would I advise a friend experiencing what I am now?" we, too, can unlock the same nurturing, helpful, supportive, motivating advice. How brilliant!

When in doubt about *anything*, whip this out, you will not regret it. It provides us instantly with critical distance and a new perspective AND it allows us to access and share our own stored-up wisdom for ourselves.

Since it's highly unlikely we'd tell a friend that they are a lonely, average, sad example of a human being, the friend advice we'd give to ourselves is probably a lot kinder compared to the bitchy inner critic we've got in our heads already. Developing a nurturing, self-compassionate inner voice is the key to choosing flexibility.

Remember back to being a kid. What made us feel better, being yelled at or hugged? By learning to stop yelling at ourselves inside our head, we can start to give ourselves a mental hug instead. Self-compassion doesn't solve problems. It just makes them a lot easier to manage. And when stress is reduced, and cortisol isn't flowing, everything is clearer and solutions are more easily found.

Choosing to respond compassionately is really the answer to every emotional block we put up. It's like watering and sunning a plant in a dark, dried-out patch. If we don't take conscious action to change our negative-bias brain and ANTs, we will forever struggle to thrive and grow. Compassion is giving ourselves support and permission to bloom.

Flexercise: The Friend POV

Practice using the third-party friend voice in aspects of your life you may be struggling with.

What would you advise a friend experiencing the same sort of relationship/single struggle that you are having now?

What would you advise a friend with the same sort of work challenges that you are having now?

What would you tell a friend who wants to plan a future like you do?

What would you say to a friend who has the same health goals as you do?

Reflect on your answers. You don't need a guru. You, my friend, are just as filled with wisdom as any guru. All you need to do is switch on that badass CEO brain of yours and tune into WCHL to access it.

Hold On or Let Go?

In order to stretch in ways we never thought possible, to create futures we haven't even dared to dream of, we have to let go of the heavy backpack of fear, resentment, anger, and negativity about ourselves and others. And that means going pro at forgiveness.

When I was eighteen, I was sitting in a bookshop in Oxford, England, a very sweet little town. I was just sitting there, having coffee, and a girl tried to steal my handbag. I realized what was happening, stood up, and went to stop her from running away with it. As I tried to grab her, she turned around and stabbed me in the forehead.

Blood started spurting out of the wound. I remember that it felt warm. Blood was suddenly everywhere, like a river gushing down my face. I kept repeating, "She stole my bag, she stole my bag." The police and ambulance arrived, and I was taken to the hospital. Three weeks after, I had to identify the girl in a police lineup, which was triggering at best. She was arrested, but I didn't feel closure or safer. For many weeks, I was terrified of leaving the house. I blamed myself for leaving my bag on the floor, thinking, *How stupid of you, Poppy. It's your fault this happened.* If I'd put it somewhere more secure, I could have prevented this trauma. I wouldn't now have the scar on the upper right side of my forehead. That girl gave me not just a physical wound but a growing emotional one. That day she took something far more valuable from me than my bag: my peace.

A wise mentor of mine said, "What do you gain from holding so much blame and resentment?"

"Well, she nearly sliced my face open," I replied.

"Do you really think she meant to hurt you?"

I thought about it. No, I didn't believe that. I was unfortunately in the wrong place at the wrong time, and this distressed girl was only trying to survive. Her actions were not about me, although they were done to me. She didn't think she had a choice but to steal, so she took that action. Her mind must have been blaring WFML, and she wasn't thinking rationally when she pulled out the knife. Her erratic behavior was the manifestation of the hopelessness and chaos in her own mind. I could relate to that.

In that moment, my mentor led me to understand the pointlessness of my anger toward her. Her actions were wrong, absolutely. But being pissed off and holding on to the event only hurt me. She didn't intend to cause pain to me personally. It could have been anyone. I had two choices: Either I could forgive and move on, raising my energetic vibrations with compassion, or not forgive, stay in rumination, going around in circles, stuck in low-vibrational emotional states like hopelessness and condemnation. I had a choice.

It was like night and day. When I chose forgiveness, I could feel the weight lifting off my shoulders, and my heart started to glow. It felt *much better*. I realized in that moment, forgiveness cuts the energetic connection we have to past events; I no longer needed to suffer from her actions.

Forgiveness doesn't mean excusing bad behavior. It's a choice to *let go* of the past, just as it's a choice to aspire to our better natures.

The gift of a very bad experience taught me a powerful lesson. Sister Elizabeth Kenny once wrote, "He who angers you, conquers you." Forgiveness is not about the other person. It's an action we do for ourselves so that we can file away the experience in a "case closed" drawer of our minds. It's so we aren't eaten up by negative emotions, since we've got plenty of those already.

For me to let go, I didn't need to write my stabber a letter that said, "I forgive you." It helped, though, if I made that statement to her in my imagination. Clinical psychologists Leslie Greenberg and Wanda Malcolm researched the effectiveness of "empty chair dialogues" to help their twenty-six subjects resolve unfinished business with people from their childhoods.[34] They found that by just imagining sitting down, talking it out, and forgiving, people had a better outcome (more resolution) than they did when they attempted to express their unmet needs in person.

Brilliant. Just by perching next to an empty chair for a chat, we can free ourselves from the burden of grudges, warm our hard hearts, tear down our walls, and majorly up our emotional vibrational states.

When I was holding on to a lot of anger and self-blame about that cruel business partner while just starting to develop the Flex method, this step was the thing that freed me from years of victimhood. If I was ever going to heal, I had to choose to forgive her. I fought with myself for days, thinking she didn't deserve my forgiveness, and would list all the things *again* she'd said and done. I was trying to validate how hurt I felt. But whenever I began to reflect, I could feel myself drop into low, toxic-vibrational energy of blame, shame, and hopelessness.

As my old mentor had guided me to forgive the stabber, I shifted my perspective on the troubling investors I had, and could finally see that their hurtful behavior wasn't about me, either. It was about their need to be that way because of their belief system, their learned behavior, their history. I didn't have anything to do with how they conducted themselves.

"What others think about me is none of my business."
—Eleanor Roosevelt

I had to choose to forgive the investors *and* myself. I was twenty-six years old with zero experience and just trying my best in the way I knew how. As Maya Angelou said, you can only do better when you know better. I didn't know better then and by offering myself this forgiveness, I began to feel somewhat proud that I had survived that journey, built what I created and didn't give up. I had to stretch *quite a bit* to forgive, and it took a while. Becoming bendy takes a lot of effort and repetition to remind our negative-loving brains we deserve it. But it works. Making the choice of forgiveness unshackled me from past memories and freed me to feel empowered to embrace the present.

Flexercise: Forgiveness

It's easy to say, "Stop holding on to resentment. Just let go of anger!" It's a trick to actually do it.

Most of the Flexercises are about looking inward. This time, look outward. Ask a few questions to stretch your perspective about the person who hurt you. Why do it? Because you need to see just how much their shittiness is NOT ABOUT YOU. You can repeat this exercise again and again and stretch different people with each go.

What was their life like growing up?

What wounds did they suffer that would make them want to hurt others?

What pressures or stresses were they under when they offended you?

These questions are not meant to excuse or condone, but rather to better understand their humanizing, vulnerable pain points. Generally, the more we understand why people do things we don't agree with, the more flexible and unreactive we are in the future.

If it helps—and it just might—turn this into a "talk to the empty chair" chat and imagine having a forgiving conversation with the person in question. Explain why the person you wish to forgive is the way they are . . . and how you don't need to be affected by them anymore.

We've all heard the saying "Living well is the best revenge."

I'd amend it to say, "Flexing well is the best revenge." By CHOOSING to Flex away from ANTs and feeling wounded, we bend our victim mentality toward a strong flexible mindset. As many wise people have said, "Life doesn't happen *to* you, it happens *for* you." You get to choose your outlook.

Stiff thoughts about reacting to harm are bitter, resentful, and vengeful. To be flexible, it requires making the choice to turn negative thoughts about someone else into loving, compassionate thoughts about ourselves. If we are serious about raising our own vibration by looking at our life with gratitude and compassion, we have to consciously decide to place the focus there. *Especially* when we feel darkness creeping in, we have to throw extra sandwiches toward the Wolf of Love.

Flexible or Stiff?

That's what it all boils down to. The baseline choice behind every... single...thing in life, micro, macro, from an isolated comment to an entire relationship, from asking small questions like "What's for lunch?" to huge ones like "What's my why?" is between bendiness and rigidity, between openness to learning and being closed to new ideas, between living a whole life and living a half-life.

The flexible mindset choice appreciates that there's no such thing as a negative emotion—feelings are just feelings; we all have 'em and they exist for a reason—and **every feeling and perspective can be changed when we put on our Flexi-glasses**.

It's about making the choice to **be more compassionate to ourselves every day and learning how best that works for us**. I understand how difficult this is, because for our whole lives, many of us have been conditioned to believe that we are not enough. We're used to being our own harsh taskmasters, shouting at ourselves through a bullhorn, *"Keep going! Do more! Bust your fat ass! Not Good Enough Yet!"* We get to choose to lower the bullhorn and **stretch toward kindness**. (And our asses are NOT FAT! And even if they were, SO FUCKING WHAT? Did Isaac Newton care about the size of his ass? Prob not, he was leading a scientific revolution.)

We get to **choose love over fear**. It is within our power to build new habits around compassion-forgiveness thinking to manifest a better future full of love and health. It takes work. Without making a conscious choice to feed the Love Wolf, the Fear Wolf will just gobble up everything, making us vulnerable to self-sabotage, resentment, victimhood, shame, and guilt.

Choice isn't about self-gaslighting or lying to yourself by crushing ANTs and choosing love. Quite the opposite! By Flexing, you bring realness and awareness about emotional experience (Connection), exploring where and how the BS started (Curiosity), and then consciously Choose an outlook that will get you unstuck from the past and open your mind to all the possibilities of the future.

For the next short while, practice asking, "What's my choice here? What choice will feed the Wolf of Love and what will have me step back into feeding fear?" Ask yourself in any times of emotional duress and take note of how veering one way or the other makes you feel on a vibrational level (what choice makes you feel sluggish, or energized?). Keep repeating the Choice step until stepping into love, compassion, and forgiveness becomes the normal without prompting. Once it begins to feel more familiar, you can move on to learn the final step: Commitment.

I'll close Choice with a quote from legendary flexible thinker Albert Einstein: "There are only two ways to live your life," he said. "One is as though **nothing** is a **miracle**. The other is as though **everything** is a **miracle**."

The choice is ours.

Now, on to the final step in the Flex: **Commitment**.

"THE MOST EFFECTIVE
WAY TO DO IT,
IS TO DO IT."

—AMELIA EARHART

COMMITMENT

Step #4 of the Flex is Commitment. For the next few days to a week, you will practice making a...

Commitment to taking action to effect change.

Commitment to upholding values, whatever they might be.

Commitment to finding the gifts that lie within struggle.

Commitment to feeling grateful and celebrating life's joys.

Stiff thoughts lead us to get stuck in worry loops and to repeat, over and over again, bad habits that were created in the past.

Flexible thoughts stretch to find new outlooks, possibilities, and understandings to create the brilliant future we want.

Dr. Mlodinow explained to *Scientific American*, "Happiness, contentment, and gratitude are not just important life goals; they also prompt us to widen our range of thoughts and actions, explore our environment, and open ourselves to new information, all of which are important to success." But I don't think we need to be happy first. For me, flexibility came first, then greater happiness and success later. Though I do believe *continued* happiness and success are dependent on my *commitment* to psychological flexibility.

It's like this: We stretch and stretch, and after MONTHS of struggle, we can finally touch our toes. Yay. Mission accomplished. But unless we keep stretching, we'll get stiff again, our toes will be a mile away, and it's like the limbering never even happened. Mental flexibility unfolds or folds up in the exact same way.

The fourth and final step of the Flex is Commitment, because we're talking about long-lasting liberation from anxiety and self-doubt. Change requires effort. New neural pathways aren't blazed overnight; new habits don't take root in a day or a week or a month. Real change only occurs through *consistent flexing*.

Although our past is the architect of our present, the future is still under construction.

Every moment going forward is about bending thoughts in the direction that takes us to a compassionate liberated direction. It won't magically happen on its own. We have to be consciously flexible in the present moment to ensure we manifest a better future.

Like anything worthwhile, it takes desire and effort to make our shiny new thoughts. The Flex is a veritable healthy-thought factory. We just have to want to keep the machines running to get endless benefits. It takes a bit of effort to broaden our horizons, have courage to challenge and then to imagine *new* happier outcomes.

Close the Case

Nothing happens if we don't make it happen. We can't get the job we don't apply for. We can't date the guy we don't text back. We can't have good mental health if we don't take action to break out of limiting thought patterns and anxious drama loops.

I was the worst at this! Something would set off my anxiety, and I would then start talking about it...and then I'd find new people to discuss the same worry with, didn't matter who, anyone with a pulse and two ears was fine. I wasn't solving the problem. I just felt compelled to find new people to rehash the drama with.

Without the sound of the filing cabinet slamming shut, our brain considers the stressful issue "open," and won't let us rest. Cue 1:00 a.m. wake-ups, 3:00 a.m. wake-ups, 5:00 a.m. wake-ups, etc. The reason we jolt awake during the night is usually because the brain hasn't been able to file away our worries. Dreams are actually a support mechanism for this; they help the brain process and make sense of unfiled thoughts.

Russian psychologist Bluma Zeigarnik noticed that we tend to forget things we've completed and remember our unfinished business. The Zeigarnik effect came from the observation that waiters can remember customers' orders before they're delivered, but as soon as the plates hit the cloth, the info flies out of their heads. Psychologists E. J. Masicampo and Roy Baumeister discovered in their research[35] that unfinished tasks are distracting and uncomfortable for the mind, but making a plan to complete them, like a to-do list, is a useful trick in alleviating the anxiety.

By talking, talking, talking, I wasn't doing, doing, doing. If I'd just taken a few minutes to write down practical things I could do about the worry, and actually done them, I would have helped my mind close the case, interrupted the rigid thought loops I was stuck in, and felt sweet relief. Taking action to stop anxiety creates a feeling of completion, clears the mind, and helps develop resilience against similar future worries, and most important, helps switch off rumination.

Flexercise: Free Your Mind

So when I talk about taking action to stop anxiety, I'm not talking about climbing Mount Everest. It can be as small-yet-significant as:

1. Open a notes app.

2. Type a few words.

3. Done!

I howled with laughter as I found this example on my phone:

```
(Current Poppy)

Really upset not invited to my friend's
Zoom Corona Cocktail party.
```

I have absolutely no recollection of whose Zoom party I was upset I wasn't invited to. On rereading, I can see the absolute hilarity to my emotions. Just shows, as soon as you write a thought down, it leaves you and then you can read it back and laugh about how silly our monkey minds can be sometimes.

Take Values-Based Action

In previous steps, I've talked a lot about the power of not reacting when cortisol is pumping. But eventually, we have to do *something*. But what kind of *something* is the next critical part of the Flex method. To stop the worry loops, we need closure. But only *considered decisions* that align with our desired values will provide us with a sense of completion we can feel proud about.

I don't mean the values we've been taught by our parents, religion, and authority figures. A lot of those values are conditioned, unconscious baggage. The biggest problem and main culprit for inflexible thoughts are people stuck living out learned values that do not actually fit their true soul-based values. If we want to step into a kinder, calmer, more confident future, we will NEVER get there unless we are making decisions to be kinder, calmer, and more confident. It's like wanting to get in better shape but not ever making the decision to exercise. Our days are filled with mostly minor but some major decisions that move us forward if we want them to. If we consciously ensure every action is based on upholding a value we care about, we will undoubtedly create meaningful aligned lives.

What I found most surprising when learning about values-based decisions was realizing I actually didn't know what my values were. I thought I knew but when I considered my list, I could see that many were learned values, ones I thought I *should* have. Here are some of my true guiding-light values below. Which ones are the most important to your soul?

Altruism	Humility
Calmness	Integrity
Compassion	Joyfulness
Dependability	Loyalty
Determination	Open-mindedness
Devotion	Optimism
Dignity	Reliability
Enthusiasm	Responsibility
Generosity	Respectfulness
Honesty	Self-acceptance

For me, enthusiasm, honesty, integrity, optimism, self-acceptance, compassion, generosity, open-mindedness, and determination are the values that I base my actions upon. You may have many others that aren't noted above.

If you're struggling to think about which values are most important to you, a helpful trick is selecting some Flexi-Mentors for inspiration and guidance. Flexi-Mentors are people who you respect more than anyone else. Consider why you respect them so much and think about what values they have prioritized to be who they are. Flexi-Mentors are the embodiment of the values we admire, respect, and wish to emulate. So if we find ourselves spiraling, it helps to consider quickly,

"What would one of my Flexi-Mentors do in this situation?" before we (re)act.

When my bitchy inner critic pipes up, I often jump to asking, "What would Oprah do?" *(Oprah is my ALL TIME Flexi-Mentor.)* I know she'd uphold the value of self-acceptance, and kindness but also inner strength, and with Oprah and her values in mind, I make my decision aligned with that.

I have go-to Flexi-Mentors for different areas in my life. When I feel disheartened about relationships, I ask, "What would John and Alice do?" They are a great couple I know who have crazy fun together and are my mentors in how to create an epic partnership. So when I'm feeling triggered by a message I've received for example, I know they'd say, "Forgive, relax, and have a laugh."

When I feel down on my luck and anxious, I ask, "What would Charlotte do?" She is this awesome woman who is such a power soul and *glows* with radiance whenever she walks into the room. Just thinking how she would act in a situation raises my vibe to try to emulate the *extra* fabulous one she takes everywhere.

My best friend is always so measured and calm, especially when things aren't going well, so when I get pissed off, I ask, "What would Suki do?" The answer is usually "Value patience and be rational. Slow down and look for more evidence about what made me so mad and whether it's worth all this anger." By doing so, I miraculously hold off on sending a scorching reply text with six exclamation points. Suki just wouldn't do it, so I take action by deciding to channel her self-control.

As we know from shadow work, we admire qualities in others that we possess ourselves. It takes one to know one. The same is true for values. If you notice and admire a value in your Flexi-Mentors, then you are capable of embodying those values yourself.

Dr. Judson Brewer told me about the concept of the BBO, the Bigger Better Offer. We will never create a new habit if we don't have an enormous carrot seducing us to create newness. The BBO has to be SO great, our brains *want* to remember the stretch toward it. The Flexi-Mentors' values are your new BBO. For example, thinking that I could be even one-tenth as fabulous as Charlotte makes me committed to breaking through my anxiety and negative thought habits when I am in social situations and channeling her. So next time you are in a situation and need to take action, ask yourself, "What would my Flexi-Mentor do?" And then do that. Huge carrots await.

We have forever learned through copying (human see, human do). We have "mirror neurons"—brain cells that turn on when we mimic actions we've observed, like walking and talking as babies—that help us learn just about everything. We don't have to stop learning through copying ever, and what's even better, we can now CHOOSE who we copy. Continue this valuable growth/learning process by choosing Flexi-Mentors and consciously activate those mirror neurons by studying them (read their books, follow their social media, listen to their podcasts, anything and everything) and enact their behavior. Flexi-Mentors help our brain recognize juicy opportunities that arise in our own life that can move us forward in positive directions.

You are the average of the five people you spend time with, so make sure you are spending adequate time with people who inspire you, even when they aren't physically there. Do it long enough, and the new habit of behaving like a calm, confident, and fabulous person will be the new normal. Make enough decisions based on what those who inspire you would do, and you're quickly on the right path to growing in alignment with those you respect, which in turn creates more self-respect.

By committing to using this method, your idols become your life-long teachers who can prevent stressful spiraling situations, and push you to feeling more confident, having greater faith in your abilities, and seeing endless possibilities.

It's not "fake it till you make it."

It's "be it until you become it."

Flexercise: Be Your Wild Self

If you can't think of a Flexi-Mentor to channel, that is OKAY! Don't stress about scrambling to find your Oprah or Charlotte. The idea is to identify values, and the embodiment of those values, to get you closer to wholeness.

Another, equally impactful way to help navigate decisions and actions is by using your own Wild Self (aka your Highest Self) as a mentor.

On my podcast, I interviewed Michaela Boehm, author of *The Wild Woman's Way: Unlock Your Full Potential for Pleasure, Power, and Fulfillment.* She defined "wild" not as the out-of-control #partygirl but as the one who is deeply attuned to every aspect of herself *without shame,* with integrity and healthy boundaries. The Wild Self isn't self-conscious and self-doubting. It trusts its instincts (which is very much like listening to our inner guidance and syncing our four brains). It's aware and respectful of our natural-born rhythms. The Wild Self *allows* us to cycle from periods of energy to periods of restfulness, times of creative output to times of rest, so we can be alive in our life as it is happening in the moment.

Clarissa Pinkola Estes wrote in *Women Who Run with the Wolves,* "When [people] reassert their relationship with the wildish nature, they are gifted with a permanent and internal watcher, a knower, a visionary, an oracle, an [inspiration], an intuitive, a maker, a creator, an inventor, and a listener who guide, suggest, and urge vibrant life in the inner and outer worlds," she said. "This wild teacher, wild mother, wild mentor supports their inner and outer lives, no matter what."

Talk about something to aspire to! To be as natural, instinctual, and gracefully accepting as a wild creature that's completely free to be itself and inspires us to vibrancy. The power and inspiration come from within.

Think of a time you felt the most connected you've ever been. You had "winning" energy, as my friend Sharmadean likes to similarly describe it. A moment when you were in your power, totally connected to your body and the world around you, when you were gloriously free and felt like nothing could stop you. Pinpoint that moment (or as close as you can get) and label that as your Wild Self you can return to.

Whenever you are confused as to what to do next, or in deciding how to act, return to that Wild Self. What would the most connected, liberated, winning you decide? This Wild Self is wholly authentic and surrounded only by unconditional love. Notice how your decisions change when you start to make them from the fearless, full-of-love Wild side (the one that runs with the wolves), not the fearful tamed self.

Find the Gifts

Searching for gifts—aka silver linings—forces our thoughts to stretch out of the rigidity of "this is 200 percent shit." Whenever anything "bad" happens, when we commit to flexibility, we open up our minds to see how that experience moved us forward. As Joseph Campbell wrote, "We must let go of the life we have planned, so as to accept the one that is waiting for us." The life we are uncovering every single minute is better than the one we've imagined, and flexibility helps us detach from any fixed expectations and disappointments to see that everything is unfolding exactly as it should. Our path is laden with gifts if we commit to look.

My mother has a brilliant ability to look for the gifts and see life as full of miracles. When my brother got rejected from a job he really *really* wanted, my mother said, "Clearly not right for you. Something better is brewing." Believing that is almighty hard, especially if we are stuck in fixed ideas about our desires. She was right, he bagged a way better job a month later. Suffering happens in the gap we hold between the expectations we have and reality. Flexing and finding the gifts in the gap resolves the pain.

The gift in disappointment isn't always obvious or immediately apparent. Nor are gifts always nicely wrapped with a bow on top; they might be hard to accept; you might wish you could send them back. I think of gifts as "growth nuggets," lessons presented to us that we really need to learn. Even if the lessons are difficult, we will benefit from learning them. If we redirect our focus toward finding growth nuggets at all times, they are guaranteed to appear, probably in unexpected places. The alternative approach is saying, "Screw this fairy tale wishful thinking/self-gaslighting. This situation is rubbish, it's just rubbish" and giving up. Well, that guarantees it will be rubbish because if we don't look for the gifts and learn our lessons, we definitely won't find them, recognize them when they come, or benefit from them.

A famous psych experiment by psychologists Christopher Chabris and Daniel Simons had subjects watch a video of six people, three in white shirts and three in black shirts, tossing a basketball back and forth. The subjects were instructed to count the number of times a white-shirted player passed the ball. In the middle of the experiment, a gorilla in a black shirt strolled into the middle of the action, faced the camera, and thumped its chest for nine seconds of screen time. As incredible as it might seem, half the subjects didn't notice the gorilla at all. The experiment shows that when we focus our attention on one thing—one job, crush, goal, desire—we can easily become blind to whatever else is happening. Hence, the name of the experiment: the Invisible Gorilla. It proved that (1) we aren't as observant as we think we are, and (2) we don't even know what we're missing out on.

Our unconscious brain is constantly looking out for new or relevant info and will only alert our conscious brain to things it deems useful, otherwise it's left undisturbed. Have you ever bought a car? Or a dress? And then suddenly noticed many other people wearing that exact dress or driving that car? This is a great example of how our unconscious can automatically change what alerts our conscious brain sends to us just from buying something different. There are not more red cars on the road, we're just more aware of them since it's become relevant information. Finding the gifts works in the exact same way. By committing to look for life's gifts, our minds will begin to naturally alert us to them, overriding the negative bias that is on a constant hunt for threats, and start to see where our opportunities lie. If we believe that every lump of coal contains a diamond, we'll find more diamonds.

"Learn to get in touch with the silence within yourself and know that everything in this life has a purpose, there are no mistakes, no coincidences, all events are blessings given to us to learn from."
—Elisabeth Kübler-Ross

Recently, a relationship fizzled out in New York, and left me quite disoriented. It was one of those connections that flew in and out so intensely, it left me wondering what had just happened. Instead of just lying there pondering why I was so upset about the split, I searched for gifts and found a bounty:

- I had even greater clarity about what I really wanted from a relationship.

- I learned what happens when I don't listen to my gut and instead get lost in my own projected fantasy.

- The loss made me realize that I was homesick for England.

I moved back home to the UK temporarily, and had plenty of time to notice and feel grateful for the gifts of reconnecting with old friends, feeling grounded for the first time in eight years of nomadic life, and spending tons of time with my parents and appreciating them more than ever, which is a gift and a blessing. On reflection I was, in a weird sort of way, grateful to the guy for breaking up with me. He gave me SO many growth nuggets.

Flexercise: Diving for Pearls

Perhaps you've been in a grisly situation that has no apparent gifts or pearls in sight, such as, "That whole relationship was a waste of time. He was just a dick, a self-absorbed, arrogant asshole, and I was an idiot for getting involved with him!!" or "NOTHING is going right for me, I hate my work, I hate my apartment, I hate my housemates. I'm just pissed at life right now."

Even when things feel bleak AF, Flex the mindset: What's the gift in feeling like you're at rock bottom?

I truly believe nothing happens in this world without a reason. Giraffes responded to adversity and grew longer necks, hedgehogs got spikier, and grasshoppers began hopping higher. Our ability to find the gift in all situations we are presented with is the key to our adaptation to living better. The emotional waves are happening *for* us, to push us to where we need to go and to tell us when changes are needed. All of our struggles are edging us closer to being better and living more in alignment. But we have to *be* present to find the present.

This is not about being fake positive. It's about accepting that there is not "only bad" or "only good," but that there is BALANCE in a life of wholeness. Some things *do* suck; there is no way around it. Your Wild Self doesn't bemoan rough patches. It accepts them, as all life is cyclical and in stages of different rhythms so it does its best in the moment. By accepting and Flexing through difficulties, we can move past them with pockets full of pearls.

Celebrate!

We shouldn't just feed our Love Wolf. We should throw it a cracking good party! Celebrate love and freedom. Whenever we take values-based action, have compassionate thoughts, set a new healthy habit, and prevent a downward spiral by using the Flex, we should light up the fireworks in our heads.

To make any change permanent, it has to be positively reinforced. Along with searching for gifts, why not gift ourselves little presents when we deserve them? Make the brain *want* to Flex over and over again and turn this healthy thought habit into your default by enjoying the carrots along the way. Sing from the rooftops. Jump around. Message me! I'm dying to share Flex stories about living a more compassionate life and finding the gifts that lie in all the situations you run into.

As legendary author and women's health expert Christiane Northrup, MD, once wrote, "It's our divine right to feel joyful and to do things in life that bring us joy!" Sadness and depression trigger disease-causing inflammation. Our immune system gets a boost when we are happy. Biologically, our bodies were designed to bliss out. We were meant to be joyful creatures because that's when everything on the inside works at its best. Dr. Northrup believes that making choices based on what makes us feel alive—from smelling the roses to dancing to singing in the shower—is the best and only job we have on Earth.

Flexercise: Find Your Bliss

Every morning, commit to doing activities and taking action that reinforces bliss. Can be as small as making coffee, walking, chatting to close friends. Five minutes, ten minutes, an hour, it's all good. Fill your day with mini blissful moments. My friend keeps a spreadsheet of things she enjoys and refers to that for inspiration when in a low mood. You can do that . . . or just list three things that give you life:

1. _____

2. _____

3. _____

Do It for Someone Else

The ultimate value to aspire to: altruism.

Social scientists have proven that we're more likely to commit to a new behavior if we're doing it for someone else.

In the UK, the government knew if they asked the whole population to stay at home during COVID-19 lockdown, it would be a tall order. They found out they'd get better compliance if they pitched quarantine as a selfless act to protect other people and our national health service over just "protect yourself." The research showed that citizens were 10 percent more likely to change their behavior if they knew it was for the benefit of someone else.

I thought it was fascinating to find out that we're not wired to be wholly selfish. I assumed the opposite. The human brain is actually wired for altruism. We are more likely to stick to habit changes if we do it for the benefit of someone we really care about.

If this works for you, explore taking an altruistic approach for self-change: Think of a loved one you'd do anything for, to make them happier. *Commit to flexible thinking for them*. The benefits are endless for you, less stress, more patience, better health, and increased energy, and the change in you will undoubtedly have a positive impact on them simultaneously.

For me, committing to walk away from fear for the people I love has been a strong motivator. When I started Flexing, my self-esteem was so low, I wasn't sure I was worthy of thinking in a different way. I didn't have the courage to challenge my brain or even consider that the messages in my mind were BS. The only thing that gave me energy to change was the thought of doing it for others. I thought of my parents and best friends and how much stress I'd put them through over the years. The late-night tears were even less fun for them than for me. After I unloaded, I felt better (temporarily), and they were left to worry. Anxiety is contagious and I was a superspreader. They didn't deserve to be infected. I realized that if I can think differently to improve my own health, I can also boost *their* immunity.

If we don't feel worthy enough to believe we deserve to be at peace, accepted, and happy, think of the people we love most in the world and commit to a life of compassion for them.

Make better decisions for them. As a result, we all enjoy the benefits. Choosing a life of self-acceptance and compassion is the least selfish path we can take. It's not easy. We are fighting against decades of learned habits and biases. But if we know we're fighting to the betterment of someone else, we will discover that our strength is limitless.

Commitment is about CONSISTENCY OVER TIME. Healing is not linear. Think "progress not perfection." Flexing for a week and then blowing it off isn't going to have a long-term impact. It's like eating broccoli once and thinking you've had all the greens you'll ever need. Sometimes we'll feel empowered, grateful, filled with positive momentum when we start and then slack off. Remember the metaphor about touching your toes! Do it daily, and you'll always be able to. So practice Commitment strategies every day—with a determined focus for three days or more to really "set" them into place—to liberate the mind of anxiety.

Make a note of what's bothering you to free it from your mind. Use Flexi-Mentors and/or your instinctual Wild Self for guidance and inspiration to take considered action for better outcomes and wholeness.

Search for pearls in the ocean because they're waiting to be found.

Celebrate your wins and revel in the small joys of life because you deserve it!

Be altruistic because life is richer and happier when we do it for others.

Sometimes, despite Flexing daily, we might feel stuck again, like we're not making any progress at all. In those moments we might want to hit the "Fuck it!" button and unravel. But that's when we have to allow for fuckups and accept that this work is full of surprises. I have to constantly check myself as my perfectionism creeps back in. I can become a perfectionist about being flexible, beating myself up when I do something stiff. But I tell myself, "Poppy, Flexing is the opposite of perfectionism: There is no right or wrong, just learning!" and then throw a pound of red meat to the Wolf of Love, and surrender to the stretch I'm in.

No one is born knowing how to play soccer or to be a flexible thinker. We need to acquire the skill with lots and lots of practice. The only raw skill you need is desire. Desire sparks action. Soccer pros love the game and then practice all the time to be great. Our emotional health is the same. Use your desire for a joy-filled life and then notice how the more you practice Flexing, the healthier and happier you become.

Each Flex step is helpful in and of itself. Sometimes using just one step singularly might be enough to get through a crisis. But together they guide us into a freedom to embrace our whole selves, warts and wonder. My great friend, Human Design expert and spiritual teacher Jenna Zoë, once said to me, "I want to achieve all my big dreams, but only if I'm creating a self and a life that is goofy, carefree, and spontaneous with all the lightness we had as children before it was trained out of us." The Flex was my way to do exactly that. It has been my method to create a playful, inspiration-filled, curious life.

When I interviewed Daniel Ryan, a hypnotherapist in New York, he explained to me that we spend most of our life in a trance, an autopilot idling mode that our brain likes because it doesn't need much energy. Flexing takes energy. We're asking our minds to stay conscious, to blaze new pathways and create new solutions, and our lazy brains would stick to autopilot if they were left in control. Intervention is necessary. No one manifests their dream life while sleepwalking and if you want to build a future that has meaning, this rests in waking up and committing to living life with conscious thought flexibility.

In the next section of the book, I'll dig deeper into how rigidity and entrenched patterns limit us in big areas of life, and how we can use the Flex to overcome problems, affect outcomes, and change our futures for the better.

I once read this great quote on Instagram: "In a society that profits from your self-doubt, liking yourself is a rebellious act."

Flexing is my rebellion and my activism. Hopefully, it'll be yours, too.

"A person who has good thoughts cannot ever be ugly. You can have a wonky nose and a crooked mouth and a double chin and stick-out teeth, but if you have good thoughts they will shine out of your face like sunbeams and you will always look lovely."
—Roald Dahl

PART THREE

THE FLEX IN REAL LIFE

"TO ACCEPT ONE'S PAST—ONE'S HISTORY—IS NOT THE SAME THING AS DROWNING IN IT; IT IS LEARNING HOW TO USE IT."

—JAMES BALDWIN

FLEX THE PAST

We are the sum of our past, everything we've ever done or felt. But do we want our future to look like the past, repeating the same patterns? If you're like me, you might be ready for a change.

I do want to call attention to the fact we'll be dealing with a very slippery character—the past. It can contort to whatever role it wants to play. Like a fantastic showman, it tells us stories that excite, inspire, enrapture, enthrall or terrify, haunt, victimize, and imprison. We should think twice before trusting our memory and letting that be our North Star. Following it like the Pied Piper might lead us down the same roads we've traveled before and hoped to avoid seeing again.

Every experience and feeling we've had is stored in our unconscious, but science has proven that our brain's filing system is *glitchy as fuck.* While reading Dr. Mlodinow's *Subliminal*, I had a rather nasty reality check realizing our brains can't store *every* detail of our memories. We recall the gist—enough to create a story that makes sense to us—and, as he explained, we fill in the blanks with our expectations, desires, prior knowledge, and beliefs. It's as if our brain cooks up a half dish and then adds a heaping cup of extras before serving it, completely changing the original taste but making it edible. The seasoning effect happens unconsciously and unintentionally. For example, our brains don't want us to remember pain clearly. If we did, women would never give birth twice.

While making the documentary *The Memory Mirage*, director Josh Freed found that war heroes on a speaking tour gradually enhanced their exploits as they retold their stories again and again from audience to audience, city to city, to the point that they sounded unrecognizable by the end. The process was unintentional. Once our brain has a new version of a story, it erases the previous one. Even the most sophisticated MRI brain scans can't distinguish between truth and fiction when people believe what they're saying. Freed said, "I've learned it's wise not to argue with my spouse about who-said-what-to-whom seven years ago. Science suggests that we're probably both wrong about many events in our memory album."[36]

Stiff thinkers are stuck in yesteryear and unwilling/unable to let the past go. They stay in a rainstorm of fixed beliefs, getting drenched and bearing unnecessary discomfort. But the discovery that our memories are often inaccurate is both strange and potentially liberating. Flexible thinkers have a real opportunity here to blaze new interpretations and associations with past events.

Whenever I used to reflect on this one past relationship, I would feel a crushing disappointment that it ended because I had enjoyed it so much, and then blame myself for its demise. My best friend Flexed me straight one day, saying, "Stop remembering him like a god! He upset you continually throughout the relationship! He said you were annoyingly energetic in the mornings among other things. This is not a relationship to pine after." I'd conveniently forgot *those* details.

Flexing the past isn't about forgetting it. It's about reducing its power, extracting the wisdom to move forward, and consciously creating something new.

Choose a New Story

New characters, new plot, new script

Our brains are compulsive storytellers, always casting ourselves in plots of our imagination. We tend to filter our mental movies through the lens of our own preoccupations; so many of my movies have been about all the ways I've been let down or let myself down, or an endless loop of drama.

For a good storyline, you need a hero and a villain. We are conditioned by the good vs. evil narrative found in everything from Disney to our parents warning us about bad people ("Don't take candy from strangers!"), to James Bond. Like a warm cup of tea or a weighted blanket, knowing how people fit into the plot and being able to predict the ending give us comfort. The villian vs. victim stories are recyling the same shit, a movie with a million sequels that are always exactly the same. It's like *Groundhog Day* in real life, and most of us are living it.

My plots were too often "poor me" stories. My teenage frustrated actor dreams would come alive as I performed my own daily pantomimes with lines like "CAN YOU BELIEVE THEY DID THAT TO ME!?" I had been dating this guy (who I'd really fallen for) and out of the blue he broke up with me. Within days, I heard he'd bunny-hopped into a new relationship and even months later, I was still recounting the horror. I called my friend Margo, a very wise screenwriter in Los Angeles, to talk about it and started off by saying, *"Can you believe…"*

"Pops, first off, I think you dated your imagination rather than who that guy really was. You hardly saw each other," she said.

Okay, that wasn't in the script. She was supposed to say, "Poor you."

Flexible thinking is about choosing to rewrite your story by widening the lens on what happened, to get a multidimensional perspective on it. For one thing, we have a tendency to make all our stories deeply personal, when a lot of the time, it's got nothing to do with us. For example, kids often blame themselves or put themselves in a central role in their parents' divorce.

For another thing, the bitchy brain likes 2D characters and thin plots. But the flexible mind expands to 3D, with complexity and depth that allow for compassion and kindness. Although basic good vs. evil battles make for exciting scenes—and they are fun to write as we lie awake at night, plotting our revenge and wallowing in victimhood— these simple, stiff thoughts shut down the realness and honesty we need to create a happier, healthier life.

Mindset and performance coach Polly Bateman described people who are unwilling to rewrite past narratives as like flies that continually bash against a window, trying to get inside. If it stopped bashing and looked around, the fly would find the wide-open door nearby. "We are so fixed on our stories that we don't look for others and discover easier routes forward," she said. "We have to work to see the open window next door. But it's not a lot of work! Just the effort it takes to turn around."

Along with good vs. evil, we've been heavily conditioned to believe in right vs. wrong. But according to Bateman, *right* and *wrong* are just cultural concepts created so we can exist in a peaceful society. Rules and laws are helpful and necessary, of course. But when it comes to the stress and anxiety about getting things "wrong," or trying to be "right," we don't need it. "Challenge the concept," she said. "Stop fighting to be right, and don't fear being wrong. The brain doesn't distinguish between what's real and what's imagined. We go with the one we like best. We take what's happened, we dice up what we assume it's about based on past conditioning from family, school and culture, and we react. We love to be right and we love to blame so we can easily end up stuck in ruts."

I giggled to myself listening to Bateman, because I'd just had an argument with a friend who was always late for everything. I grew up learning that being late was rude, disrespectful, and a sign that you don't appreciate the person you're meeting. When I called her out on her consistent lateness, my friend thought I was being oversensitive and told me to not take it so seriously. Everyone was late for everything in her family, so she saw it as no big deal and it didn't mean anything aside from bad time management. I guess neither of us was right or wrong; I shouldn't interpret the tardiness to mean she doesn't care about me, and my friend should make a bit more of an effort to be on time next time.

It's both terrifying and liberating to think that experiences we "know" to be right or wrong can be just made up in our head.

Our new movie can start at any moment. The minute we choose a Flexi-thought—"What's the evidence?" or "My memory about that might not be accurate" or "The window is closed but there might be an open door nearby…"—we are already in a new story, and can change the script to whatever we want. The Flex brings back our power in the present moment to forgive the past, stop acting out rote lines and scenes, craft a new narrative…

…and commit to a new *inner voice.*

The way we remember our past is highly influenced by the language we use.

Elizabeth Loftus, one of the world's most influential psychologists, has shown that by changing the language of how we recount our past, we can change our relationship with it. In an experiment, she screened videos of cars crashing and then asked viewers what they saw. The participants who were asked, "How fast were the cars going when they smashed into each other?" reported higher speeds than participants who were asked, "How fast were the cars going when they hit each other?"[37] Just one word changed the response.

Furthermore, when participants were invited back a week later to talk about the video, the "smash" group was more likely to remember seeing lots of broken glass (there wasn't any) than the other group. It's extraordinary how memory is affected with just a subtle language change. And thanks to science, we can take advantage of this knowledge in our own lives. Hurrah!

Flexercise: Change Your Words, Change Your Narrative

Use language to your advantage and retell your past story in a way that empowers you. This is a very powerful exercise because your brain believes everything you tell it.

To turn "failure" into "growth," edit stiff-thinking words and replace them with elastic ones.

American architect, designer, author, and futurist Buckminster Fuller once said, "There is no such thing as a failed experiment, only experiments with unexpected outcomes."

So, replace unhelpful words like "failure," "fuckup," "screwup," and "disaster" with the word "unexpected."

Stiff version: "Deciding to make those products when the company was low on funds was a complete disaster."

Flexi-edit: "Making those products was an experiment with an unexpected outcome. It will really help me think through future experiments more thoroughly."

Stiff version: "It was a complete disaster when I crotch-dived an A-list actor on my first opportunity as a TV reporter. What a fuckup."

Flexi-edit: "It was quite unexpected that I missed the seat, and I learned forever after to look before I sit."

Try it. Write down all your "failures" and exchange that word for "unexpected." Really takes the sting out and, most important, places you back in a curious, forward-thinking mindset. Flexible.

Are You Stuck in the Past?

We are often controlled by events that happened ages ago

Being stuck in the past is exhausting, for one thing. It's like our unconscious is chained on the hamster wheel from hell. To find out if you are on that treadmill, read the statements below. How many ring bells for you?

1. "I keep making the same mistakes."

2. "I don't know why I did that!"

3. "I'd better not fail."

4. "Don't ask me, I'm no good at that."

5. "This stuff always happens to me."

6. "All men/women are…"

7. "I'm afraid of…"

8. "I'm a terrible failure."

9. "I shouldn't have done that."

10. "I'll never forgive them/myself."

11. "I'm *still* pissed."

12. "I'm feeling self-conscious."

13. "I don't know why this triggers me so much."

14. "I overreacted."

15. "I like/don't like that [before I've even tried it]."

If half or more of these statements sound right, it's likely that you are stuck in the past. But don't beat yourself up! *It's not your fault!* It's actually pretty normal. Here's why:

Being stuck in the past is about survival. If our ancestors had a past memory of being chased by a lion, they quickly learned what to do when put in the same situation again, RUN. By using established pathways, our brains save time and energy. As cavemen, we needed to conserve as much energy as possible to deal with the hardship of life. So even just a faint clue a lion might be approaching would cause an automatic reflex to seek safety. Thanks to past memories, we've survived many a future threat.

BUT nowadays this isn't so helpful: If we have a childhood memory of, say, being scolded by an authority figure and learned that throwing a tantrum made it stop, doing that behavior again as an adult isn't going to serve us well.

Using past memories to save energy and help us survive: epic.

Using past memories to inform emotional reactions: fail.

It's about efficiency. By relying on past memory over present thought, our conscious mind has space to think about other things. For example, walking into the supermarket, our unconscious knows it's been here before, and immediately opens that memory file. Instantly, we know to grab a cart, move through the aisles, grab our stuff, and go to checkout. Simultaneously, we can chat on the phone about much more important things, like the fact that Moe and Charlie hooked up last night or what's new on Netflix. Without blinking, we've gone shopping, come home, and unpacked bags, all without expending a single conscious thought on the entire process. We are just repeating actions we've learned on autopilot. Very helpful and convenient for shopping but not ideal for life! It's a bit disconcerting that we spend close to 90 percent of our day on autopilot practically living life from past memory.

It's about certainty. A major reason we find ourselves repeating patterns, even when we know they aren't good for us: Our unconscious *loves* the familiar. Our brain *craves* delicious certainty. It's on a constant mission to show us again and again that what it believes *is* right. Affirming what we "know" to be true is our brain's safe place.

Look at it this way: A football game would be chaos if there were no rules, right? We feel safe and reassured by rules, and we want them to be the same every time we leave the house. The problem is, the rules (how to relate, how to react, how to behave) our brain is constantly confirming might be harmful, hurtful, and limiting.

The brain will ALWAYS push us toward certainty because an uncertain future can be terrifying to contemplate.

This is the mantra of rigid thinkers: "Better the devil you know than the devil you don't." They would rather stick with the predictable past, even if it blows. Clinging to the past *is* tempting, like sleeping with an ex. Or going for the same type of partner every time, even if they're toxic. It still feels somewhat safe, only because it's familiar and provides that "oh, yeah, this feels like home, I've been here before" sensation. This familiarity can be like a wolf in sheep's clothing.

We might have *some* awareness of repeating patterns of thought or behavior because we make the same mistakes and bad choices over and over again, cycling through relationships, jobs, diets, friendships, that all seem to take a similar road to nowhere. But it's hard to break those patterns. I have thought, too many times to count, **This time, it's going to be different.** But this quickly slides into **Why does this always happen!** Even though we optimistically believe change is on the horizon, our emotional habits march us to the same beat, down the same road.

Unless we *consciously reframe the past and make new, better choices*, it will continue to act like a persistent nosy neighbor who keeps knocking on our door with fresh muffins, which is to say, biologically impossible to resist. Being stuck in the past isn't anyone's fault; everyone wants to say "yes" to hot muffins. We were never taught that our unconscious mind clings to established patterns like a scared toddler to his mom's leg. Or the fact that our bitchy inner critic is a gangster at finding all the evidence to confirm our fears.

Freedom awaits, though. The fact that you are reading this book attests to your commitment to finding it. Flexing allows us to override the old, and replace it with new courage, compassion, and action to design a new future.

One of the most profound books about challenging old beliefs is *The Four Agreements* by Don Miguel Ruiz. It gave me another life-shattering lesson about how we grow up with "agreements" we didn't actually agree to—such as the language we speak, our names, our religious beliefs, how to behave, what's right and wrong, beautiful and ugly, good and bad, etc. When we realize just how much of our lives are ruled by these agreements, we can begin to decide consciously which to keep and which to renegotiate. It is critical that we activate our ability to choose what we want to hold on to, and what we need to let go of, which beliefs lift us up and which weigh us down.

"We have many agreements that make us suffer, that make us fail in life. If you want to live a life of joy and fulfillment, you have to find the courage to break those agreements that are fear-based and claim your personal power."
—Don Miguel Ruiz

Flexercise: Dump Old Faulty Beliefs

Write these headings on five pieces of paper: *MEN, WOMEN, AUTHORITY, WORK, MYSELF.* Then write any word that comes to mind about the headings. Don't think too hard. Just write.

I asked a friend who'd dated three cheating BFs in a row to do this exercise, and here's what she came up with.

MEN: untrustworthy, liar, hurtful

WOMEN: kind, nurturing, easily manipulated

AUTHORITY: question, scary, unfair

WORK: sporadic, pressure, not there yet

MYSELF: scared, lost, lonely, strong

The reason this exercise is revealing is because the words that first come to mind show your underlying beliefs around these topics. Immediately, my friend could see that her beliefs about MEN and AUTHORITY had shaped her reality. She dated similar men who validated her core beliefs. "Jesus, I had no idea how negative I am about pretty much everything," she said.

Being curious (step #2) about our beliefs gives us insight that wakes us up to the cause of our suffering.

This exercise comes from the Queen of Wellness, author Louise Hay. During a reader Q&A, a woman told Hay that she hated her job because no one listened to her. When she tried to be assertive, she was met with annoyance. If she gave up and stayed silent, she felt invisible and unimportant.

Hay asked the woman to complete this exercise. Next, Hay asked her how many of the words and phrases she wrote down related to her experiences growing up. The woman was amazed by the abundant overlap between her office now and her childhood home.

When you do the exercise, take away any judgment from what you write. There are no right or wrong answers. You're looking for *clues* about your long-held faulty beliefs, and how they might have come to be. Through this awareness, you can forgive yourself a million times over. It's not your fault that you have them. You inherited them. But now that you're aware of them, you have the power to let them go.

Why Are We So Haunted?

The past leaves a mark on your permanent record

The brain is truly miraculous. It has unlimited capacity to store all of our memories from the sponge years. However, it tends to prioritize the more emotionally traumatic ones. Very ANNOYING. Polly Bateman uses the example of a playground insult. One kid says to another in the sandbox, "Those are hideous shoes!" A confident kid might respond, "I love these shoes, piss off!" But most children will react to criticism with shame, fear of being kicked out of the group, and an intense inner pressure to conform to feel loved and accepted. *Playground teasing at six is an existential threat... kicked out of the tribe for hideous shoes...never to be seen again.*

The fear, shame, and rejection over ugly shoes our mum probably forced us to wear gets stored in our "watchtower brain," as Bateman calls it, which just wants us to survive. In this case, survival means fitting in. But long after our child brain protected us from the shower of shame by begging our mum for new shoes, our adult brain tells us in EVERY context that we'll avoid shame by wearing and buying the right stuff. Perhaps some Instagram influencers who are obsessed with dressing and looking "right" are just grown-up children trying to fit in, desperate for a sense of belonging.

The ancient Greek philospher Aristotle said, "Give me a child until he is seven, and I will show you the man." Psychological research proves he was onto something there. Young children are not controlled by their past because they don't have one yet. That's why they meet everything with wonder, presence, and curiosity, and without self-judgment. As we grow up, our fearlessness is swapped out for conditioning and fears. By seven, our foundational beliefs for life are arguably formed and set. "We were all born as blank slates," said Bateman. "We've got our own genetic differences, of course, but emotions and thoughts flip on and off in our brains only because of the sum of our unique experiences. Just recognize that any strong reaction [in adulthood] has a root somewhere to an unhelpful reaction we learned as a child to a situation we didn't understand or weren't equipped to deal with yet."

Our memories dictate how we interpret life and what meaning we attach to what could be meaningless events. I've talked about pattern matching before, but just a quick recap: It's the mental process triggered by an event of attaching emotional meaning to it based on our past experiences.

Event → past emotion → reaction on autopilot.

For example, someone criticizes our shoes, and we instantly feel shame, but only because our brain's internal Google searched its database for a historical match, opened the file, and read that receiving such criticism is shameful. Without awareness of these automatic reactions, we are powerless to stop them. As a result, we feel boatloads of unnecessary shame, and might develop a shoe addiciton as an atttempt to lessen the shame. Our shoe shelf may fill up, but we can't buy relief from stored pain.

Even when our thoughts are clearly unproductive, in some convoluted way, they are trying to be protective. We have to appreciate that we have always been doing the best we could with the information we had at the time...and, most likely, so did our parents. They didn't know that freaking out when a son falls off a bike or saying "shush" during a crying fit or praising a girl for her happy smile or putting a lock on the pantry would trigger emotions in a child that turned into a story that would affect their life forevermore.

It only takes a split second for our brain to dredge up ancient fear and pain. So fast, we don't realize it's happening, and then we just react to it. A woman I admire immensely, Britteny Floyd-Mayo, the founder of Trap Yoga, told me a story about her childhood fears returning in adulthood to damage a close friendship. "I grew up in foster care and had been living by myself at fifteen," she said. "When my hot water was turned off, I stopped going to school." Her Spanish teacher, a woman six years older than Britteny, invited her to use her shower because she knew Britteny wouldn't go to school otherwise. They grew close and the Spanish teacher became a mentor and champion for Britteny.

Ten years later, Britteny's career started taking off and her mentor seemed to withdraw from her life. "My parents abandoned me, and when she started stepping away, I immediately assumed this was just *another person* in my life who wanted to leave me. It's my default reaction, always," she said.

She suffered in silence until one day, she found the courage to confront her mentor. As it turned out, Britteny had misinterpreted the situation. Her former teacher was devastated to learn Britteny thought she was abandoning her. She explained that she did step back a bit, but only to make room for Britteny to grow and come into her own. "My mentor saw me as *graduating*," she said. "I was suffering unnecessarily. I'd felt neglected and mistreated but I was just reliving trauma from the past. It was not the present reality at all." Having the courage to be curious, investigate further, and be flexible freed Britteny from the trap of past assumptions.

Polly Bateman again: "There are only three basic triggers you will ever experience. Anytime you feel upset or irritated, think back to see what root cause is being triggered: *Am I safe? Am I loved? Am I enough?* How we behave every day of our lives is the surface to these roots," she said. "When I see people reacting to the three root causes of anxiety, I remind them, 'You're not that eight-year-old that got rejected in the playground anymore.' We have to work on getting to know ourselves and what is true in this current day."

Every single one of us has stories that might seem minor in hindsight, but they define us to this day. A friend of mine, an early bloomer who towered over her classmates in first grade, was told by her teacher, "Don't hug the other kids because you'll hurt them." She shared, "To this day, I hesitate to hug people. It's been thirty years!"

"Life gives you people and places to
show you where you're not free."
—Peter Crone

Unlocking the cage of the past is a constant negotiation. The past will always be seductive, as it's all-knowing certainty. Becoming radically aware of our past patterns and beliefs takes courage but it's the only way to begin reframing. It's not easy to challenge the old and be curious and open to new information. But staying stiff, assuming you know why, what, and when, will be all of our downfall.

Flexercise: Use Your "Get Out of Prison" Card

To get out of autopilot reactiveness to the past . . . FLEX!

CONNECTION. Accept the feeling as it comes up. Don't mindlessly react to it. Let it happen. Notice it. Defuse it! "Today I am feeling . . ." To unstick yourself from the feeling of the trigger, energize the rewiring process, stand up, sit down, run around, dance, belly breathe, unclench your jaw, and activate the body in some way.

CURIOSITY. Search your database as best you can for historical instances of this feeling. What is this current situation reminding you of? Start by just thinking about the last time you felt it, even if it was a day ago. And then try to hop to the time before that, and so on, until you get ever closer to the sandbox moment itself.

CHOICE. Consciously decide you are ready to rewrite the narrative on this reaction. Choose to step into compassion and forgiveness by reframing the experience by putting it in a new perspective. Ask yourself, "Where and who can I forgive?"

COMMITMENT. Change your future by responding differently to the stimulus and taking values-based action. Consult your Flexi-Mentors and consider what they would do next. I ask myself, "What would Oprah do?" or "How would a person who thinks she's good enough and has self-appreciation react?" What would my Wild Self, a creature who has no shame, do? And then I just do *that* to react in alignment with the future I want to create.

Recycling Relationships

Yup, even your romantic attachments are dictated by your childhood

Research on "attachment style" goes back to the mid-twentieth century with British psychologist John Bowlby. American-Canadian psychologist Mary Ainsworth took Dr. Bowlby's theories further in her famous "Strange Situation" study.[38] She put a mother and her toddler in a playroom together, and then had the mom leave for a few minutes. Dr. Ainsworth studied how the toddler reacted upon the mother's return to the room and classified the relationships into three main types. Sixty percent of the relationships were "secure"; 20 percent were "anxious"; 20 percent were "avoidant."

- **Secure.** These toddlers were upset when their mum left the room. They searched for her and allowed themselves to be comforted by her when she came back. These kids' emotional needs were met by their parent; they received consistent love and attention, felt safe, and took comfort gladly.

- **Anxious.** These babies were super upset when Mum left, and when she came back, they weren't sure how to react, with anger, relief, or joy. These kids' needs were insufficiently met; they could have been neglected, felt unsafe, or/and been shown love inconsistently.

- **Avoidant.** These kids didn't seem to care that Mum left and paid more attention to their toys when Mum returned. Later on, researchers defined two subcategories for avoidant attachment: avoidant-fearful (recoiling as if afraid from the parent) and avoidant-dismissive (purposefully ignoring the parent). All avoidantly attached kids' needs were inconsistently met by somewhat neglectful parents who were dismissive of their children's distress, and possibly abusive.

But here's the key point: Our attachment to our parents when we were toddlers foreshadowed our relationship styles as adults.

Which Relationship Style Pings You?

Secure	Anxious	Avoidant-Fearful	Avoidant-Dismissive
Satisfying	Stressful	Like walking on eggshells	Distant
Supportive	People pleasing	Possessive	Noncommittal
Forgiving	Clingy	Obsessive	Uncomfortable if your partner tries to push it forward
Accepting	Needy of reassurance	Suspicious	
Reliable	Possessive	Demanding	
Boundaries are clear	Jealous	You crave love and validation and are terrified of rejection.	It's unbalanced, with you wishing he/she could be more independent.
You can express freely how you feel.	Too permissive of the partner's bad behavior		
During bad times, you lift each other up.	Always on the verge of ending (in your head)	Arguments are loud and hurtful, and lead to tears and makeup sex.	Distancing is easier than talking about problems.
During good times, you celebrate together.	Fantasy-based; the partner is idolized, not seen as a real person.	When it ends, you say, "I'm going to be alone forever."	You shut down when emotional demands are made.
The connection is real (not a fairy tale).	You bite your lip instead of saying how you really feel.		Fights end with storming off or exploding.
When it ends, you say, "We were good while it lasted, but it ran its course. I wish him/her well."	Is full of tears and desperate outbursts		When it ends, you say, "It was more trouble than it was worth."
	When it ends you say, "He never really loved me."		

It might come as no surprise that my relationship style was anxious, which indicates I had an anxious attachment to my parents. I used to end romances before they even began out of fear that my partner wasn't that into me. And when it ended, I'd say, "He never liked me anyway." On first reading through the list of characteristics linked to anxiously attached people, I started laughing because I literally ticked every single box.

Diary entry: 17th October 2017
(current Poppy)

I've known this guy for barely any time, and I'm fearful I'm going to get hurt. I know this is all self-inflicted, but the terror I feel is unbearable. Why has he made me worry and cry so much? I think I'm terrified of relationships. This fear of abandonment before it's even happened, the need for consistency is bottomless. It's so weird being able to see how psycho I'm being, and wondering whether it's me or if I'm being triggered. Perhaps it's best if I just politely end it, write a note and say I think that's the best idea. Even writing this makes me calmer. That's what I'm going to do . . .

Horrifying! Back then, I didn't know what I didn't know about where my anxiety in relationships came from.

Obviously, no one changes overnight, and I still struggle from having an anxious relationship style, but now I recognize when it's overtaking me. That awareness allows me to jump quickly to Step #3 of the Flex and to consciously choose not to let fear rule me. When I date now, as soon as I leap to, "I should just break this up, he clearly doesn't like me," I have to talk to myself in the third person, a defusing technique Dr. Joan Rosenberg recommended, and say, "There is no evidence he's not that into you, Poppy. Stay in your power!" I would shower the guys I was dating with worshipful adoration, as if they were some Greek god who'd come down from Mount Olympus to ask me out, because that fit my romance narrative, also formed in childhood. Now I make an effort to appreciate my value and remember it's just a guy, not the best thing since squeeze mayonnaise. Nor is he a villain who might dump me for no reason. Flexing gave me the awareness to challenge my anxiety, stop dating my imagination, and bring the relationship back to reality.

You are not bound for all time to the anxiety and avoidance you might have experienced as a powerless child, or the resulting attachment style, or the current relationship style. Freedom from our past starts with awareness and then beginning to make different decisions to what our auto-pilot brain tells us to do. We are not to blame for our relationship style. It's based on how we first encountered need and fulfillment, usually from our parents or main caregivers. Bring zero judgment into this gathering insight. It's just information to take in, reflect on, and learn from. Again, don't blame caregivers! They did the best they could with what they knew/were dealing with at the time. Release the blame all around.

Is it *Really* Possible to Let Go of the Past?

Unlocking the cage

Can we really let go of *anything*? Dr. Steve Hayes said, "We can't erase our unconscious." We don't need to erase it, though. The brilliant thing about the Flex is that letting go doesn't mean forgetting the past. It's about reframing and stretching it so you can make peace with it. With *curiosity*, we can recognize how unreliable our memory is, and then we *choose* how it influences us. Will we stay trapped in fear? Or will we reframe it to empower ourselves going forward?

> "We all have a story. The difference is: Do you use the story to empower yourself? Or do you use your story to keep yourself a victim? The question itself empowers you to change your life."
> —Sunny Dawn Johnston

Let's talk about a victim mentality, a great thing to let go of.

It's a very stiff mindset that causes a stubborn cycle of "bad things always happen to me," and coming up with endless explanations and blame. Many of the walking wounded don't even realize they have a victim mentality. It can be surprisingly subtle. Robert Leahy, PhD, director of the American Institute for Cognitive Therapy, taught me the signs:

- **Feeling powerless** to solve a problem or cope effectively; e.g., "I can't deal. I don't know what to do. I've tried and nothing's working."

- **Seeing every problem as a catastrophe**; e.g., "It's a complete fucking disaster!"

- **Thinking others are purposefully trying to hurt you**; e.g., "They wanted this to happen to me. People want me to fuck up!"

- **Believing you alone are targeted for mistreatment**; e.g., "Of course, they didn't invite *me*. They excluded me on purpose."

- **Holding tightly to a victim status**; e.g., "You don't understand because you didn't have a neurotic mother like I do."

Oh, boy, could I relate to this very stiff, stuck-in-the-mud mentality. Rather than committing to action that could heal my wounds, I often stayed a victim to get sympathy. Author Jessa Crispin wrote in *Why I Am Not a Feminist: A Feminist Manifesto*, "There are advantages to being labeled the victim. You are listened to, paid attention to. Sympathy is bestowed upon you." This is why the victim mentality is hard to break. Believe it or not, it's secretly meeting a basic need to receive love or reassurance.

I craved validation for the pain I went through, and comments like "So sorry, Poppy, you've really been through the wringer!" were like oxygen. But whining about my problem loops, catastrophizing, and taking everything personally, I began to realize that receiving sympathy was never going to be enough to bandage my cuts. I wasted years choosing to remain a victim, but if anyone accused me of having a victim mentality at the time, I would have immediately rejected the idea. FYI: Defensiveness is another sign of a victim mentality. Byron Katie wrote, "Defense is the first act of war." If you feel like you need to defend against other people, you might have this subtle stiff mindset.

I had a victim mentality, but I am not a victim of abuse, violence, or neglect. Many people have gone through much worse than me. No matter the difficulties in our history, whether "victim" deserves to be in quote marks or not, we all have a real fear of letting go of past grievances because it gives us a feeling of "letting someone off the hook" for things that are not forgivable. But by reframing what forgiveness is, we can free ourselves of another's karma. It's not about saying what they did is okay; it's an act of energy up-leveling for us. When you stay trapped in the wrongs, the perpetrator wins. Choosing to let go doesn't change what happened. It *does* change our reactiveness. The sweetest revenge is forgiving as we cut energetic ties.

What does this mindset have to do with the past? Like all faulty beliefs, a victim mentality is learned in childhood. Perhaps we watched a parent use this strategy, or receiving sympathy made us feel heard and seen. "Blaming others" and "not being to blame" kept us safe once, and our mind likes to repeat anything that achieves this. Brené Brown once said, "Blame is simply the discharging of pain and discomfort."

Our brain is highly susceptible to falling into a victim mentality because it protects our ego. There's a seductiveness to never being at fault.

But if you have done nothing wrong, you have nothing to learn. Victimhood is a state of arrested development. Children are blameless. Adults take responsibilty because healing can only happen when we stop farming out feelings onto others. So staying in victim mode actually *self-sabotages* and locks us in the past.

If we want to pick up pearls, we have to be accountable. On her podcast, life coach Brooke Castillo described receiving an email from an old client listing all the things she didn't like about her. "Immediately, as I read this list of things that this other person had said about me, I felt myself get defensive," she recalled. "Uh oh, I'm going right into that victim mentality. Poor me. How could they say all this about me? Oh, my gosh. I can't believe they did this to me." She had to take a deep breath and, rather than spiral, she read the list of insults and responded "I agree" to some of them. In that moment of ownership, she made a choice. Instead of playing the victim and turning the email writer into a villain, she decided to use curiosity to see if she could find any truth in the criticism and gain insight. She found many gifts in the slam email.

Victimhood is therefore an avoidance strategy. If we refuse to take responsibility and *nothing* is our fault, we don't have to do any emotional work. Mark Manson, author of *The Subtle Art of Not Giving a F*ck,* wrote, "Victims seek to blame others for their problems or blame outside circumstances. This may make them feel better in the short term, but it leads to a life of anger, helplessness, and despair." As such, a victim mentality keeps you stuck in low, low, low vibrational energy.

Short-term gains turn into long-term damage. Blaming others only cements living in the past, relinquishing control and remaining a child forever. It provides no opportunity for change and keeps us on the sidelines of our own lives. Sure, we will be spared having to explore uncomfy emotions and can probably get away with very bad behavior just by saying, "They made me do it! It's not my fault!" But if we want to be the pilot of our life and not just a passenger, it's time for a conscious change and a Flex.

Flexercise: Ending the Blame Game

Think of someone you blame for causing pain in your life. Now answer these four questions. Be honest! No judgment!

What good is it doing *for me* to hold this blame?

How does holding on to blame, anger, hatred, resentment, sadness, self-pity help me in my life?

How does holding on to these negative emotions hurt me?

Am I ready to let go of this blame?

Every emotional reaction we have in the present has been learned from past experiences. No one can make us feel angry, shameful, guilty, or embarrassed, but we make ourselves feel these things by attaching our own interpretation to events. By blaming others, as in, "You made me so angry," we remain powerless to our emotions. But by taking responsibility for our part in the creation of our feelings, we are empowered. It also gives us a measure of control to remember that the present has little to do with how we feel; it's all residue from the past that needs to be cleaned.

The upside-down version of a victim mentality is when we blame ourselves for everything. We believe we are the cause of all our problems, as in, "It's all my fault!"

Shocker alert: This shame, self-hate, low-self-esteem-generating stiff mindset also comes from the past. It's *another* coping strategy (as well as an automatic negative thought) for dealing with the uncertainty of life. If we believe we are The Ruiner of all that is good, at least we feel like we have some control when things go wrong. And then the hand-wringing and apologies start. A lot of upside-down victims apologize for apologizing too much!

Self-blame is a nasty habit of taking on *too much* responsibility for the past when more often than not, what happened is not in our control or down to stuff that had nothing to do with us. Overpersonalizing the past, making it all about us, distracts us from seeking the truth. A useful way I learned to counteract this was inspired by Don Miguel Ruiz and choosing to make a new agreement with myself not to take things personally. By choosing to take other forces into account, we let *ourselves* off the hook for things that are not our fault.

Flexercise: Red Button, Green Button

This visualization exercise is based on the work of British psychotherapist Terence Watts, founder of BrainWorking Recursive Therapy, to help people overcome lingering resentment toward someone they are struggling to let off the hook.

Imagine there's a red button to your left, and a green button to your right.

Picture the person you resent in your mind. If you press the RED button, nothing will change, and you'll stay stuck with resentment, anger, and pain for the rest of your entire life.

If you press the GREEN button, you can move forward without the offender's influence, free from hurt and bitterness.

When you imagine hitting the button, hit it HARD. Smash it. Feel the impact on your palm. Dr. Watts says, "Hit it hard to show you mean it!"

Ideally, most of the time, you'll hit the green button to swing open the cage of the past and claim emotional freedom. But on the rare occasion you want to hit the red button, accept that you are choosing to stay with anger and resentment *this time*. Make a conscious choice to hold on to past negativity or let go of it. We don't control what happens, but we can control how we choose to respond.

Post-Traumatic Growth

Turning pain into gifts

I first heard the phrase "post-traumatic growth" from Zelana Montminy, PhD, a behavioral scientist, positive psychologist, and author of *21 Days to Resilience: How to Transcend the Daily Grind, Deal with the Tough Stuff, and Discover Your Strongest Self.* "We all know people who have gone through hardships, but some were victimized by them and haven't really elevated or been able to grow from them. They are stuck," she said. "But if you're able to approach your stressors and challenges with a certain lens and able to grow and learn and strengthen from that, that's what resilience really is."

That's what flexibility is, too.

To turn damage into growth, *connect* by accepting our human frailty. We're just human beings who have been afraid and alone, but we can *choose* to forgive and begin to heal. The lessons we need to learn will keep coming up until we really learn them, so be *curious* about what those might be. The next time we fall into old patterns of self-blame (which is likely, given how our bitchy inner critic LOVES victim storylines), *commit* to self-compassion by saying, "Today, my brain must have been very scared to react that way." Quick language Flexes change how these memories are stored and keep us moving forward without the weight of regret and shame. The reward for all this acceptance, forgiveness, and understanding is the magic of a future we can't predict but trust will unfold to teach us what we need to learn.

The past is a known, a stuck pattern with a predictable ending to an already-written narrative. You can either relive it, or let go. With a conscious retelling, we can open up to an unknown, unexpected future with endings that you can't possibly have imagined, with gifts lining the journey.

The process of finding our lessons from the past is like winning points in the Mario Kart Tour through life. They are the gifts of emotional release and they create growth nugget opportunities to be *grateful* for our past—because when we spot them, we're given the chance to upgrade our thinking and behavior.

My friend who grew up with an emotionally abusive mother was eventually able to see what gifts that gave her. "I think my mother taught me to be independent," she said. "To get very good with money because she was terrible. She taught me to survive. When my boyfriend was panicking about COVID-19 and going into lockdown, I was completely fine because I grew up learning how to comfort myself when things were unsafe around me. Just listing these gifts feels really good, actually."

Another wonderful friend, an acting coach, lost her leg in an accident when she was young. When I asked her if any gifts came from that traumatic event, she said, "I can't believe I would ever think this, but losing my leg was the best thing that ever happened to me. It gave me freedom to decide what I wanted to do in life instead of taking it for granted. My accident and the people I met in recovery changed my life for the better." She's the opposite of a victim, a pro gift finder, and a radiant Flexi-Mentor of mine.

Committing to finding the gifts of the past is itself a gift. It offers us a peaceful way to remember. Erasing isn't required. Instead, we can wade into that pool of wisdom, and dip into it at our will to feel reassured that we are all survivors.

Since Flexing, I make a conscious effort not to fall back into my old identity—even after multiple tequilas. When I start to trip down memory lane in a negative way, recounting past hurts and falling back into stiff narratives of villians and victims, I catch myself. Flexible minds live in the present, staying curious to what's happening, and don't predict the end before it's begun. My mantra is "Expect the unexpected but keeps your wits about you." It reminds me to use the wisdom the past has gifted me, but to focus my current thoughts and feelings on the way things ARE now and not how they WERE then.

Our storylines can change with every decision we make and I am far more excited about what could happen next. Making peace with the past is about accepting it for what it is, the pressure that was needed to form our unique human crystal. No two humans are the same, just like no two crystals are. Our journeys and the pressures and challenges we have endured only seek to create more beauty. When we are able to extract ourselves from the environments that created us, we can focus on sparkling.

Some Finer Points...

Remember the four C's to Flex free of the past.

- **Connection.** Your body is the best compass. It's a constant source of wisdom that's always available to steer you into the future, if you give it a chance. Every day, ensure you are strengthening the connection to your body by energizing. If going for a small run or dance break is too much, even a belly breath or a gentle walk outside will create an energetic shift to give you more power to reconnect and help forge new neural pathways over the old, past ones and tap into your inner guidance system.

- **Curiosity.** Sometimes, all you need to avoid the autopilot mode of misinterpreting the present, overreacting, and making assumptions, is to stop, think, and say, "Wait, why am I turning *this* situation into *that*?" or "That's an interesting thought; I need some more evidence before I can believe it," and, as always, "Is this true?" Identify your naughty ANTs; whether they're overgeneralizing, all-or-nothing thinking, or fortune-telling, stamp them down.

- **Choice.** As Don Miguel Ruiz said, "If you want to live a life of joy and fulfillment, you have to find the courage to break those agreements that are fear-based and claim your personal power." Courage starts with making a choice to break the patterns that have us going around in circles. I choose to forgive the past and I choose to look for more compassionate explanations to the situations I am in. I use language that propels me forward into love and away from fear, like "I expect the unexpected" and "Don't take it personally. Anything is possible." This prevents my bitchy inner critic from assuming she knows everything.

- **Commitment.** Instead of reacting how my scared inner child wants to, I take action based on what either my Flexi-Mentors or my Wildest, full-of-love self would do. It's helpful to find a Flexi-Mentor that has had a similar past and transcended it. A friend of mine had a very challenging childhood with both parents struggling from addiction and their Flexi-Mentor was Dr. James Doty. In his book, *Into the Magic Shop*, he writes about the moment he let go of the past and forgave his parents and went on to be a world-changing thought leader, high-flying CEO, and founder of the compassion center at Stanford. He is a shining example of someone who Flexed with forgiveness and compassion and created an entirely new future.

Our past got us this far. It's our winning formula that has created the unique person we see in the mirror. But now, by Flexing, you can move forward with the option to do things differently instead of reliving what was. The band Oasis said, "Don't look back in anger." Look ahead with joy and excitement with the knowledge that you have already survived every single one of your worst days. We no longer need to live unconsciously following the beat of the drum we were given but we can set a new rhythm for ourselves. A rhythm that's going to help us thrive today and forevermore.

"The worst is survivable. The goal is not to imagine that bad things don't unfold, it is to see that we are far more capable of enduring them than we currently think."
—Alain de Botton

"ONE OF THE GREATEST REGRETS IN LIFE IS BEING WHAT OTHERS WOULD WANT YOU TO BE, RATHER THAN BEING YOURSELF."

-SHANNON ALDER

chapter ten

FLEX CULTURE

In a commencement speech in 2005 to the graduating class of Kenyon College, author David Foster Wallace opened with this parable about culture: "There are these two young fish swimming along and they happen to meet an older fish swimming the other way, who nods at them and says, 'Morning, boys. How's the water?' And the two young fish swim on for a bit, and then eventually one of them looks over at the other and goes, 'What the hell is water?'"

Culture is like an ocean we bathe in daily, hourly, every minute, and no one can exist without being touched by it, from the way we dress, eat, speak, behave, and think. I think we can all agree that it's been a toxic dunk lately. Cultural forces have a lot to answer for for our skyrocketing stress and anxiety. The mental health epidemic is a symptom. The cause is our culture putting us under so much water pressure.

It's a daily battle to choose enoughness when our culture tells us that we are all shamefully inadequate. We live in a world that promotes:

Be Successful = Have lots of money, lots of fabulous stuff, lots of friends, lots of travel.

Be Acceptable = Be pleasing, always. Don't be weird, or be weird in exactly the right way, like "kooky."

Be Awesome = Be your #bestself at all times, even if you're tired, down, or sick. Smile and just be 100 percent awesome, always.

Be Healthy = Look good in yoga pants while holding a green juice or cup of matcha pretending you like it.

Be Purposeful = Must know your life goals and have a plan by twelve…or you're doomed.

Be Effortless = Just be phenomenal in every area, always, but don't try too hard, make out like things just happen.

DON'T BE A FAILURE = If you're not a married millionaire by thirty, just give up.

Our cultural conditioning says that to be "happy," we can't have any problem of any kind. We have to be wealthy and fit with a great job and cool friends, while also maintaining a PERFECT life balance. But even then, we still have to strive to "be better" than who we are at any present moment. If we aren't self-improving or getting ahead, we'll be left behind. Be more. Give more. Do more. Don't stop driving until you get "there." Hustle, hustle, hustle. But don't worry! Don't fear! Don't stress! That'll only slow you down, turn people off, and make you sick.

Our culture does everything to make us feel unsafe, remind us that we don't belong and we aren't enough despite how hard we try. No wonder poor mental health rates are so high! We are all absolutely fucking *exhausted* from constant chasing and acquiring. The illusion that self-worth comes from buying stuff keeps us in a "grasping" state, as Buddhists say. Our expectations for life have been stuffed like a turkey, leaving us feeling like rotten failures when reality falls short. It is unsurprising that so many of us secretly live with fragile egos and low self-esteem.

Again, it's NOT OUR FAULT that we are struggling with this. Western society can feel like a compassion desert. Flowers can't grow in barren soil; humans can't flourish in a toxic culture. It's not our fault but it is our responsibility to collectively Flex to redefine success and shift our needy-greedy culture toward one of compassion and self-acceptance.

"Compassion is the basis of morality."
—Arthur Schopenhauer

Teaching children to prioritize kindness over acquisition can remake the world. Kids' minds are endlessly flexible. Their imagination turns teacups into rocket ships. The sponge years were when most of us absorbed the messaging that turned our stretching minds into stiff ones, and makes life feel like a constant slog now. Grades and scores were rewarded, not acts of kindness. We are trained and tricked away from expansive thought to fit into a status quo of the education system that teaches all kids to learn in the same way. Triangle, oblong, semicircle, or hexagon type people learn to believe there is something wrong with them because they aren't square; schools only praise squaredom. We're so young, we don't challenge the fact that we *like* being a hexagon. But the desire to belong and feel safe is so strong, we chip away at our hexagon selves until we look like squares. Stiff squares. Self-acceptance? Doesn't stand a chance. And then we wonder why we don't know who we are or how to feel at peace years later.

Flexible thoughts ask us to question our cultural conditioning, to connect with our hexagon or oblong selves again, and to return to childlike wonder where curiosity is our default.

Stiff thinking sticks with the status quo to feel safe, which is limiting and imprisoning.

The status quo has tremendous energy to perpetuate itself. We have to actively energize and educate ourselves to stretch our internal world. If we don't challenge unhealthy culture norms, we'll sleepwalk into reinforcing them. We all have a part to play in what type of water we swim in together. So let's make a point of stretching culture to empower all of us to swim, belong, and feel accepted (not just the elite few).

I truly believe that if more of us adopt flexible thinking, the greater our chances of changing the toxic culture. We can Connect with our feelings instead of blindly reacting to them; stay Curious and open to ideas that might be wiser than the ones we were conditioned to believe; Choose the Wolf of Love in all of our interactions and decisions; and Commit to uphold individual values of compassion, forgiveness, and self-awareness. Just like our plastic brains, our culture can be reshaped and rewired by habitual thoughts and behaviors that promote flexible thinking. We all have the responsibility to steer culture in a way that SUPPORTS our mental health.

More

The never-ending need

The main driver of the Culture of More is the belief that having more of everything (things, friends, "likes," respect) will keep us safe, make us feel like we're enough, protect us from rejection, and secure our place in the tribe.

Sounds like a great plan and made sense in caveman times. More food = more chances of surviving and someone wanting to have sex with you. But where has this evolutionary drive brought us? We're in a rat race to nowhere, on the hamster wheel from hell.

Connect to how that feels. The rat race made me feel like a frazzled ball of stress for ten years straight, at the end of which, I was a small shivering ball of worry and a walking ad for feeling inadequate.

Wanting is not inherently bad. We were born with desire. But our culture has taken the desire for things and pumped it full of steroids. It's all too easy to cross the toxic invisible line between a healthy desire for a comfortable life, and the unhealthy obsession with having more endlessly—and the terror of not having enough. In a recent study[39] by researchers at Princeton University about whether high income impacts happiness and "life satisfaction," more money did NOT mean more happiness. Of course, having more money made life easier. But if people had enough to cover their bills and had some left over for fun, their life satisfaction was equal to that of the wealthiest subjects.

Even though Princeton researchers proved that "enough IS enough" and the Notorious B.I.G. spoke from experience when he said, "Mo' money, mo' problems," we stay stuck in the conditioning that we can never have enough.

Putting corporate profits over people isn't worth the opportunity costs that are arising. Really, who benefits from dieting? The dieter, or the weight loss industry? Who benefits from the anxiety plague? People who are suffering, or Big Pharma? We are rapidly depleting our natural resources—our health and well-being, as well as the stability of the planet—so that corporations can make surplus profit on our insecurities.

If most of us can objectively recognize that the Culture of More is making us sick, that it's harmful to us as individuals, to society, and to the environment at large, why don't we get off the hamster wheel? We KNOW advertising plays to our desires and fears, we know a new car isn't going to create bone-deep confidence. We know we won't *really* look like that model in the ads. We always have a *choice*. We can listen to the conscious, savvy, grown-up thought: "I know a new car isn't going to heal my deep wounds and silence my inner Regina." Or take the Band-Aid approach and listen to the yearning, frightened child-mind from the past: "I'll feel inadequate without it, and maybe, this one time, it might make me feel safe." Which one is more likely to contribute to a life of fullness?

In Alain de Botton's TED Talk called "A Kinder, Gentler Philosophy of Success," he said, "We have been inspired to consciously or unconsciously look for 'love' in the cultural arena of success driven by capitalism, where no true love exists and, instead of blaming culture when we don't find what we're looking for, we blame ourselves and assume it's because we aren't good enough, not because culture has led us to Burger King when we asked for a salad."

Buying things also acts as a handy coping mechanism because it provides us with a seductive distraction, an escape, from stress and anxiety, while simultaneously causing more of it.

Our culture doesn't encourage us to question our default settings, though, because it profits when we're grasping and buying, when we're forever worried about living up to who we think we have to be and pissed off that we're not getting there quicker. We're nailed daily by the cultural "not good enough" hammer to motivate us to consume more in the hope that this will one day make us okay.

I grew up in a financially insecure household, so unlike my friends at school we had no fancy holidays or many new toys. When we (very rarely) went out to dinner, Tom, Ed, and I always chose the cheapest items on the menu, thinking we were helping the situation. We were so wary of putting more financial pressure on my parents that even a side of fries seemed like an extravagance. At friends' houses, their freezers were packed with tubs of Ben & Jerry's (an ice cream brand my mother deemed too expensive), toy boxes overflowed, and wardrobes were the stuff of my dreams. I'd come home in a daze of wonder (and high on candy), and Mom would say, "Don't get used to it." By age ten, with equal parts guilt and anger, I vowed to not stop working until I reached the sort of success where I, too, could make nonstop Ben & Jerry's my reality.

My mother taught us to find solutions to our problems from a young age, and that if we wanted to do something, we'd best figure it out for ourselves. I learned from my father that hard work was painful, so I understood this to mean that if I *wasn't* in pain, I wasn't working hard enough. "Figure it out" and "Work till it hurts" became my core beliefs. As you know, I got my first job at sixteen and haven't stopped working since.

I wasn't the only one who was taught to "go harder." Culturally, "Do More" is portrayed as a virtue, not a cause for sickness. Many like myself have to make a real effort to Flex the need to stop being the hare that burns out and gets sick. And be the turtle that takes her time and enjoys the race. The rebellious Flex against mainstream culture is to *slow down* (but that also doesn't mean never challenging your limits). Knowing why you want "more" is helpful in moderation. Are you driven by fear? Not-enoughness? Or does working hard and attaining more make you feel alive in your heart and mind? Being flexible is about stretching in new, previously unexplored directions. There are many ways to go. As long as we're mindful about motivation and we get adequate rest, there's value to seeing how far we can go.

Flexercise: Bend "Get More, Do More!" into "I Have Enough. I Am Enough"

I have to do this one over and over again to unlearn the belief that happiness and acceptance exist on the other side of "more." Just recently, I was offered a work opportunity that would have taken me away from home for years but paid *very* well. I was torn about what to do. So, to make a wise, conscious decision, I Flexed.

CONNECTION. I paused and used the belly breath to calm my frazzled energy over this quandary. By switching over to WCHL, I connected with my body and my four brains and started reprogramming my anxiety-driven desire for "more."

CURIOSITY. Once I'd created some mental space, I tapped into my internal guidance system and began investigating: "Do I actually want this job or do I feel pressure to want it?" I started scanning for evidence of cultural bias, negative bias, confirmation bias. What was the root of my need to say "yes"? I could see that I was being influenced by my childhood fears of not having enough and my thirst for external validation (which I will probably always be a bit susceptible to).

CHOICE. What decision would bring me closer to self-compassion and love? If I was to feed the Wolf of Love, I would say "no" to the job, and stay close to family and friends and the soul-nourishing work I was already doing. A "yes" would be fear-based on the negative thought that I'd never get a better offer.

COMMITMENT. My top two values—love and connection—would not be upheld if I were on a flight every day for the next two years. It would perhaps look "good" on Instagram, being so busy. But it wouldn't *feel* good for my heart or health. My Wild Self, aka the person I am beneath all the conditioning, the one who listens to her instincts and is not influenced by cultural bias, would say "no" to spending her life in airports and lonely hotel rooms.

I declined the job and reminded myself that I have enough as it is and to stay optimistic about the future, and hope for better offers.

N.B.: Within weeks of saying "thanks but no thanks," another opportunity came that matched nearly all I'd hoped for! This is a bit of my *woo woo* self coming out, but I honestly think the universe gives us tests to see if we are ready to step up into vibrating higher and being more aligned with who we want to be.

Scarcity

The terror of going without

We evolved to have a scarcity mindset. To survive in caveman times, we had to compete with other tribes or people within our own tribe to grab whatever food we could in the moment, because it might not be there tomorrow. In lean times, one person's survival depended on another's demise.

But we're not our ancestors. We are not battling to the death on the Serengeti for the last antelope. And yet a scarcity mentality hangover from our species' earliest days continues to throb in our brains. We've been programmed to think that if Lucy gets a raise, or a boyfriend, or a new kitchen, it might mean there's less for us. Or, treacherously worse, for one race to enjoy its privilege, another must be suppressed. No wonder we have such extreme anxiety levels. We have deep conditioned fears that we'll soon fall behind if someone else strolls ahead.

Look, I know in my heart and in my intellect that when Tashia uploads her engagement pictures on the Gram, it has nothing to do with me and my life. But I still have to combat the scarcity feelings that bubble up like, "Oh, no, another good man down, less around for the rest of us." I quickly counter it with, "This doesn't mean I won't find someone or that I'm not good enough." Jealousy and competition are such low-vibration energies, they drag us across the floor, and they keep us stuck in rigid thought. Our "winner takes all" culture amplifies black and white thinking. Our brains love the dichotomy. "I'm safe" vs. "Fuck, I'm in danger!" Good vs. evil. Right vs. wrong. Hero vs. villain. Winning vs. losing. Have vs. have not.

Being a part of a large family, I learned very quickly that when food was offered, I had to eat as MUCH as possible right away, because if not, someone else would polish it off within ten minutes. Having two brothers will do that. The "grab now or go without" fear lingered for years and had me overeating everything like my survival depended on it. To this day, family-style dinners make me feel a bit anxious and have me eating four times as much as I need, just in case there isn't any left over. But I'm Flexing this.

Getting upset about another's promotion isn't going to take it away from them, but it does further bind us to our fear.

The US has an up-by-your-bootstraps culture that leans heavily on blaming individuals for their circumstances, creating envy and fear of failure (and scarcity). But the truth is, there are many other factors at play, like luck, privilege, and prejudice, that determine who gets ahead. Maybe Josie's promotion wasn't based on her merit, but on the fact that her father owns the company. I am not suggesting we should walk around as victims or undoing others' wins, but compassionately taking into account that circumstance has a big influence over how "culturally successful" we are may relieve some of our burden.

Scarce thinking is stiff because it has a 2D outlook on the "win" and it assumes we all want the same things when, actually, we all have different hopes and desires. Josie might get a promotion, but Charlie who sits next to her might get a new puppy that brings just as much, if not more, happiness. Culturally we are only encouraged to compare bank balances, not the whole picture.

The opposite of a scarcity mindset is one of abundance, that there is plenty of whatever we desire to go around. Everyone gets their time in the sun. We have to Flex into reminding ourselves to have more patience and trust in the ebbs and flows.

Human Design expert Jenna Zoë uses the music industry as an example of how we can adopt an "abundant mentality." When you download a song, that doesn't stop someone else from listening to it. If anything, the song rising in the charts might encourage more people to listen to it. Listeners win, the artist wins, the platform wins. Win-win-win.

When we live with an abundance mindset and agree that someone else's gain isn't our loss, we stay happier and can feel more gratitude, celebrate all of our successes, vibrate from a higher consciousness, and boost our health at the same time.

Flexercise: Bend "They Win, I Lose" to "Everyone Wins!"

Just last night, I bumped into an old friend at a party who told me about all these projects she was doing, and I immediately felt threatened. But just as quickly, I challenged it: *Hey, brain, Flex FFS! Why are you feeling threatened?! Away with the scarcity and move into abundancy.* BTW, it's kind of awkward to Flex mid-convo but worth it because it completely flipped my energy and allowed me to enjoy the rest of the night.

CONNECTION. I connected with the physical manifestations of jealousy, the rapid heart rate and tense shoulders. I focused on unclenching my jaw and breathing through the wave for ninety seconds. I accepted that I had been triggered, and micro-shifted my energy by straightening my posture and relaxing my shoulders down.

CURIOSITY. There was no evidence to support my jealous feelings. I flipped through Byron Katie's questions.

Did I know for a *fact* that her win would be my loss? No.

Could I be 100 percent sure this was true? Nope.

How did this thought make me feel? Small, envious, jealous, low vibe, limited, fake.

Who would I be if I didn't have this thought? Open, loving, happy for her and for me, supportive, much more aligned with my Wild Self who doesn't give a crap about "influence."

CHOICE. I chose to repeat the mantra I learned from Comparison Coach Lucy Sheridan: "Good for you, and good for me." Someone takes a huge slice of cake? No problem! We can make another to share with everyone. "Not now" doesn't mean "never." Our time will come.

COMMITMENT. I switched from "WHY is this happening?" to "WHAT can I learn?" and, wow, did I instantly find a huge shiny gift in the situation. My jealousy was showing me a desire I had for myself. I deep down wanted to be working on something similar. With this gift of a realization, I could swap out jealousy for gratitude and be appreciative of what I'd learned and feel excited about my next steps. My Wild Self smiled at me, saying, "Be proud of your journey; everything is unfolding in the way it should be." It's easy to lose our sense of ourselves when we are impressed by others and our cultural bias takes over. The compassionate commitment allowed me to walk back into the path, energy warm and uplifted.

"Be thankful for what you have, you'll end up having more. If you concentrate on what you don't have, you will never have enough."
—Oprah Winfrey

Swoon

What's love got to do with it?

I grew up imagining my romantic life would be exactly like the relationships I saw in rom-coms, perfectly sweet and quirky with a cheeky frisson of sexual tension until my soulmate and I flew off together in a hot air balloon, amid a bevy of doves spelling out "I Love You" in the sky. Just really normal stuff.

My romantic idealization and conditioning started in childhood with *Cinderella*, *Snow White,* and *The Parent Trap*, reinforced later on by *Notting Hill*, *Meet the Parents*, and *Maid in Manhattan*. The main characters were chased by honorable sexy men, and then they lived happily ever after. The End.

You can imagine how, when my quarter-life crisis happened, I was a bit alarmed that no Prince had shown up yet. My anxieties started piling on and I kept asking myself, "Why am I going through this alone?" Why hadn't an honorable, sexy man proposed to me, or, for that matter, bought me a drink? I reconciled the gap between my reality and my romantic expectations by deciding that *I must be failing* at living up to Princess standards. Maybe if I just hit the gym more and worked harder, my very own Luke Wilson (circa 2001) would appear, along with a ring. I know you'll be surprised to hear this, but Luke never came, just chronic exhaustion and burnout as I said goodbye to the last glimmer of self-esteem.

Consciously, I told myself, "It's ridiculous to compare real life to the romantic fairy tales in movies." There were no dating apps in Neverland. But I did it anyway. How could I not? I'd been swimming in cultural romantic idealization for decades.

My vision of "love" was admittedly narrow and *very* stiff. I was adamant that it *had* to play out in the way I had learned. But when I started Flexing, I began to notice some holes in these fairy tales I held so close. For starters, why was the "ever after" part of the story always left untold? How did things *actually* work out for Cinderella? Did her Prince help her process the death of her mother, her fatherless adolescence, and the physical and verbal abuse of her stepfamily? Does Snow White have recurring nightmares about the multiple attempts on her life or wonder why *her* Prince was into snogging with a pseudo corpse? Or how did marital life play out for *Pretty Woman*'s Richard Gere and Julia Roberts? No emotional fallout from her having been a sex worker, and his having been someone who hired her? Cultural romance is glossy because it glosses over realities of having a past, having brain biases and insecurities that don't magically disappear after the big kiss scene.

Long-term emotional health concerns are not part of fairy tales, as we all know. A troubling aspect of our "always be awesome" culture, as it pertains to romance, is that love should only get better and better, and that once we find our soulmate, we'll be bursting with joy forever after even though we all know—some of us all too well—that 50 percent of all marriages end in divorce. One hundred percent of my relationships had ended badly or sadly. So why was I basing my very real hopes and expectations on made-up stories? I needed a new frame of reference, and to stop the self-blame, pronto. The world of poison apples provided no relevant advice in a world of Bumble. The reality is, no one is without insecurity. No man has unshakable confidence. No woman has perfect hair ALL the time.

I am no expert on relationships, to be sure—romantic, platonic, straight, or queer—but in my study of flexible thinking and interpersonal connections, I've come across some discoveries worth sharing. It's been *extremely* healing to acknowledge how warped my understanding of them was in the first place.

The main message is that finding love will instantly solve all our problems. It's tenacious, which is why *The Bachelor*, a cultural phenomenon, is still on the air and going strong. But don't believe it. Love itself doesn't fix us, but it can reveal to us how to heal ourselves. I learned from the Fairy Godmother to us all—Oprah Winfrey—the fascinating nugget that "relationships are mirrors" that turn up to show us our flaws, fears, beliefs, and patterns. They can be our greatest teachers, if we let them.

I once dated a guy and his enthusiasm was a bit overwhelming and verging on unbelievable. He was SO excited about *everything* and added a dozen exclamation marks in a single text. "Coffee?" "YESSSS PLEASE!!!!!!!"

I told a friend, "He's just too enthusiastic for me, I don't know if he is for real!!!!!"

She said, "Are you talking about yourself?"

Okay, she had a point. He was a mirror right there. I was equally guilty of exclamation overuse and being SO EXCITED, people thought I was lying. We can easily look for and find common traits with our partners, big or small, including ones we'd rather not admit.

But what my Flexi-Mentor Supreme Oprah was really getting at is that our relationships reflect our deepest fears *and* our heart's desires.

If we look at it and say, "It's so unstable," the reflected fear is, "I am not safe." The heart's desire is to feel safe.

If we say, "It's not giving me the love I need," the reflected fear is, "I am unloved." The heart's desire is to feel loved.

If we say, "I worry that he/she/they are going to find someone else, someone better," the reflected fear is, "I'm not good enough." The heart's desire is to feel worthy and wanted.

Every relationship is sent to us to show us what we need to learn, and how we need to heal and evolve to our highest selves. If we are fortunate, we will have many relationships and friendships that support and challenge us, asking us continually to learn, heal, evolve, and become better humans along the way. When a relationship is flexible, it stretches both people to better understand themselves and each other. If a relationship doesn't allow and encourage growth, it's stiff and stuck.

Disney conditioned me to think a certain way about love and left me bitterly disappointed by what I found in the real world.

The Flex had me look at relationships differently, much to my relief. They're not fairy tales but actual experiences with the soul and sole purpose of helping us evolve, grow, become a better person.

When the next one rolls around, I won't be fretting about whether he's The One. I'll focus on why we have come into each other's lives, the lessons we need to teach each other, and learning them. Who needs a ring when we can find so many *gifts*?

Overload

The feeling of being buried alive

We have created an always-on culture of nonstop texting, tweeting, snapping, 'Gramming. A big reason people feel overwhelmed is because we *are* inundated by data, images, and all forms of content. There is always something new to watch or read, and if we try to absorb it all, we are probably suffering from "infoxication," poisoned by an overdose of content.

At times, I have been a flat-out information addict. One weekend, I decided to delete Instagram, and I found myself reaching to open the app dozens of times a day. My hand moved by itself! Checking social media has been ingrained in my unconscious alarmingly. Steve

Jobs and Bill Gates, creators of addictive tech, clearly knew the risk to young minds, and refused to let their own kids have devices until their mid-teens. They just sweetly left the rest of us to become the addicted guinea pigs. Forty-three percent of millennials check their phones every twenty minutes and a typical phone user taps or swipes their phone more than 2,500 times per day.

Our information onslaught doesn't let us think deeply anymore. How can we? We're too busy keeping up-to-date with the world's chatter. We have culturally induced attention disorders because of our constant distractions. Information overload forces us to bounce from one thought to the next, always skipping on the surface, resulting in a shallow society.

As for how this info flood is impacting our emotional health, the less our thoughts have depth and breadth, the stiffer they become. We have no chance to express or explore, no opportunity to stretch with care. Just swiping, swiping, swiping. To be great and flexible thinkers, we have to create uninterrupted time and space away from the constant noise and distraction to connect with our feelings, challenge old beliefs, and make considered new choices—*to think for ourselves*. We need space and a break from cultural infoxication to use Curiosity to consciously consider *What do I want, like, or care about?* And not just click the "Most Popular" icon every time.

Not only are we info addicts, we are also dealers. We supply quick fixes on social media that feed the need for more.

Arguably, we should be more flexible because of our access to *everything* on the Internet. But, as my friend Sharmadean Reid says, "You've got to know what to Google." If you ask the wrong questions, the search engine will give you page after page of uselessness. And the variety of opinions out there doesn't actually make us more open to new ideas. In the 1960s, French psychologists Serge Moscovici and Marisa Zavalloni studied what we call "groupthink," and found that groups of participants that held light views on a topic became more extreme in their opinions after speaking about them.[40] The research shows how social media fuels us to become more stiff and rigid in the way we think because we're being encouraged to constantly share our opinion and find others who agree, intensifying our POV.

Groupthink and Google are fine for certain things, but they don't necessarily accommodate flexible thinking. Google can't help you decipher that your adult anger could be connected to the time your aunt forgot your sixth birthday. We have to find the confidence to be our own search engine—our brain's data banks—and develop the ability to interpret the intel, and not rely on technology to feed us info and tell us what to think. We have to know when to look for answers inside our own head instead of relying on a machine or listening to strangers. Take back the control of which information you are allowing in and what information you are politely leaving at the door.

So we have to be our own Marie Kondo, and clear our minds of garbage content. To figure out what to keep and what to throw out, I've created the grid below, adapted from Stephen Covey's *The 7 Habits of Highly Effective People*. Reorder and prioritize the info that sparks JOY and sideline the rest for when you have the brain space to process it.

	URGENT	NOT URGENT
IMPORTANT	**QUADRANT ONE** Extreme weather reports A text from your cat sitter saying she can't get into your apartment and the kitties are starving to death Notifications from LifeLock and/or your bank	**QUADRANT TWO** Email about free yoga on ClassPass Your astrology app alerting you to Mercury retrograde starting Texts from the boss with a list of to-dos.
NOT IMPORTANT	**QUADRANT THREE** General catch-up texts from friends, family, and significant others Winks and waves on dating apps	**QUADRANT FOUR** Humble-braggers on social media Quizzes on BuzzFeed *The Bachelor* gossip on *The Daily Mail* online

Quadrant One: Keep.

Quadrant Two: Keep.

Quadrant Three: Keep but put on hold. An email from an ex might *feel* urgent, but the world will not stop spinning if you take an hour to reflect before you reply.

Quadrant Four: Throw away, or risk infobesity (a lovely term for stuffing our brains with junk).

Bad news sources are at the top of my "throw away" list. Being an informed person is like taking a daily scroll of terror. Is the world falling apart more than ever, or does it just read that way? Or is the media taking advantage of our wiring to be easily frightened? We are like puppets to the media's clickbait, dancing to strong, external forces that trigger an emotional response. How many articles or tweets did we read today with a negative slant? How many were positive? Are we better informed by reading 100 terrifying tweets or would 10 be enough?

Authors John Tierney and Roy F. Baumeister, in *The Power of Bad: How the Negative Effect Rules Us and How We Can Rule It,* believe that negative news cycles keep us in a state of constant anxiety and recommend a "low-bad diet." They acknowledge that 100 percent good news is impossible, so they suggest shooting for a negative-to-positive ratio of 1:4. For every single bad/scary article, read four good/uplifting ones to neutralize the "negative effect." There are some positive news sites like The Happy Newspaper, Positive News, and Good News Shared, which I cling onto and make a point of surfing.

We are what we consume, so how can we challenge and reprogram our inherent strong negative bias when we only read doomsday news? Our brain will always go to the bad first, so we have to jump ahead of it by consciously seeking the positive. Practice on Yelp or Amazon when reading reviews. Instead of going straight to the one-star slams, practice Flexing by reading at least four five-star reviews first to balance out the negative before you decide whether to buy.

"[A]lways look on the bright side of life."
—Eric Idle

#Happiness
The pressure to feel perpetually thrilled

I know this section may seem ironic considering the title of the book, but I am also highly aware of all the toxicity that lies behind Happiness Culture. It's been cramming that goal down our throats for over a decade and at times causing more anxiety than it's curing.

"Depression rates are higher in countries that place a premium on happiness," according to social psychologist Brock Bastian. After following so many "How to be happy!" blogs and podcasts until I was practically reciting the words and wondering why I wasn't feeling happier, I wasn't surprised by this. In fact, by trying so hard to be happy, I felt worse, thinking something must be wrong with me.

Dr. Bastian carried out studies that proved *expecting* happiness causes the opposite. For one, he asked a group of people to solve a puzzle (they didn't know it was unsolvable) in a room full of motivational posters and happiness paraphernalia. Compared with the control group in a room with neutral decorations, the first group dwelled on their failure far more.[41] "We're finding that overemphasizing happiness—the importance of seeking positive emotion and avoiding negative emotion—has implications for how people respond to their negative emotional experiences. We think we should be happy like we're expected to be, and when we're not, it can make us miserable," Dr. Bastian told an interviewer at the World Economic Forum.

A big problem with the happiness industry is that it promotes the idea that it's a thing that you can achieve, and that once you get there, all will be super, peachy keen for the rest of your life. The viral meme "just choose happiness" suggests that it's as easy as ordering a vanilla iced latte! I used to think, *Fuck, I must be choosing unhappiness. Where and why am I going so wrong?*

Do not take on guilt or shame for not feeling happy.

Humans experience a full range of emotions, not just the "good" ones. When I interviewed breathwork practitioner/coach Kathleen Booker on how she defined happiness, she said, "Happiness often doesn't arrive with a smile." That's why I titled this book *Happy Not Perfect*. It was only when I realized the "happiness" I was once chasing was actually "perfection" in disguise, and that was making me sick, could I begin to change my thinking. When I stopped trying to be perfect and happy and just embraced being authentically me with a whole spectrum of emotions, I ironically felt happier than ever. It's a quieter happiness than I used to imagine. Happiness now means self-acceptance and being reconnected to my Wild Self. In this calm, confident state of mind, I do laugh a lot, and from a deeper place.

I spoke to human behavior expert and cofounder of the Princeton Review Adam Robinson about the pressure to feel happy (the beer commercial kind), and the misery of thinking we're the only one who fails at it. He told me to open Google and type, "Why am I so..." and "Why is everybody else so..." The drop-down searches aggregate the most popular searches globally and provide data-driven factual insight into what's really on people's minds. This is what popped up:

Why am I feeling so:

Why am I feeling so tired

Why am I feeling so cold

Why am I feeling so emotional

Why am I feeling so sleepy

Why am I feeling so low

Why am I feeling so down

Why am I feeling so dizzy

Why does everyone:

Why does everyone else get to be happy

Why does everyone else's life seem better

Why does everyone expect so much from me

Why does everyone evaporate in infinity war

Why does everyone eat ham on Easter

Why does everyone eat fish on Good Friday

Why does everyone end up leaving me

Robinson said, "This shows you the macro reality we are living in. This is so sad, Poppy. Everyone right now thinks that everyone else is happier than them, when actually we are all feeling just as confused on the inside." When I saw the search "Why does everyone else's life seem better?" I immediately thought about social media. Social media #happiness makes us believe it's the ultimate emotion we should be striving for and feeling the entire time and if we feel anything else, something isn't right with us. As we know by now, suppressing emotion only intensifies the feeling behind our stapled-on smiles and "I'm fine" responses. We can feel shame for not being "as happy" as we're being brainwashed to believe we should be. Dr. Bastian did another study that found the subjects who felt social pressure *not* to feel sad and fearful had the greater risk for depression.[42]

Dr. Zelena Montminy started out as a happiness researcher, and then, as she told me, "I became quickly disenchanted with our obsession with happiness in our culture and realized that, like with balance, the happier people want to be, the less happy they really are. We've [got] all these things on our to-do list of how to be happy. Vision boards, meditate. And none of us can really get to it all. So we end up feeling like failures at the end of the day."

She decided to shift from her research on happiness toward the study of resilience, or how to bounce back from difficulty. "If it's not happiness specifically that leads to all these positive outcomes for my mental health, then what is it?" she asked. "Everything shifted for me when I figured out that people who've overcome hardships were the most content. And so it's the skill set of resilience that actually matters."

I loved this reframe! Imagine if we worshipped overcoming our troubles as much as we do happiness? Rather than beating ourselves up when we hit a rocky path and feel uneasy (rightly so), let's move in the direction of celebrating opportunities to elevate ourselves through compassion. Let's appreciate how our emotions provide sweet gifts of learning and opportunity for growth.

Flexercise: Define Happiness for Yourself

I ask everyone to define happiness and have yet to get the same answer.

Albert Einstein said happiness is "a table, a chair, a bowl of fruit, and a violin."

Psychologist Mihaly Csikszentmihalyi wrote in *Flow*, **"The joy we get from living, ultimately depends directly on how the mind filters and interprets everyday experiences."**

Charles Schulz wrote, "Happiness is a warm puppy."

Johnny Cash said, "This morning, with her, having coffee."

And you? A strong sense of self? A flexible mindset? A belly laugh? Love and connection? Celebration? Gratitude? A cozy cat? A sunny day?

Write down your definition of happiness: _____

Reflect on the feeling and bask in it when it comes. Otherwise, forgive yourself for not feeling perma-happy.

Canceled

And just like that, you're gone

We all want to feel safe, loved, and enough. So it's not too surprising that the most cutting cultural punishment is to make someone feel unsafe, unloved, and not enough via *exile* or *imprisonment*. In some cases, just the threat of banishment can push culture to where it needs to go, like shaming abusers and racists. The #MeToo, body positivity, and Black Lives Matter movements called out offenders so we can reach higher ideals as a society.

But cancel culture, as we have come to know it, is a stiff mindset of good vs. evil and right vs. wrong. Flexible thinking allows for shades of gray.

To clarify, Cancel Culture isn't calling a friend and canceling dinner three times in row (which *is* fucking irritating). It's living in a world where the rug can be pulled out from under us at any time. Some canceled people *are* better off in exile—or in prison. But some perhaps don't deserve to be erased. Taylor Swift tweeted about it recently: "When you say someone is canceled, it's not a TV show. It's a human being. You're sending mass amounts of messaging to this person to either shut up, disappear, or it could also be perceived as, 'Kill yourself.'" This is dangerously alarming in our anxiety culture.

A project or partnership can be "canceled" overnight. Having founded two companies and worked across several TV networks, I know how precarious the business and entertainment worlds are. You might be a hit today and gone tomorrow. We might experience it going for a third job interview, being told we're at the top of the list, and then never hearing from the company again. A single unreplied-to text can trigger our worst black-hole fears of being unseen and unheard. It's hard not to take being ignored or disregarded personally when, in our own head, we're self-canceling with insecurities.

Breakups can set off the most traumatic feelings of canceling, at least for me. When I was ghosted, I found it even more troubling than when my investor wanted to cancel me from my own company. Being romantically erased was like reading a billboard that said, "YOU ARE NOT WANTED."

Our Cancel Culture puts us on edge, makes us afraid to post or say the wrong thing and leads us to think we should be perfect or game/life over. I call it FOSO, fear of speaking out. It happens about expressing any viewpoint that's even slightly divergent from the masses.

We don't necessarily have to *agree* on everything. But being open to different opinions is essential to keeping a flexible mind.

The writings and teachings[43] of neuroscientist V. S. Ramachandran shed light on why so many people remain stiff in their thoughts.

He explains the brain is a gatekeeper. If a thought comes up to the gate that is different from what the brain is used to, defensive mechanisms put up their shields to protect the brain from this kind of foreign thought invasion. This is why we jump to defensiveness and stubbornness: The brain feels safe when its beliefs are confirmed as "right." For this reason people like to hang out or follow people who think the same as them. However, when the opposite happens, some shrinks call this phenomenon "hot cognition," because the challenging thought sets off wildfire in the mind. When our brains are burning with opposing views trying to enter, our sense of security is engulfed and sets off a feeling of "Fuck, I'm in danger!" which triggers extreme resistance.

So the next time stubbornness and a refusal to listen come up in a relationship or on Twitter, take a moment to acknowledge what's really happening: a protective biochemical process that's turning us into blockheads and bulldozers. With that awareness, and some belly breaths, we can mindfully calm the mind and open our ears, instead of reactively canceling someone. Listen, and then, even if we disagree, simply say, "I hear what you're saying." Repeat what they are saying back, word for word, to prove it. And just like that, we've calmed their defensiveness and Flexed ourselves out of tension and into a mutually respectful interaction.

Since Flexing for two years, I have looked back at all the ghosting, and rejections I've faced, and noticed that they mirrored my own self-canceling. I had unconsciously found individuals who confirmed my worst fears, of course, the seduction of the familiar. I walked straight into their webs, compelled by my own faulty thinking. But the cancelers gave me gifts full of lessons in the end! They made me see what I'd refused to look at, how low my self-worth really was, and how self-cancellation was preventing me from living an authentic life. I tried to shape-shift into a version of myself I thought they'd like better and lost myself in the process. I was gifted the opportunity to hit rock bottom and rise again to heal, learn, and grow.

By Flexing, we don't have to live in fear of other people's rejection, because we live with confidence in the knowledge that our actions are aligned with our highest values and an expression of our whole self. When we seek to act in accordance with values like compassion and kindness, we can fearlessly move through the world.

Cancel Culture is, by default, "hot cognition" judgmental group-think that is sometimes a crazy witch hunt and sometimes a valid response to objective offensiveness. For individuals, though, the threat of extreme societal rejection is another fear to add to our long list of "Reasons We're So Anxious." I would not want to watch my life ruined for a tweet, and I wouldn't want to ruin someone else's over it. We're human. We all mess up. Let's be flexible about nuance. Let's enhance the culture of forgiveness, and commit to compassion and listening. It's okay to be wrong; it's okay to be different. Having a contrarian opinion isn't cause for a public flogging. Rather than abandoning people—which does not promote growth and freedom of thought—the flexible approach prioritizes challenging groupthink with Curiosity, asking questions like, "Can you tell me more about why you think that way?" It allows for redemption through Commitment to higher values. Little drops of water create an ocean; if we individually focus on Flexing away from reactiveness to greater openness and acceptance, we will soon be able to turn the wider tide.

Body Shame
Ever feel your body isn't good enough?

Cultural forces have a lot to answer for when it comes to how we view our bodies. I read in my twelve-year-old diary, "I am so fat at the moment," and it made my heart sink. I didn't learn this shame from my parents, because they had always been neutral about that. I learned about my body through the media I consumed with my friends. From an early age, I wondered why no one on TV or in the magazines had the rolls I had.

According to a recent study, nearly 80 percent of US women don't like how they look. Adolescent girls overwhelmingly believe being thinner would make them happier, healthier, and better-looking.[44] The media's thin ideal causes unhealthy comparisons and a higher risk for eating disorders like bulimia.[45] Dr. Northrup noted in *Women's Bodies,*

Women's Wisdom, "More than half of girls as young as six to eight years old think their ideal weight is less than they currently weigh." A significant percentage of girls start dieting by seven. Thirty million people in the US have some form of eating disorder, and twenty million of them are female. Of course, we begin to reject ourselves when we see no representation of our shape and size in the media. No wonder so many of us have low self-confidence and negative body image.

I battled for years believing that my imperfect body and chubby cheeks made me horrifically unattractive. I dreaded being invited on vacation for fear of wearing a swimsuit. I was neither skinny nor curvy. In my eyes, I was a blob. I was absolutely sure if I just lost weight, I would be happier and better-looking. I didn't just want to change my shoes to be accepted, I was desperate to change my entire body.

The irony is real: The same magazines that tell us to self-love also tell us to self-hate with their lack of body diversity (this is changing!). We turn the page to be reminded we don't belong and are not accepted here. The irony is, women who I would assume had infinite confidence because they were literal models felt just as insecure about their bodies as anyone else.

The rise of the body positivity movement has been hugely impactful by showing and celebrating the diversity of body types. The Flex has been critical in helping me overcome cultural pressure to look a certain way. This is one of my greatest challenge areas, especially if I'm sleep deprived and overworked and my bitchy brain is firing off some of the meanest comments ever. Before the Flex, I basically printed my biggest insecurities on a mental T-shirt and wore it constantly. But now I'm getting better at challenging them: "Unattractive, you say? By whose standards? Compared to an unrealistic expectation in a fashion ad? I'm a grown woman! Of course I have cellulite!"

I believe that one of the most damaging consequences of body hate is detachment, like we don't exist from the neck down. We begin to hate our body so much, we would prefer to pretend it isn't there. By doing this, we figuratively lop off our inner guidance system. In the early days of my recovery when I felt huge body hate, I focused on just Connection. Before I went to sleep, I placed my hand on my belly and breathed for a few minutes. While inhaling, holding, and exhaling into my belly, I would imagine sending love to each body part, love to those areas I had been so mean about. I'd send gratitude to my legs for helping me walk, to my tum for digesting my food, to my uterus for the children I'd carry one day. The connection step has helped me gradually come to accept my body and appreciate her role in influencing my energetic frequency. A few jumping jacks before a meeting I'm nervous about gives me a full energy makeover.

I no longer use fashion magazines as my ideal and instead fill up my social media feeds with women who make me feel great. No longer will I equate my value as a human being with numbers on a scale. My Wild Self, as she roams the terrain, does not consider her size, only her strength. Using only one metric to determine health and happiness is stiff, rigid tunnel-visioning. Flexible minds have a multidimensional approach to self-love and acceptance.

If our brains can send a message to our fingers to wiggle them, then it can also send love, kindness, and acceptance!

Less Than

Ever felt inferior?

Our culture has an unofficial but widely accepted caste system that exists on racial, gender, sexual orientation, and class lines. To not take into account how culture affects people based on the color of their skin, for example, is dangerous, naive, and ignorant. As a person who was born into racial privilege, I've always considered it my responsibility to use it for the benefit of others. One of the driving objectives with Happy Not Perfect—the app and the book—has been to democratize mental health information. You may wish to keep going beyond this book and find your own mentors or even begin therapy, but my hope is to at least provide a set of tools to help you with discovery.

Our brains suffer the same hurdles, but those who've been oppressed have had to contend with racism, homophobia, and sexism ON TOP OF unconscious biases and the hurt, anger, shame, and resentment attached to all of it. It's an incredible and essential time in history for flexible thinking, uprooting rigid beliefs, and healing old wounds, as individuals and as a society. I stand with any movement that sets out to stretch negative thoughts and faulty beliefs so much that they lose shape, and the reforms of equality, compassion, kindness, and love are the new normal. When our cultural conditioning (not to mention our past history) tells us we're inferior, we must consciously challenge and powerfully change that message for future generations to come.

I've learned—am still learning—to Flex my thoughts of inferiority as a woman in a world built for men. Threads of doubt do have a tendency to worm into my unconscious, no matter how consciously I affirm my female power. When I was raising capital for my two businesses, it was obvious why only 2 percent of venture capital goes to women; for the most part, men control it. Consciously or unconsciously, men favor men. This is normal, actually, for like to favor like. I would also consciously or unconsciously favor people who reminded me of myself. We all do it. If I was an investor and LOVED to bike, let's say, it would be near to impossible not to be influenced by my personal bias and favor unconsciously or consciously a startup about cycling over a random fishing company.

You can therefore see the issues I faced pitching to men about female-skewed fashion and wellness companies. When I would start my pitch, take my heart out of my chest, place it on the table beating, and begin the sell, their eyes would glaze over. After I finished with spirit fingers, a song, and some high kicks, a few of them would say, "You should speak to my wife/daughter." *What does that mean? Does the daughter have investment capital?* With Happy Not Perfect, it took me three times as long as my male counterparts who had smaller markets and were making less money to get start-up funds. And once the men did invest, they questioned every decision I wanted to make. Men are allowed to learn from mistakes, but women only get one chance.

Dr. Northrup calls the impact of sexism "degradation of the feminine." She cited examples like getting the side-eye when breastfeeding in public, the difficulty in wanting to be attractive but not so sensual that we have to deal with unwanted attention ("and then [be] blamed for it," as she said), and hiding the fact that periods exist. In business, I tried to overcompensate by being overly forceful and opinionated, like a dude, but also mindful not to be a demanding diva, either. But the effect was inauthentic and just served to alienate my team.

It helped to look at how my Flexi-Mentors had handled being a woman in a culture dominated by men. Dr. Northrup in particular helped me see that in order to heal my internalized sense of inferiority, I had to take responsibility to change my conditioned beliefs that our bodies are messy, smelly, provocative, and that our emotionality is a hindrance when it's really a huge advantage. She wrote, "Most modern civilizations are characterized by the belief that the intellect is superior to emotions, the mind and spirit are entirely separate from the body, masculinity is superior to femininity, and nature is something to be exploited for her resources." However, "[o]ur current worldview is only about 5,000 years old. Before that, peaceful societies flourished for thousands of years. In these societies, women held high positions, art flourished, and religion included the worship of the Goddess."

There is no reason why we can't return to Goddess worshipping ☺, but we can't sit around and wait for this to happen. It begins with our appreciating ourselves and being the change we wish to see.

As a woman, it's okay to embody the version of womanhood we want to emulate and to put our own needs first over the cultural monster we seek validation from.

Right now, I am really struggling with how culture reinforces the message that women should be married and with child by thirty. I'm not sure if it's my biological clock or my cultural need for acceptance that's ticking. This worry could also be inflated due to the fact that I'm writing this book during lockdown in COVID-19 and wondering whether I'll ever meet someone in real life again. I had one Skype date during quarantine. It was thirty minutes of awkwardness that I could have done without.

But I accept my feelings. I forgive myself for giving a shit about marriage and kids and remember to constantly question whether I really desire these things or if it's my culturally conditioned ego chatting loudly.

This is why I love the Flex method! When I'm feeling deeply inadequate compared to the cultural optimum—and the nonstop wedding/honeymoon/baby posts on the Gram—instead of spiraling into prolonged anxiety and sadness like I used to, wondering if I'm going to grow old alone, now I have something better to do. I get to Flex myself right back up and touch base with what my soul wants.

Flexercise: Bend "Future Spinster with Cats" to "Whatever Happens, Happens"

Culture can squash inner wisdom. To decipher whether the desire "I want to get married and have kids" is coming from my inner wisdom or cultural messaging . . . I Flex.

CONNECTION. How do I feel? *Today my gut feels anxious that I might wind up living with my parents forever and become* that girl *people feel sorry for. Today, I'm embarrassed that I'm writing a book about mental health but am still full of anxiety.* Then, I energetically shift by making a cup of tea and taking a walk outside.

CURIOSITY. *Is this true that I'm a loser and an impostor for having spinster fears?* Um, no. I have zero evidence that this worry is legit. I do know these fears are being amplified by cultural narratives, though.

How do I react to having these thoughts? I'm anxious! Regina is firing insults that get uglier by the day. I lose confidence and energy and sink into a slumpy mood.

Who would I be without these thoughts? I would be excited about the future, knowing that what is right for me will not pass me by. I would be enjoying my freedom, focusing on my writing, helping others and feeling grateful for the opportunity!

Which faulty thinking habit is at play here? All-or-nothing thinking and assuming I can predict the future.

CHOICE. I choose to forgive myself for being dragged down by the rom-com standard. It's easy for anyone to fall into the trap of thinking they're doing life wrong. I recognize I have the power to create a new thought and *choose to find a new perspective*.

COMMITMENT. To break the crystal-ball fortune-telling automatic-negative-thought habit, I ask myself what my Wild Self would do. My internal she-wolf (of love) would NOT be worried. She would be excited about what delicious magic the future might hold and set out on a trot to find it. To a friend experiencing the same feels, I'd say, "Live for yourself today. Because one day, you'll long for the freedom you have now." Using that perspective, I felt an even greater energy shift-up. I committed to the daily affirmation "Everything Poppy is unfolding is for my own good." It may sound kooky, but compassionate soul-talk-with-self works. It helps to leave the fearful ego behind, and trust in one's inner guidance that says, "It's going to be okay."

One hallmark of our culture is fear of change. "Same" feels "safe" because it's known. But the essential irony of playing it stiff and safe today, is the fact that you're reducing your chances of being safe tomorrow. When the world moves, we've got to move with it or risk being left behind. Just think, do I want to be Netflix or Blockbuster? Flex or end up a curmudgeonly oldie, shaking their fist shouting about "what it was like in their day."

Some people might stay stiff until they are ready to stretch or are forced into it. It can be crushing when people we love aren't willing to Flex. My father, for example, has spent years saying, "I am just anxious, this is just the way I am, I can't change," and my mother and I would want to pull our hair out. We would send him podcast after podcast, book after book of research to show him his stiff thinking is scientifically unproven. It is our human right to be flexible and evolve, but he would find the one sentence that confirmed 0.000001 percent of stiff thoughts and ignore the entire library saying the opposite. He is gradually coming around to the idea of flexibility and accepting the hard, cold science to prove that it's possible. I will force him to read this book, too, so...*Hi, Dad! Will you please now accept you can change and are not just "an anxious person"? Thank you. I'll see you in the kitchen for some belly breathing and Flexing later.*

We might feel alone as we try to heal and change. Some people take longer than others to start stretching. One thing is for sure: No one can be forced, change only begins when someone is ready to *choose* to Flex for themselves and commit to it with action. We can invite everyone and anyone to join us but if they refuse, there's not a lot we can do but inspire by example without judgment. We can't change others, but often the change in ourselves has a profound effect on those around us. Be the force that pushes our culture toward equality. Be the person that opens the door to new pastures for everyone else.

"Success is liking yourself, liking what you do, and liking how you do it."
—Maya Angelou

"I'LL TELL YOU WHAT FREEDOM IS TO ME: NO FEAR. I MEAN, REALLY, NO FEAR!"

—NINA SIMONE

FLEX CONFIDENCE

The word "confidence" comes from *fidere*, Latin for "to trust." When we have trust/belief in ourselves to meet life's challenges, we have confidence. For example, I'm *confident* that I can start a company. (For that matter, I'm *confident* that I will never be a professional chef, as I can barely fry an egg without burning it.)

In terms of the Flex, confidence means quieting our bitchy inner critic and raising the volume of our inner guidance system. It seems doable enough, and yet so many of us really struggle with believing in ourselves. My self-help books on confidence could fill a wee library. Lack of confidence is epidemic and unsurprising due to our negative bias and a culture that erodes self-trust by telling us we can buy confidence. It doesn't encourage us to grow it within. But, through Flexing, we can do that for ourselves.

The odd thing about confidence is that we all started out with it at 100 percent. As babies, we didn't worry about whether we deserved to be heard or care about how silly our first steps looked when we face-planted in front of the family. We were born with total curiosity, no fear of judgment, and zero hesitancy to scream for what we needed, be it food, sleep, cuddles, or a clean diaper. A baby is born knowing they are good enough, and they can cry if they want to!

So what happened? We were conditioned to have fears and doubts. Our baby selves' blissful confidence—"Hello! Look at me!

Listen to me! I'm here!"—was quickly overturned in the sponge years when we started building a model about the world and our place in it. We developed opinions, tastes, beliefs, values, boundaries (or not), and behaviors. We learned how others perceived us, and what our strengths and weaknesses were. We learned how to get attention and love, and what got us into trouble. Parents, siblings, teachers, friends are all co-builders of our self-model, for good or ill. But if our co-builders said things like...

"You don't deserve that!"

"You're naughty."

"You're lazy."

"You're ugly."

"No one likes you."

"Don't shout! Don't cry! Be a good girl."

"You can't do that."

...then that is what became our concept of self. We learned, from our co-builders, to criticize and doubt ourselves.

> "The way we talk to our children
> becomes their inner voice."
> —Peggy O'Mara

Children take the word of authority figures as fact. They don't have the capacity to challenge yet. So the messages we absorb in the sponge years turn into the programmed core beliefs we spend the rest of our lives playing out and looking for evidence to confirm. Instead of doubting the messenger and the message, we learn to doubt ourselves.

In the adulting process, questions like "Will I succeed?" "Do they like me?" "Am I good enough?" "Will others approve?" or "Will things go horribly, horribly wrong?" took prominence, and overshadowed our natural-born confidence like a cloud on a sunny day.

For a lot of the Anxious Generation, the cloud just won't go away. In part, we can find cause in our well-meaning parents who hovered and swooped in to save the day whenever we faced the slightest hint of trouble. "Don't worry about screwing that up, darling. I'll make your science project for you!" they said. "You don't have to go on the school trip if you feel anxious. I'll have a word with the teachers." Sound familiar?

We were conditioned to be intolerant of hard feelings, and never developed the skills to move through them. Helicopter parents lifted the weight for many of us and our muscles stayed weak. The truth is, we would have been fine without so much loving intervention, but we were never given the opportunity to learn that. Confidence grows through doing, sometimes failing, learning that facing failure is how we grow, and trying again until we get it right.

Confidence lies on the other side of conditioned fear.

I have yet to meet someone with no fears, but I have met many confident souls who are better than others at managing their unpleasant feelings.

If I'd understood that my lack of confidence came from my over-bearing fear of feeling less-than, perhaps I wouldn't have beaten myself up so much and assumed something was wrong with me. I fell into the trap of believing in the "illusion of confidence" our culture propagates. Social media, as we all know, fosters the illusion. We're exposed to countless #girlsnightout pics of happy people who look like life is a piece of cake. But how many posts do we ever see that say, "So nervous about going to this party! Will anyone talk to me?"

My giveaway sign that I'm anxious AF and suffering severe droughts in confidence is when I talk so much, you might think I was on drugs. The thought of a conversation silence fills me with such dread that I defensively ramble. The person usually squirms away, leaving me with even less confidence as I turn the squirm into evidence that I'm not worthy of their time. I've begun to see I'm less alone in thinking this than I once thought. I've met celebrities, business leaders, frontline workers, and all sorts of people I assumed were successful because of their overflowing, innate buckets of confidence. But when I scratched lightly to get below the surface, I found a vulnerable, insecure soul who's faking it like the rest of us.

Stiff thinkers are trapped in "I can't...what if I screw up or embarrass myself?...People will think less of me." Underneath, it's all about being afraid of rejection, not enough, or unlovable.

Flexible thinkers challenge the faulty beliefs and brain biases that hold us back, so we can move forward and say, "Perhaps I can...only one way to find out...I trust myself."

It's not our fault we have low self-esteem, but it *is* our responsibility to stretch out of that mindset by choosing trust over doubt, and love over fear. Becoming aware of faulty programming is the first step to freedom and the debugging/upgrading process.

About those fears...per my tea party of experts, I discovered we all carry the Big Three to varying degrees:

1. Fear of failure

2. Fear of rejection

3. Fear of not being enough.

For example, the dream of writing a book might be snuffed out by the fear of failure, so the pages remain blank.

The desire to apply for a dream job might be clouded over by the fear of rejection, so we never send in our résumé.

The yearning to get up and dance might be squashed by the fear that we'll look like a wiggly, jiggly socially awkward banana, so we stay seated in the corner.

We can stop letting fear hold us back, since all of these situations *can* be Flexed, freeing us to start writing, go for the job, and dance like an oblong yellow fruit.

I've added two niche fears that I've noticed among my peers: fear of other people's opinions (FOPO) and the fear of bad outcomes (FOBO). One could argue they are shades of the Big Three fears, but I think they're unique roadblocks, so I'm keeping them separate. (It's my book and I'll subhead if I want to ☺.)

When we Flex our fears and come through them in one piece, confidence is waiting with wide-open arms on the other side.

Failure doesn't really exist.

Outcomes are just opportunities.

Rejection isn't about us.

The opinions of others are not our problem.

We ARE enough.

Confidence is available to us when we are unapologetically ourselves. When we embody acceptance and detach from certain ideas of how things should be, we become irresistible to the world, and our future breaks wide open. We all contain a Wild Self inside who has unbridled confidence and is waiting to connect.

Failure Does Not Exist

The brain doesn't lose, it learns

My sage on the elasticity of the mind, Dr. Leonard Mlodinow, believes that flexible thoughts are made possible when we look for new ways to think about old things. Instead of staying stiff, we can challenge ourselves to reframe ideas, thoughts, and events, and stretch how we see them. He has said that every human mind is innately flexible, we just need to practice stretching it into the shape that best works for us. Hurrah for us, fellow Flexers!

A useful Flex reframe of "failure" is "the brain never fails, it learns." In Dr. Mlodinow's collaboration with Deepak Chopra, *War of the Worldviews: Where Science and Spirituality Meet—and Do Not,* he described the intelligence feedback loop of learning to ski. When beginners start the sport, they fall down. Great. That's an essential part of the learning process. Every time we fall, the body figures out something new about how to balance with two planks of wood attached to our feet, and it makes adjustments. Falls aren't failures. They take us, one bruise at a time, toward mastery. When Mlodinow himself learned to ski, he actually forced himself to fall. Otherwise, he found himself skiing in a really stiff way. By purposely falling, he took away his fear of it and, therefore, had more confidence to try out new things and allow his muscles and mind to learn even quicker.

Thomas Edison, another legendary Flexer, once said of his many dashed experiments when inventing the lightbulb, "I have not failed. I've just found 10,000 ways that won't work." Edison probably didn't know he was practicing "exposure therapy" to minimize the fear of failure by doing so much of it that it no longer affected him. "Our greatest weakness lies in giving up," he also said. "The most certain way to succeed is always to try just one more time."

Fear of failure is what keeps us from having the confidence to try again—or to try AT ALL.

But fear is just a signal from the WFML station, a burst of static that only lasts ninety seconds. If we can breathe through it, and remind ourselves of the huge dangling carrot, the Bigger Better Offer of learning something new, we can overcome the fear.

If we can be like Edison, and make Learn Something New our North Star, the meaning we've attached to "failure" can be rewritten. We didn't face-plant on the slopes; we learned a new skill. We didn't make a worthless lightbulb; we got one step closer to changing the world.

And then when we commit to trying again, we can CELEBRATE our efforts. Dr. Judson Brewer wrote that the brain will not create new habits unless it's incentivized to. It is extremely hard to break through fear if we don't reward ourselves every step of the way. I tested this out again when I was trying to get into a daily exercise routine during quarantine. No gyms were open, so I had to think of other ways I could move my body and stay fit. I decided to build a habit around running daily but it was going to be a challenging task as I've always *hated* running. I decided to reward myself by listening to my favorite music only when I was running, so if I wanted to enjoy some great tunes, I would have to get my running shoes on. I surprised myself with how quickly I began to look forward to my runs because my brain craved that burst of feel-good vibes from the music. Learning this habit turned into a Step #1 practice, as while I was running, I felt like it was a practice to upgrade my energy and connect with my body.

Flexercise: The Failure Flex

It's really all about CHOICE here, in choosing to adopt a Growth Mindset where failure equals advancement.

EXPECT GROWTH PAINS. Swap the terror of failing with the power of growth, even if it's a tad uncomfy. As psychologist Jessamy Hibberd told me, "Because growth is a good thing, we think it's going to *feel* good, and be easy and straightforward. But growth comes from stepping outside of your comfort zone, out of autopilot mode, and it does feel a bit daunting." But only at first, she assured me. The first time you fall down and realize you can get back up, you're less afraid to fall again. Choose to lean into the discomfort of fear.

DON'T EXPECT INSTANT IMPROVEMENT. Growth isn't always as fast as we'd like it to be. But if you feel like you're not progressing, keep asking, "What can I learn from this experience?" and let go of old statements like "Why does this happen to me!?" The growth area might not be what you anticipated. You might learn practical information to change and get better. You might gain self-knowledge or the self-trust you needed to do something even more awesome. Your Wild Self doesn't waste energy feeling frustrated about not getting exactly what he or she hoped for and anticipated. It keeps going with both eyes open, endlessly curious, searching for whatever is out there in the world to learn. It goes bravely into every new adventure, knowing that gaining experience itself is the point and gift, and the outcome doesn't even matter.

Outcomes Are Opportunities
Being successful is a state of mind

FOBO is the fear of bad outcomes (not fear of body odor, which is legit, too!). FOBO kills confidence like bad breath kills a date. This fear is a critical driver behind most anxieties, like the social anxiety of knowing you should go to the party but being terrified you'll find no one to talk to. FOMO scares you into going out, FOBO scares you into staying home.

This fortune-telling automatic negative thought (ANT) inspires what Dr. Joan Rosenberg calls "bad emotional math." We attach a meaning to one shitty time at a party and create the equation: parties = misery + embarrasment. One bad outcome = the same bad outcome for eternity. This is simply not true, and a terrible miscalculation that causes severe FOBO.

One bad experience does NOT mean they'll all be bad. Nor does an anxiety-riddled past mean we are stuck in a lifetime of worry. This is very stiff thinking. I'm reminded of a talk I gave in Boston at a corporate event about the science of neuroplasticity and the possibility of change, and a young woman came up to me in tears after. It was the first time anyone had told her that anxiety was malleable and didn't have to be a life sentence. "I was born an anxious person. I always have been and thought I always woud be." I asked her how she came to have this idea that a life of anxiety was inevitable. She said, "My mother told me that she passed on the anxious gene to me." Although there is a genetic link to anxiety, genes are not destiny. Childhood influences do have an enormous impact on the way our belief systems are first formulated. But beliefs *are* 100 percent changeable. They are not destiny.

With curiosity, we can disprove what we are convinced are immutable facts. To Flex, we have to embrace our power to see a multitude of potential outcomes, not a single, scary, sad ONE and ONLY.

Just yesterday, I sent an email to a group that, in the past, has been deeply ambivalent about my work, to ask for their support on a new project. I had put off sending it for weeks. Since they'd rejected me before, I was afraid/expecting that they might do it again #FOBO. I was tired (a key factor in my slipping back into stiff thinking), and so before I hit send, I called a friend to process my fear. "I need them or the project will never get off the ground. But I'm just so worried they're going to be dicks about it and not support me!"

She said, "You have no idea how they are going to react. Your negative bias and fearful inner critic are doing all the talking right now."

I started laughing. I TAUGHT HER ABOUT NEGATIVE BIAS, and she was throwing my own words back at me. And she was right: My past experience was coloring my feelings and I really didn't know how this request would be received, since it was entirely different from the last time. I took a few deep breaths and committed to being my brave instinctual Wild Self. What would she do in this situation? She'd move forward with no fear, accept any outcome, and then move on. So I worked hard to send a very professional, enticing email that presented the facts sans emotion, and hit send. Then I did my best to detach as I waited for a reply. I didn't wait long! Within two hours, everyone had responded *positively*. Shocked would be an understatement!! Had I not Flexed, I'd have been a victim to FOBO and not put myself forward.

Science has proven the power of expectations via the Placebo Effect: If a patient expects a pill to work, it does, even if the pill contains no actual medicine. A recent study[46] testing migraine medication found the placebo to be 50 percent as effective as the real drug after a migraine attack. The lead researcher, Ted Kaptchuk, a professor at Harvard-affiliated Beth Israel Deaconess Medical Center, said about the study, "Even if they know it's not medicine, the action itself can stimulate the brain into thinking the body is being healed."[47]

The other side of the same coin is expecting something bad to happen, and it's more likely to. This is called "a self-fulfilling prophecy," a phrase attributed to sociologist Robert Merton. In 1948 he defined it as: "a false definition of the situation evoking a new behavior which makes the originally false conception come true."[48]

The "law of attraction" manifesting crowd said that we attract our greatest fears. The scientific crowd agrees.

The more we fear something, the more activated our unconscious is to look out for it and find confirmation for our faulty beliefs. What we focus on gets louder and the more we rumble through our fears, the more vigilant our mind is at spotting them.

Physiologically, fear of pain (a bad outcome to be sure) increases it. Neuroscientists at the University of Colorado at Boulder hooked up their subjects to an MRI brain imaging machine and told them that they'd be subjected to a high or low heat stimulation that was going to hurt. The subjects who expected the high heat experienced more intense brain activity regardless of how much pain they were subjected to. *Actual* pain didn't matter. The key factor was expectation.[49] We suffer far more by thinking than by doing.

The other danger of FOBO is our power in ensuring bad outcomes just to prove to ourselves that our fears were right (even when they need not be!). Harvard Medical School professor and clinical psychiatrist John Sharp, MD, wrote in *The Insight Cure*, "Your unconscious loves to be right. One way we can be right is to make sure things go wrong, as in, 'I *knew* this was a mistake!' or 'I *knew* I'd blow it!'" In a sick way, our ego wants us to fuck up just so it can say "I told you so." Sharp wrote, "It's human nature to confirm your beliefs, even if they are wrong and hurtful."[50]

Dr. Sharp mapped out the progression of how fear of bad outcomes turns into reality. It starts with the ASSUMPTION, such as, "No one is going to talk to me at the party." That flows into PERCEPTION, walking in there and seeing people in tight circles, engaged in their conversations and believing it's impossible to break in. That flows into ACTION, standing at the far end of the bar, putting up walls, not even trying to engage. Finally, that turns into EVIDENCE, as in, "I *knew* no one would talk to me! I was *right!*" which sets us up nicely for the next Assumption-Perception-Action-Evidence flow. Each time we take this vicious cycle, it wires more deeply into our brain.

When Dr. Sharp works with patients to flex FOBO, he asks them to imagine different outcomes in any given situation. Man walks into a bar... woman speaks up in the classroom...candidate has a job interview... and *then what*? After the patient offers the first, autopilot response, Dr. Sharp urges them to come up with another outcome, and another, from the banal to the outlandish. When we practice visualizing a positive outcome, we are training our unconscious brain in the right way to spot the good things in a future situation. Olympic teams have been taking advantage of the science behind positive visualization for years and imagining playing their best game to enhance their future performance.

After setting positive intentions, to Flex FOBO farther, we have to practice fully detaching from the certainty of stiff expectations.

> *"If you expect the battle to be insurmountable, you've met the enemy. It's you."*
> —Khang Kijarro Nguyen

Burn the security blanket of FOBO to a crisp. Just eradicate it and venture out into the world bare-assed naked where anything positive can happen, and it probably will! As Deepak Chopra says, allow yourself to experience infinite potential. #ExpectTheUnexpected

Per Dr. Sharp, the map out of FOBO starts by setting an INTENTION, an attainable goal, as in, "I *intend* to talk to two people at this party." That flows into PREPARATION, or whatever we can do to achieve the goal, say, buy a bottle of wine and give it to the host (convo #1) and ask to fix someone else a drink (convo #2). Within five minutes of being there, we've already realized our intention. We could just go home happy at that point. Or, we could live in the moment and EXPERIENCE what is actually happening, not what we *fear* is going to happen. Challenge yourself to stay for another five minutes and see if anything opens up. And finish up with EVALUATION, the party postmortem. How'd it go with the wine giving and challenging yourself to stay a little longer? What different Intentions and Preparations could alter future Experiences? And then, by doing an Evaluation, we learn that the outcome is always up for interpretation. It's our call how we perceive situations.

The same Intention-Preparation-Experience-Evaluation movement works in just about any context, like, say, a job interview. Set the Intention of expressing yourself well. Prepare the night before by visualizing that you nailed the experience, rehearse answers to likely questions, do some breathing exercises to calm nerves and keep WCHL playing, write a list of values you appreciate about the company and how you would fit in. Experience the interview in the moment by actively listening and not letting your mind wander. Evaluation is a mental replay of what worked and what to improve on next time, as well as following up with the interviewer to ask for feedback. This is the secret to any success: stretching your amazing, plastic brain to continually learn, grow, grab opportunities, and find those growth nuggets!

I had a bad case of FOBO about public speaking. It related to my perfectionism. One flub was like falling through the floor in my mind. I was more afraid of how I'd beat myself up afterward than making a mistake itself. I started to nearly hyperventilate before any public speaking gig, and I would have stopped doing them if I hadn't Flexed daily to release myself from the fear of expectations.

When I was interviewing Britteny Floyd-Mayo of Trap Yoga, she shared a great technique she uses with her children to teach them about building confidence and Flexing out of FOBO. When they are nervous for school, she'll ask them to say, "Wouldn't it be nice..." and list all the things it would be lovely to experience that day. "Wouldn't it be nice if recess was twice as long" and "Wouldn't it be nice if I aced my test." Voicing their desires immediately switched their focus to what they *wanted to happen* that day and moved them away from focusing on any fears they were having. I have since adopted this strategy for myself to defuse FOBO. "Wouldn't it be nice if my presentation today went well!" The "wouldn't it be nice" approach is a gentler way I find to place positivity into intention, without putting pressure, and less intense than an affirmation my brain might reject as a full-on lie.

A lifelong habit of FOBO won't go away with the snap of our fingers like on *Sabrina the Teenage Witch* (if only). It takes a lot of Flexing to stretch the brain away from negative expectations and/or debilitating high expectations toward no expectations and just positive intentions. But as Flexing becomes second nature, we learn to embrace and appreciate the glorious mystery of endless possibility, growing our strength to handle anything life throws at us, which is, actually, the definition of confidence.

Even if the branch breaks beneath us, we have the strength to fly and find a new branch. It is so easy to forget the wings we have. But if we risk doing what we're most afraid of, we'll learn that twigs break *for* us all the time so we can find Bigger Better branches and develop stronger wings!

Flexercise: The FOBO Flex

Don't let the fear of bad outcomes kill your confidence. Flex to know you've got this!

CONNECTION. You are not in danger. You are afraid that you might be in danger. Big difference. Burn off the FOBO fear by raising your energy vibe from anticipatory dread to nervous excitement or chilled anticipation. Either utilize your belly breathing, focusing on your exhales being longer than your inhales, or before a party, I put on beat-y music and jump around to activate my happy hormones and endorphins. After a pregame dance party for one, I can bounce into the party, the job interview, the first time meeting new investors, and bring the higher vibrations with me. (N.B.: If you try this, choose your music wisely. If you play something dreary like the soundtrack to *Titanic*, be careful your energy doesn't take you down with the ship.)

CURIOSITY. Never take your fear seriously without investigating it. Asking questions is your friend always! Which ANT is being naughty right now? Where's the negative bias? How did I learn to fear this outcome? What can I do differently this time? What's the worst that could happen? Then create a worst case (will never happen) survival plan to show yourself that you still would be okay even if disaster strikes. Can I control this or not? Who would I be without the fear?

CHOICE. FOBO is a product of the Wolf of Fear. With awareness, choose to feed the Wolf of Love by repeating the mantra "I choose to expect the unexpected" in the face of any rising worry. As soon as you hear the slightest sounds of predictions and assumptions forgive yourself for being a human with confirmation biases to overcome. Shimmy back to choosing to stay present and experience life as it unfolds.

COMMITMENT. Take action with the help of a Flexi-Mentor. What would your most confident authentic friend do? Keep in mind that the *appearance* of confidence might be a smoke screen. Some people can exercise their bodies into perfection and dress beautifully, but that doesn't mean they walk with confidence. You can be a size 2 or a size 22 and feel the same fear. The person with *self-acceptance* walks in confidence.

And even that person has *some* doubts. One of Dr. Rick Hanson's greatest lessons was teaching me to gaze at other people's foreheads when I meet them and remind myself that there's a human being inside who is dealing with their own battles that I know nothing about. It makes walking into a party or a job interview a lot easier when you can get out of your head, stop reading from your FOBO script, and focus your attention on the person or situation in front of you. This allows you to be present in the room (not lost in your own thoughts), open to anything and compassionate to others. Long story short, we are all scared shitless and no one has it together *really.*

Rejection Isn't About Us

It's about the other person

Right off the bat, we have to acknowledge what is behind the fear of rejection. It's the terror of not BELONGING. We're social animals and feeling like we belong and are accepted by a community is high on any list of human needs. Being part of a whole is hardwired in our brains. Our evolutionary instincts drive us to seek social acceptance for survival. If the tribe likes us, we get to stay in the cave and live with plenty of resources available. If the tribe rejects us, we're cast out to die alone.

Any kind of rejection triggers consciously or unconsciously our worst fear of being cast out. But when we seek acceptance from others at the expense of being ourselves, we pay a price for it in stepping outside our integrity and diminished confidence. It's kind of sad, really, because so much of "self-love" self-help tells us to "just do you." If only it were that simple! Not only is it extremely hard to *be* a lone wolf, it's even harder to be one who values herself.

American sociologist Charles Horton Cooley coined the term the "Looking-Glass Self" in 1902.[51] It means we base who we are on our perception of how others see us. Every time we feel rejection and turn it into self-hatred, we're taking a figurative Looking-Glass Selfie.

The crack in the Looking-Glass Self is that, even on our best day, we don't know what other people really think of us. We don't live in their heads. We can't read minds. It's simply impossible to know if someone might reject you. We humans, with our hubris and storytelling skills, invent reasons that we deserve to be rejected based on who we are, what we look like, what we sound like, and what we've said and done. But without evidence of why someone rejects, we can't really know what it's about. In almost every case, the reason is their prejudice and belief system and has nothing to do with us. Say you wore red glasses to a job interview, and the interviewer has a personal hatred of the color red. They can't hear or see you, they only see what they hate. You don't get the job because of a stranger's aversion to your favorite color. It's not about you. It's about their nonsensical prejudice.

"If you can't love yourself, how the hell are you gonna love somebody else?"
—RuPaul

Others' Opinions Are Not Your Problem

A pound of salt, please

Fear of other people's opinions (FOPO) is being afraid of what others think to the degree that we disregard our own feelings when making important life choices. I've struggled mightily with this. Some telltale signs:

- Agonizing so much about whether people are going to agree with our decisions that we can't make them without feedback

- Deleting posts that don't get a certain number of likes within a certain time frame

- Doormat behaviors—agreeing to ridiculous favors—just so they like us

- Hiding a secret love or fandom because people might mock us for it

- Making excuses if others judge us for something we said, did, or wore

- Editing ourselves, all in a blatant attempt to prevent judgment

It's healthy and human to care what other people think of us. It's unhealthy when we care so much that we can't do anything without validation.

How we look, what we wear, what we do for a living, whom we date, which movies we see, books we read, food we eat, places we go, are all up for social judgment. We can try to "win" approval from our vast networks with filtered, face-tuned, curated online versions of ourselves. Each *like* gives the brain a hit of primal belonging. But when we don't get approval, it feels like a slap of primal judgment that triggers ALL our worst fears of being failures, rejects, and not good enough. For perfectionists, the sound of crickets is particularly wounding. We try so hard to prove our worth to ensure belonging and acceptance, when external validation doesn't come, our worst fears are confirmed that maybe we aren't "good enough or lovable enough." That's why a lukewarm response to a Gram post can be self-esteem-crushing.

It is no wonder we're in a constant state of low-grade "survival mode," when survival means approval, approval comes from the appearance of worthiness, and approval is by no means guaranteed. (Especially true on Instagram with its algorithm that screws you over if you post when no one's looking…the Insta-algorithm is threatening our survival? What has the world come to!)

So many times throughout my life I have let other people dictate my choices. Some completely ill-informed school career adviser told me psychology wasn't a serious degree (um, what!!?); I studied politics instead, and spent years dragging myself to politics classes and hating it, while reading psychology books in my free time and loving them.

I can list at least five boys I avoided dating because I cared too much about what people might think. How did that work out? Way too many nights watering my plants instead of having fun and getting to know new people.

We can't disregard *all* judgment or advice. But choose confidants wisely. Not all advice is equal! Consulting a beloved friend is a lot wiser than basing our self-concept on the opinions of people we don't know and can't trust.

My queen Brené Brown admitted to being cut deeply after reading highly personal attacks in the comments section under her articles and videos. To soothe herself, Brown dove into an eight-hour *Downton Abbey* binge. (It's always a fantastic remedy, I must say.) While watching *Downton*, she stumbled across a quote from President Theodore Roosevelt that inspired her to write: "If you're not also in the arena getting your ass kicked, I'm not interested in your feedback." Wow, I think we all need to hear this on a daily basis. Feedback is not born equal and should not be treated equally. If you are not also living vulnerably, baring your soul, opening yourself to equal attack, too, then you can keep your comments. Thanks and #byeeeeee.

Brown stopped reading the trolls' comments. She drew a line between credible sources and not: If the source is visible, vulnerable, and creative, it's valuable. If the source is anonymous, destructive, and tears down the accomplishments of others, it's worthless. This was like reading words of gold and has also schooled me ever since. I refuse to throw criticism at ANYONE who is making an effort to contribute something good in the world. Getting out of bed and trying anything is such a fucking accomplishment because it means you've slayed the dragon of fear of public shaming. I commend anyone who puts their head above the parapet. Brown's words also empowered me not to take on critical comments. It's very easy and cowardly to hate from the couch and tear people down for doing something out of the ordinary. It's harder to be kind and supportive. Those are the values I'm Flexing and living.

When we obsessively ask for feedback and opinions, we want encouragement but attract judgment. I have called Mum a lot to ask for feedback. "What did you think of that interview I just did?" I ask, and if she comes back with anything but positive feedback, I'm upset! But I asked her. Why? My insecurities were looking for validation and encouragement that I should be giving to myself first. I'm gradually learning to go inside myself and find connection before going outward. I am no expert on this though and it's one of my greatest challenges, but I try to ask: What are my First, Second, Third, and Fourth Brains telling me about how that interview went? before I resort to calling my mother.

We all know when something's a bit of a mess or all right, and yet we look for the opinions of others to convince us and distract us from what we know inside.

It's amazing how little we defer to our own opinion and yet we know ourselves best. Or do we? Flexible thinking is our befriending process back with ourselves. When I started getting Curious about my thoughts and why I craved feedback, I could see my mind was crawling with ANTs that made me jump to "the whole interview was *terrible*" even if I slipped up on one word. They blamed me for things out of my control, like if the interviewee was closed down. When I began getting curious, I didn't need so much reassurance from other people to exterminate these ANTs. I was able to do it myself. When you get better at identifying which naughty ANT is at play, they start to dissolve as quickly as they appeared.

Sometimes, we don't seek judgment and opinions, but they are thrust upon us. This isn't necessarily a bad thing, either. I am often really grateful to those who share their thoughts. I have swerved away from many a wrong decision purely down to others making me aware of things my narrow vision couldn't see. Other people can help stretch our thoughts and actually increase our flexibility, and when that happens, it evolves us and them. But again, all advice isn't created equal.

"I understand what you're saying, and your comments are valuable, but I'm gonna ignore your advice."
—Fantastic Mr. Fox

Flexercise: The FOPO Flex

Confidence is a function of trusting your own judgment and being able to put the opinions of others into perspective.

CONNECTION. Be honest, label it, and wait for the judged feeling to pass, and defuse it further by saying, "Today, I am feeling anxious about what other people think," and then energetically shift by pulling your shoulders back, straightening your back. Accept, breathe, energize . . .

CURIOSITY. Always consider the source of the judgment as well as the judgment itself. Is the person just projecting the advice they ought to give themselves? Are they compulsive stiff thinkers, giving an opinion that reinforces their worldview? Stay curious about where the ideas come from and whether they are worth listening to. Put the opinions to the test against your inner guidance system. Does this feedback feel right to my Wild Self? Align with my values? If not, ignore it.

CHOICE. My mother used to tell me that whatever you talk about is your reality. So if you talk about problems, that's what you get. Same for the questions we look to others for reassurance about, like "Do people like me?" or "Am I safe?" These questions immediately encourage us to look for reasons why they don't or why we're not. The Choice we have to make daily is to consciously choose to ask better questions when looking for feedback. Instead of asking, "Why am I cursed with this shitty job?" ask "What can I learn from this job to improve my work going forward?" If we talk about problems, ask questions that make us look for more problems, our life is nothing but. If we talk about solutions and ask questions that lead us to discover more of them, life feels more hopeful and doable.

COMMITMENT. Self-compassion is a FOPO cure. Those who are kind to themselves are found to be less affected by negative feedback. It keeps your inner tree trunk sturdy because you have learned the skills of self-appreciation and kindness. If your mind holds on to criticism like glue and stores judgments from others in your unconscious insecurity bucket, commit to poking holes in it to let those insecurities drain. Be your own inner cheerleader, your own hype bae—picture your Wild Self running free, hooting positive truths. Some of mine are:

"Poppy, you're doing what's best for you right now!"

"Poppy, you've said the right thing!"

"Poppy, you got this! You've done it before!"

I use the awkward third person because it's been proven to be motivating. Researchers from Michigan[52] found that third-person self-talk works in a similar way to the Friend Perspective. You get a degree of separation, and it makes the brain think you're encouraging someone else, which triggers our altruism superpower.

So, as soon as you hear another's opinion, invite your cheerleader/hype bae to the mind-stage and drown out the trolls in the cheap seats.

We've heard a lot of "YOU DO YOU, BAE." I'd like to edit that slightly to "YOU *KNOW* YOU, BAE," so don't let any little shits tell you otherwise. Get to know your "true (Wild) self," and your own opinions will feel clear and genuine. By being authentic and self-assured, you give others permission to be, too. Start the domino effect. If you know yourself, are clear on your values, and have self-compassion, FOPO dissolves, and you'll react to every judgment or criticism like 🐵.

....

You ARE Enough

So why compare?

When I met then–prime minister Theresa May to receive an award in British Parliament for my work with mental health in England, I was throbbing the entire day with Impostor Syndrome. *Who am I to get an award? I haven't done enough.* My bitchy inner critic Regina was taunting me with nightmares that PM May was going to say, "On second thought, you don't deserve this award after all."

My fear of being found out as a fraud/Impostor Syndrome (IS) has been one of my biggest anxieties and a huge part of my journey. I devoured *The Imposter Cure: How to Stop Feeling Like a Fraud and Escape the Mind-Trap of Imposter Syndrome* by psychologist Jessamy Hibberd, PhD. As she told me, "Whenever you care about what you're doing but you're not sure how you're going to do it yet, it's natural to experience some discomfort. Impostors misinterpret that discomfort. They think, *Oh, God, I'm not up to this. I'm not going to be able to do it. If I were confident, I wouldn't feel like this.* They don't realize that it's completely natural to feel uncertain of yourself, but you've just got to kind of go for it anyway."

According to recent research, 70 percent of people at one time or another have Impostor Syndrome.[53] Take the quiz below to see if this is something that may also plague you. It's based on the Impostor Phenomenon Scale[54] created by Drs. Pauline Rose Clance and Suzanne Imes, the psychologists who originally identified the condition in the 1980s.

Quiz: Do You Have Impostor Syndrome?

Rate each statement on a scale of 1 to 5: 1 being "God, never" and 5 being "all the fucking time."

1. Before a test, I'm convinced that I'll fail, but then I usually do pretty well. ① ② ③ ④ ⑤

2. To other people, I come off as a lot more competent than I really am. ① ② ③ ④ ⑤

3. Praise feels terrible! I'm convinced that I'll never live up to it again. ① ② ③ ④ ⑤

4. If I've accomplished anything, it's only because I got lucky.
① ② ③ ④ ⑤

5. I'm just waiting for the day when my boss, friends, and partner realize I'm not nearly as impressive as they think I am.
① ② ③ ④ ⑤

6. I remember every detail about my screwups. My victories are kind of blurry. ① ② ③ ④ ⑤

7. Whatever my accomplishments might be, I know I could have done better. ① ② ③ ④ ⑤

8. I start out every new project with the expectation that it'll be worse than my last. ① ② ③ ④ ⑤

9. When I look around at my colleagues and peers, I compare myself unfavorably to them, even if an objective observer would think that I'm more accomplished. ① ② ③ ④ ⑤

10. As doubtful as I am about my abilities and despite how I discount any recognition, I feel horrible if I don't beat out others in any kind of competition. ① ② ③ ④ ⑤

SCORING

20 and under: You are among the 30 percent of people who DON'T feel like a fraud.

21 to 30: You've got a moderate case.

31 to 40: Your IS interferes with your life and thoughts.

41 to 50: Full-on IS, high frequency and high intensity, crushing confidence daily.

"Impostors have two rules," said Dr. Hibberd. "When they do well, it's down to external circumstances like luck. Whereas if anything goes badly, it's a personal failing and completely on them. They can't take on board their success. They're constantly seeing all their faults and not believing that they're any good. There's a gap between how they're doing and how they see themselves."

This can happen to anyone. Any. One. Even the most unlikely suspects. I was shown this in dazzling colors when I first attended the *Vanity Fair* Oscar party in 2017. I could not BELIEVE I'd been invited, all thanks to my friend Krista, the magazine's West Coast editor, who'd scooped me up like a mum in LA when she saw that my Calamity Jane personality needed some guidance. I felt like Cinderella going to the ball.

I walked in and *fucking hell*, EVERYONE was even more beautiful than the pictures. Instant confidence plunge. Whenever I feel socially anxious, I have a habit of beelining to the food and I chow down on anything I can find. In this situation, I found an In-N-Out burger with onions on a gooey bun and I started gobbling it like I hadn't eaten in weeks. (N.B.: No breath mint is powerful enough to cover up those fried onions.) On finishing, I realized none of the other guests had touched the food yet.

Fuckity fuck.

I was the only one who dove in headfirst, reeked of onion, and spilled ketchup on my dress. Excellent. My fear of being not good enough in this crowd was crippling enough without burger breath. I decided that the best option would be to hug a wall and watch the party from the side. And then while I was admiring the room sucking furiously on my mints, I had a major aha moment. These beautiful, rich, and famous people appeared to also suffer from cripplingly low confidence, *and it looked just like mine*. They were anxiously circling, looking for someone to talk to. They were nervously readjusting their dresses and secretly checking their breath. They talked too loud, too fast, exactly what I did to overcompensate. Everyone was shuffling around that party nervously, feeling unworthy compared to the next, more famous star.

I know so many women who are conventionally stunning and make a good living on their appearance, and have heard them say, "I look like shit." On the other hand, I have friends who haven't brushed their hair in weeks, don't care for makeup, and walk into every room like they're the hottest thing since climate change. But, granted, that's not the norm.

Sadly, the norm is to feel inadequate, look only at what's wrong with us, and constantly compare ourselves to others unfavorably.

Dr. Hibberd said that impostors need to own and internalize their successes. "It's not being arrogant or having an inflated ego," she said. "It's about really seeing the full picture of your life, taking on board the good things that are happening and your central part in them, rather than discrediting it." I've started to save positive feedback (IRL praise and online comments) in a "compliments corner" on my phone, and make it a practice to read it regularly, celebrate it, and feel grateful for it. Instead of brushing off compliments, I work hard to try to receive them like gifts, with a sincere "thank you." It's a challenge to learn to BELIEVE them; bit by bit, more self-appreciation means less self-doubt! Energetically, when we celebrate ourselves, it becomes easier to keep emitting high-frequency vibrations that others around us can enjoy. It's a win-win. You're a higher-vibe person who can lift others up even more if you appreciate and celebrate yourself. It's selfless! A little trick I like to do is celebrate myself for completing really mundane jobs like tidying! I straighten up my apartment and I'm like "YES, POPPY!" Get the small things full of confidence and the bigger things fall into place!

A big factor influencing our "less than" fear is the outsourcing of a rubric to measure "enough." Life became a lot more confusing after likes became digital. Our sense of self-worth was more vulnerable to turning into a numbers game. It should go without saying that we should not equate our personal value with a metric, like Instagram likes or a bank balance; that has nothing to do with who we are as people. But in recent times, some people find it easier to compare numbers than nuances of character and that needs to FLEX.

Fear of Missing Out (FOMO) is a shade of "not enough" fear. We might see photos of pretty people in flower crowns and fringe bikinis at Coachella and become convinced that every person in the world is having more fun and more sex than we are. A friend of mine told me she spent days researching flights and accommodation at Burning Man. I found this strange, since she is the type of woman who would rather walk twenty blocks than take the subway because she hates people and dirt…but the seductive pics on Instagram were enough to shimmy her into thinking she would #love the Burn. I have yet to hear details about her trip, but considering she organized to be airlifted out after one day, I'm guessing, not good.

Once upon a time, it was useful to compare. It helped us shape our wants. But our world has put comparison on steroids from comparing OOTDs, avocado toast, yoga headstands, and holiday cards. It's sabotaging our confidence about every tiny thing we might take pride and joy in.

We all know Facebook is heavily curated and that people aren't having nearly as good a time as it seems. But we're not only stacking ourselves up against Lucy from down the road, we can also begin to compare ourselves to underwear models who "eat" pizza continuously on Snapchat. *They* can eat dairy and carbs and look like that! *What's wrong with me?* According to a recent study of 117 eighteen-to-twenty-nine-year-olds, comparing yourself to others on Instagram is linked to depression. And the more strangers you compare yourself to, the worse you'll feel.[55] It shouldn't be called Instagram. It should be called Comparagram.

Lizzo once posted, "I don't think that loving yourself is a choice. I think it's a decision that has to be made for survival; it was in my case. Loving myself was the result of answering two things: Do you want to live? 'Cause this is who you are going to be for the rest of your life. Or are you gonna just have a life of emptiness, self-hatred, and self-loathing? And I choose to live, so I accept myself." I bow down to her self-compassion, and the fact that she's starving her Wolf of Fear. With self-love, she's risen above comparison into a class all her own.

The only way to gain confidence and feel "enough" about ourselves is through self-acceptance and expression, being wonderfully, wholly ourselves.

Flexercise: "Not Good Enough" to "I Am a Unique Kind of Goddess"

Polly Bateman has worked with dozens of people who struggle with feeling good enough and she warns against positive affirmations like "I'm awesome!" and "I'm fantastic!" "Some positive affirmations are nothing more than polishing a turd," she told me. "Unless we own it, we know we're lying to ourselves."

Science confirms this. As I'd later learn, per a 2009 study by researchers at the University of Waterloo in Ontario, Canada, positive self-statements like "I am lovable" can make confident people feel better. But for insecure types? It actually can serve to make our insecurity worse if our brains feel we're chatting complete BS. It's hard to affirm what you don't believe.

Bateman suggested instead of saying, "I am a GODDESS!" if you don't quite believe it yet (you will soon), try, "I'm all right, and I'm all right with that."

Or say, "I'm learning to accept I'm a unique kind of goddess." Our unconscious mind has a much better chance of absorbing and stretching to accommodate an attainable ideal, so write your own affirmations and mantras that feel natural and impactful for you. I love reminding myself that feeling insecure is HUMAN. Even Earth goddesses feel it. Just remember to accept and infuse it with higher-vibrational energy through movement or breathing, aka Step #1: dance, jump, walk, twerk, or return to the breath. The breath is always our friend in changing how we feel.

Humans are born fearless and then we quickly learn fears through conditioning and absorbing faulty messages by trying to understand the world and creating our self-concept.

To overcome fear, we can stretch our minds using the Flex techniques to question and change our autopilot responses.

By adapting to a new perspective, we can become better at seeing fearful moments as a growth opportunity to become more accepting, trusting—and grow our confidence in our ability to deal with anything and everything life might like to throw our way. We only ever get better at facing fear when we do it more often.

With a growth-nugget, gift-searching mindset:

Failure turns into learning.

Fear of bad outcomes opens a door to the glorious mystery of life.

Rejection gives us invaluable insight and positive redirection.

Others' judgment teaches us what to value for ourselves.

Feeling "not enough" gives us the ultimate opportunity to learn the power of compassion and gratitude.

The next time fear takes over, remember some advice my mentor and friend Adam Robinson, educator, author, chess champion, and founder of the Princeton Review, told me: "There are only two places for your attention ever to be. Either on the task at hand, or the person in front of you." Our brain can't be in two places at once, so when our attention is on the person in front of us, we can't feel our own fear. By getting out of our heads and redirecting our focus, we are free from our fears. With freedom comes the confidence to help someone else deal with their fears. When we take the steps to build our confidence, we effortlessly pay it forward. We become contagious in a good way ☺.

"It's impossible to be stylish without confidence, you see."

—Jane Birkin

"I CHOOSE TO MAKE THE REST OF MY LIFE THE BEST OF MY LIFE."

—LOUISE HAY

FLEX THE FUTURE

The most triggering topic saved for last: the future. Our wishes, hopes, and dreams exist there, but so do our fears. Our aspirations and our anxieties sit like twins at the gates of the future, one beckoning us to come in and the other telling us to go back. Which one shall we listen to? Some see the future as a dark, unknown place, like a distant forest we have no choice but to enter.

But if we're Flexing, we can change our understanding of this forest that's waiting for us. With upgraded biases, we're able to notice new things on the journey like birds, flowers, streams, opportunities, and adventures (and not just keeping a lookout for traps and wrong turns). The forest remains the same place, but with different outlooks and perspectives, it feels like a new world.

Since the Flex is a perpetual work in progress, I have to stay *very* focused on it. Without constant intervention and practice, old programming will always try to tug me back toward anxiety.

Wherever I go, whatever I do, I know I have the tools to Flex my way through. The energy I give right now in this present moment, the seeds I sow, is what will grow into my future. The future is just the consequence of what we decide now, so if I consciously plant sunflowers, I'm much more likely to get sunflowers.

It sounds too simple, right?! But our brain only gives us two choices/channels. To walk with fear playing WFML, "I'm in danger and the future is scary!" or to surrender to love playing WCHL, "I'm safe and everything is unfolding for my greatest good." Unless we set the intention of planting our flowers now, without even realizing it, our negative bias will take over and unintentionally we'll wind up growing a whole lot of shitty weeds and wonder why "things never go my way." But that's not going to happen. We now have the gift of awareness, so together let's help each other commit to choosing love over fear, and make decisions that turn murky futures into fabulous adventures. You in?

All the Possibilities
They're truly endless

One of my Flexi-Inspirations is Lori Gottlieb, PhD. In her *Maybe You Should Talk to Someone: A Therapist,* Her *Therapist, and Our Lives Revealed*, she wrote about facing the future by taking control of the present. "Uncertainty, I'm starting to realize, doesn't mean the loss of hope," she wrote. "It means there's possibility. I don't know what will happen next—how potentially exciting!"

A critical reframe open to all of us is choosing to accept the unknown as *exciting*. "We tend to think that the future happens later, but we're creating it in our minds every day," she said. "When the present falls apart, so does the future we had associated with it. And having the future taken away is the mother of all plot twists."

This is a tall order, because the human brain is OBSESSED with certainty. A predictable conclusion floods our completion-loving minds with the hormonal equivalent of hot chocolate. It feels warm and gooey to know what's going to happen. We value certainty more than ever as our world is changing so quickly around us and that can make us feel unsafe.

Growing up, my teachers and mentors advised me to write a plan for the future—"By thirty, I'm going to be married, have a baby, a starter house, and a car"—to essentially write my own predictable plot to a comfy ending. This kind of "future" is taking stiff thinking to its ultimate conclusion: living in our childhood and cultural conditioning, pattern matching from the past on autopilot, blocking new avenues of thought, and being ruled by fear.

Five-Year Plans therefore can quickly turn into exercises in futility, not flexibility. They never quite work out the way we hope because life isn't as predictable as stiff thinkers would like it to be. By creating fixed expectations and being stiff and inflexible about realizing them, we cause ourselves unnecessary pain and disappointment because we shut ourselves off from divergent paths that might lead to greater joy and learning than we could have planned. If set-in-stone #goals are derailed, stiff thinkers (like me pre-Flex) have a habit of blaming themselves and immediately assume they're failures or frauds just for not quite reaching a made-up finish line.

A Flexi-Future has goals and plans but no plotted, predictable ending. It's not locked in a cage or forced down a narrow tunnel because it's "what we know" or "what we want no matter what." It doesn't define a final destination (career, marriage, kids, house, car), or set out to achieve fixed material goals. The Future's true purpose is the process: to Flex our view of what our goals are. What do we really want and need to be happy, safe, loved, and feel like we're enough? By *redefining goals* away from fixed outlooks and focusing on becoming our truest, bendiest, wildest self, we can Flex an exciting, unexpected future (which is better than anything we could have imagined).

Just to make this clear: The Flex isn't a prescription for the conventional "good life," but a method and framework to help us experience life to the fullest, with great openness and eyes trained for magic. A flexible future is knowing that there are unlimited ways to become the living embodiment of our chosen values, which is our purpose and completely individual.

Honestly, given the choice between a stiff future and a flexible one, I can't imagine anyone wanting to stay limited and rigid in a HALF life of doubts and fear worrying about not getting what they think they "want." There is so much joy, peace, and adventure to experience if we connect with our bodies, stretch our minds, and live a WHOLE life moving and bending with what comes our way.

Concerns will always move in and out, of course. Death is the ending of all of our stories. But what we make of the stuff that happens before, that's up to us.

Making the Future Happen

I have always been good at "making shit happen" aka #manifesting, but being a serial entrepreneur is different from consciously creating a life in alignment with values and truest desires.

I've seen some people try to manifest, say, a snazzy car, just because, on some level, they believe that having one will make them feel "socially approved." Fast car = "successful" and "others will like me," just like I wrongly thought manifesting perfection would be validating for me. But if your goal is approval to gain a sense of belonging and safety, why not manifest the root of the desire, self-acceptance, instead? If you have self-acceptance, a trait that is so magnetic to others, no accessory is needed to create belonging, that deep sense of peace and security in who you are. Flexing cuts out the BS "thing"—the car, the big gas-guzzling bill, and the pressure that goes along with it—to get to what you *really* want, your emotional needs met.

> *"We are all children searching for love."*
> —Leonard Nimoy

Not to say it's wrong to want a car. There's no inherent ugliness in want, unless it's only about ego, and even then it's not ugly per se (we all have a degree of ego!), it'll just likely leave you feeling empty. Spiritual adviser Michael B. Beckwith said "true manifesting" is desiring to be a better version of yourself, rather than desiring for things to fill an appetite that will never be satisfied. He believes the greatest "true want" we can have is to be the most complete expression of ourselves, the most accepting of our whole self. Until we break from our learned conditioning ladled on by society and family, he said, "[w]e will always want from an immature place."

The Jewish-mysticism teaching Kabbalah describes a desire as pure if it's for the greater good so many can benefit along with you. For example, when my friend talks about wanting a raise to pay her kids' college tuition, it's an altruistic desire, high-vibration energy, a pure desire. She's wanting for more than herself. I desire to earn money to pay my staff more and make them comfortable, help out my parents, shower my friends with generosity, support charities and causes, and enjoy certain comforts for myself to then share with others. When desire is about joy and celebration for ourselves and others, it feels better and heart opening compared to when it's driven by status hunger to prove worthiness. With the Flex, we can stretch our mind toward desiring innate worthiness, not worthiness attached to accumulation.

Our soul doesn't care about money, it cares about love and belonging. If we manifest "more money" instead of "more love," we might get a promotion but wind up breaking our relationship. And then where are we? Business psychologist Douglas LaBier, PhD, wrote in *Psychology Today*, "Our security, success and well-being now require strengthening communal values and behavior; working towards common goals, the common good. Acting on self-interest *alone*, especially in the pursuit of personal power, steady career advancement and money...well, that's a non-sustainable way of life. Even when it 'worked' it left a hollowness inside, that people longed to fill but didn't know how."[56]

What I have found in my own life, is that #makingshithappen without awareness was actually my just manifesting #shit, and it made me miserable.

More than ever, the Flex has helped me turn the page on this, and my interest lies in creating a future that makes my soul sing, my heart sing, and helps the greater good. BUT I've only been able to start soul creating since doing the work to get to know my soul in the first place. Plato wrote, "Know thyself." Aristotle wrote, "Knowing yourself is the beginning of all wisdom." Self-awareness takes effort. How can we create a life we love if we don't really know who we are to begin with?

Flexercise: Know Yourself

As Lori Gottlieb wrote, "Part of getting to know yourself is to unknow yourself—to let go of the limiting stories you've told yourself about who you are so that you aren't trapped by them, so you can live your life and not the story you've been telling yourself about your life." So to really know yourself, your values, and your desires and create the future you want, start answering these questions:

1. What are five things that put a smile on your face no matter what?

2. If you could change just one thing about your life, what would it be?

3. In your life, what matters the most to you?

4. What are your greatest strengths?

5. What do you believe is possible in your life?

6. What is your proudest accomplishment in life?

7. When you have free time, what do you like to do for fun?

8. What does a perfect day look like?

9. When was the last time you felt truly happy? Where were you? With who? Doing what?

10. What makes you feel excited in the morning?

11. If you had more time, who would you want to spend it with?

12. What can't you know enough about?

13. If you could change anything about the way you were raised, what would it be?

14. Is there something you've dreamt of doing for a long time? Why haven't you done it?

15. We learn from mistakes, yet we're often afraid to make one. How is this true for you?

16. If joy became the national currency, what kind of work would make you wealthy?

17. Do any of the things that upset you a few years ago matter at all today? What's changed?

18. How different would your life be if there weren't any criticism in the world?

19. What lessons in life did you learn the hard way?

20. How often do your biggest worries and fears come true?

21. How would you describe yourself?

22. What is the most important quality you look for in another person?

23. If you could tell your younger self one thing, what would it be?

24. Who do you look up to and why?

25. In one word, what is standing between you and your biggest goal?

Your answers are full of so much wisdom. Only you can tell yourself what you *really want* for your future. Have common themes emerged? How different is your perfect day compared to your everyday? Can you spot any negative biases or faulty beliefs that are based on zero evidence? What advice can you find and act on? What changes can you make in the present based on these answers?

Set Intentions

Design your future

As Krishnamurti, the Buddha, Oprah, Deepak Chopra, Maya Angelou, Polly Bateman and thousands of other flexible thinkers have said in a variety of ways, "Name it to claim it." When we set intentions over fixed plans, we are naming what we'd like to experience and who we'd like to be inside our own heads.

When I was chatting to my mum about this, she said the greatest problem she finds with her clients is that they tend to focus on *what they don't want.* Recently, one listed her desires for the future starting with "I don't want to be anxious," "I don't want to be poor," and moved on to "I don't want my ex-husband to keep being so difficult." The old saying "What you focus on gets louder" couldn't be more apt. All this client was doing was telling her brain to "claim" difficult ex-husbands, anxiety, and poverty. By putting thought into what we are trying to move *away* from, all we are doing is strengthening neural pathways and confirmation bias that make us move *toward* them.

Michael B. Beckwith described thoughts as "units of mental energy that turns into behavior and experience." New research[57] from Canada bears this out. Scientists have discovered that we have more than 6,000 "thought worms" per day that start in one place and continue to a conclusion. If we can mindfully focus and direct our thought worms toward flexibility about our future, that is exactly where we want to go.

To design your future...

Set goals and also values. If you don't point your surfboard in a direction, it will either stay still or get washed up with the tide, traveling in a direction other people want. A slight change in direction can completely change the destination where we end up: Just imagine what happens if a plane shifts two degrees west; the slightest shift can completely change a journey and landing. It is critical we have overarching goals to work toward. BUT this isn't about just naming "five-year plan" numerical goals like salary, net worth, number of kids or cars, the age you'll marry, the square footage of your future home. It's the opposite of setting "quantity thoughts" that sit stiffly in the future, but instead setting qualitative goals that have values attached. Sensation precedes manifestation so life coach Ambi Kavanagh encourages using the present tense to help you start *feeling* what the future might be like now. Why wait for tomorrow to raise your vibrations, feel like the person you want to become? By doing so, you'll know what to look out for. This work can get tiring quickly because it requires you to stay aware, and we usually prefer to live life unconsciously.

Here are some examples of qualitative goals:

- **Career:** "I have a job that fulfills me creatively. I wake up excited to go to work. I meet smart, supportive people who bring out the best in me. I feel positively reinforced by my compensation and feel respected by my colleagues and bosses. At the end of the workday, I bring home all that emotional satisfaction for the benefit of my family." (The quantity thought: "I want to get a job that makes me a shit-ton of money.")

- **Relationship:** "I am in a relationship that is passionate, loving, loyal, expansive, and honest. We are excited for each other and prioritize our relationship. We challenge each other to stretch and grow." (The quantity thought: "I want to get married by thirty and have three kids.")

- **Self:** "I am living the life that lights up my soul and makes me excited to get up in the morning. I feel joy, celebration, gratitude, and kindness daily and have plenty of time and freedom to explore, learn, and grow, along with doing all that good stuff with the people I care about." (The quantity thought: "I've got a cool million in the bank and can do whatever I want.")

Set emotional intentions. As David Hawkins clarified on his Scale of Consciousness, when we experience emotions like peace, acceptance, and love, we vibrate at a higher frequency. Try saying affirmations like, "I am feeling peaceful, I am feeling full of love, I am becoming more accepting of myself daily and excited for all the things coming my way." Our psychology impacts our biology and when we feel these light emotions, we can begin to alter our reality. It's easier to get the "gets" (like "get a promotion" or "get married") our ego might want when we are living in higher vibrations. By focusing on upping our emotions, it can become a little shortcut to manifesting the other things. Another reason why Flexing is so key to building brilliant futures: The framework focuses on shifting you into higher emotional states with more energy to achieve your heart's desires with maximum bendiness.

By focusing on designing a life based on high-frequency emotions, we are also taking ourselves away from stiff restrictions, and freeing ourselves to see many possibilities that might look different from what we originally think we want but feel even better. When we aim to feel more love and acceptance, it's funny how the path ahead often appears much clearer and less sticky!

Set positive action. Research has shown that there are exercises we can do to train our brains to spot juicy opportunities that will take us in the direction we want. The exercises aren't woo-woo crystal cleaning or cacao drinking (although I love those activities ☺). They're called "values tagging," also known as making an action board. Executive coach Tara Swart, author of *The Source: The Secrets of the Universe, the Science of the Brain,* explained how this works. Actively designing a visual board of images of the types of situations we want to be in "[i]mprints important things onto [our] subconscious and filters out unnecessary information," Swart told CNBC. "The brain assigns a higher 'value' to [the] images on the board…the more you look at [them], the more those images move up in importance."[58]

If we tell our brains what to look out for, we're more likely to recognize when life-enhancing opportunities arise. If our brains *aren't* primed by "values-tagging," we're more vulnerable to letting our negative biases take over and we miss noticing those golden opportunities. As said, when we allow our confirmation bias to keep us focused on moving away from the things we don't want, we limit our ability to move toward the things we want.

"We are looking to create something that will inspire and manifest in your future through actions, rather than merely a vehicle for daydreams of second homes abroad and lots of money," Swart clarified. So it's not about drooling over #things. It's about using images to inspire action to take you on the road to higher-vibrational frequencies like love, acceptance, and pride. Part of this method is immersion therapy. "When you repeatedly look at images related to your goals, your brain no longer sees them as new," she said. "The process reduces the [physiological] fear response to any new situation or person, making you more likely to take healthy risks, collaborate, and embrace opportunity." So action boards help to recognize and capture opportunities because they help us reprogram our learned biases and create what I call a "future bias," if you will, a bias that trains our brains to look out for steps to a more emotionally joyous future.

Images are powerful and so is language, as we know. A daily gratitude diary helps similarly train our minds to be on a friendly alert to find the blessings in our life and to keep us in a higher vibrational state. Every time we take note of the good things, we are curtailing our negative bias from searching for bad things and learning to have a more positive bias. The exercise of a daily gratitude journal is as important to me as washing my hair. I use the gratitude step on the Happy Not Perfect app before I fall asleep every night. Instead of letting my mind chew over worries, my mind is immediately focused on celebrating my day.

With action boards and gratitude diaries, we can teach our brains to become more alert to life-enhancing possibilities (gifts, magic, lessons). When we combine these activities with daily flexing, it's a game-changer.

The future forest offers many paths and the truth is, it doesn't really matter which one we pick because each one will present unique challenges that the Flex can help us bend around. But having a clear sense and being able to visualize our "true wants" and values helps us spot better opportunities and make better decisions to ensure we're building a future journey that's aligned with our unique desires. The intention-setting process and the physical act of writing, imagining, or pinteresting creates space to consider ahead of time so when the offers come in the moment, you already know your answer. Will this take me toward the future I want or away from it?

And, of course, go ahead and include some materialistic objects on an action board. And, sure, get excited about some yummy creature comforts. Like always, the brain needs BBOs (bigger better offers) to be incentivized to work hard and spot growth nuggets and take advantage of them. If we reward ourselves and celebrate progress with occasional metaphorical cookies like a new car or new shoes—we know they aren't great for us in terms of soul nourishment, but we can't help but admit they taste delicious!—they can reinforce joy and self-care. We all need cookies in life but knowing they are just cookies and not the whole nutritious meal is the trick! Balance virtuous values building with some physical world pleasures!

Let's be real, when I was worrying about just getting my rent covered, I found it really hard to think about designing the future. So, with an eye toward the future, be compassionate toward where you are at right now.

As Maslow said, basic needs must be met first before self-actualization can begin. There have been times when I've wanted to work on my action board, but I literally have had to work until midnight to get money in my bank account to cover the basics. Vital self-care, getting by, having a safe physical space, is priority number one. *Then*, when you feel you can relax and have mental space and breathing room, engage in futurework. My friend who has two young children waits for them to go to bed, makes herself a cup of tea and works on her gratitude diary on a Sunday night when she knows nothing else is needed.

Flexercise: Checking In

Every month or at least a few times a year, ask this single question: "Am I on a train to the destination I actually want to go to?"

A friend, a leader in his field of design, called as I was working on this box, and I asked him this question. He said, "My career couldn't be going better, but I'm so sad. I'm sick, my body is telling me to stop. I need to get off this train! I can't do this anymore." He was living a life his younger self wanted, but his current self, in that moment, realized his "true wants" weren't being fulfilled. We change and this is why the Flex is always a work-in-progress.

Taking stock monthly or a few times a year helps us keep up-to-date on how our "true wants" change. As we evolve and grow, so do our wants. This is fundamentally the reason why five-year plans are ludicrous, because we change! By regularly engaging in futurework, we improve our ability to refine what we want in the future. For example, I dated this guy for a hot second recently and, although it didn't work out, it was such a brilliant experience in telling me what I *don't* want in a future relationship . . . in just three dates! Perfect. Every "no" we face—in relationships, jobs, or friends—is a data-collecting experience to make us better future Flexers!

"We must give up the life we had planned, in order to have the life that is waiting for us."
—Joseph Campbell

Let Go

Learn to surrender

Once you have clearly shown your unconscious a direction you'd like to travel in, the only thing you can do now is allow the journey to unfold by letting go of any ideas you might have about *how* it's going to go. The extent of how easy it is for you to let go is directly related to how controlling you are. It is *very* easy to become a micromanager of life. But being controlling doesn't make the future happen any faster, or better. It's like getting stressed in traffic. Banging on the steering wheel doesn't make the car move faster.

Designing the future is just like baking a cake. Eighty percent of the process is fucking messy. Flour gets all over the floor, butter melts in the microwave, the batter gets lumpy. But we TRUST that, after we whack it in the oven, given enough heat and time, it'll rise. And won't be "done" any faster or better by checking it obsessively.

We have to TRUST that if we put the right ingredients into our lives—making the best decisions we can based on intentions and values with the information we have in the moment (like using the Flex method)—our lives will rise. All we have to do is let it happen and as that famous saying goes, "The world works in mysterious ways." Author Michael A. Singer called this idea "surrendering." In *The Surrender Experiment: My Journey into Life's Perfection*, he wrote, "Because I had inwardly surrendered each step of the way, no scars were left on my psyche. It had been like writing on water—the impressions only lasted while the events were actually taking place."

When things unfold unexpectedly, because life decides to take a detour, surrendering releases us from anxiously sitting in the backseat, getting cross and saying things like, "Why is this happening to me?!" We are instead able to accept the U-turn, reduce stress, and take comfort in the knowledge that we'll get there when we get there and detours only take us to a better place in the end. As Polly Bateman has told me many times, "Don't get too involved in the HOW."

Visualize the person you want to become, Flex your way through hot moments and decisions, and let the journey unfold to get you there. Surrendering is one of the most life-changing skills I've ever learned but is a continual challenge. I often need to repeat the mantra "I surrender, I surrender, I surrender" when things start going Pete Tong (British slang: Google it). And then I Flex.

Flexercise: The Surrender Flex

Recently, a friend turned cold on me and I was madly trying to think what I'd done wrong, worrying I'd upset her unintentionally and fortune-telling that our friendship was over forever. My old wounds began pulsating and Regina started telling me, "Maybe she just woke up and decided she didn't like you anymore. This is it."

What could I do . . . *but Flex* with a special focus on letting go.

CONNECTION. How did I feel? Taking a deep breath, I said, "Today, I feel upset and rejected." I sat with the feelings and then I went for a short run to shift my energy.

CURIOSITY. Why is this so upsetting to me? I explored all the ways I could have caused her to ice me out, like anything I had said or done accidentally. When I was still at a loss, I began to identify old insecurities around people not liking me. My brain was using this incidence to confirm old fears and old toxic core beliefs about not being enough. I identified the naughty ANTs causing this spiral: paralysis by analysis and bad emotional math (now equals always). I had thought myself into a knot as to why she hadn't called me back and was starting to tell myself crazy tales about her having always secretly disliked me. By confronting my creative storytelling brain, I was able to dismantle the plot.

CHOICE. I had the choice to continue to feed my Wolf of Fear and think up more mean stories about why my friend didn't call me back. Or I could feed the Wolf of Love, value myself, and remind myself that I know I am a good friend and it will pass. With awareness, I had to choose to play a new narrative, one that wasn't about obsessing over the need for external validation but instead appreciating myself and internally validating.

COMMITMENT. The growth nugget from this situation was clear: to practice unattachment. I'd called and messaged her, and now I had to let go of the outcome. It was a lesson in not trying to control the future and self-appreciating in the present. What would I tell a friend to do in this situation? "If someone decides to ice you out, then that's their decision for whatever reason. All you can do is love and care for yourself."

I stopped calling to see if she was all right. I wasn't upset any longer because I wasn't self-blaming or blaming her. I moved away from grasping for this friendship and focused on people who did want to call me back. With the fear-antidote of surrender and letting go of control, I saved myself two weeks of worrying over nothing. She finally called me to apologize for her silence and tell me she'd been navigating hell at work (my bitchy brain couldn't have got it more wrong). When she surfaced, I could focus on her recovery from a stressful period, instead of adding to it with needing her to soothe my hurt ego. My unattachment and surrender was a boon for both of us. Letting go of the need to understand why or be in control and just focus on appreciating our values takes away so so so much stress!!

Overcoming Future Dangers

Some troubleshooting tips to keep the future flexible . . .

Prioritize yourself. The most important relationship in a Flexi-Future is, no surprise, the one we have with ourselves. But we also need to nourish our relationships with friends, family, colleagues, and partners, who might, without meaning to or knowing, diminish that primary relationship.

Ambi Kavanagh told me a story about accidental self-negation when she agreed to join her fiancé and his family on a daylong hunting trip. "I really didn't want to go," she said. "I went anyway because I felt that I needed to be liked. But when you go along, and don't speak up, you give your power away and you live out of alignment with yourself. And whenever that happens, your relationship falls out of alignment, too. The most important relationship is the one with yourself, and to nourish this, you must value your needs and desires and speak your truth more than the desire to people please."

Of course, we all do things we're not gung-ho to do for the sake of relationship harmony. That's just being flexible. Some compromise is required. But compromising your values to "go along to get along"—as many have been taught to prioritize—is self-negating (and I was addicted to this sort of behavior before Flexing). A by-product of the intense self-awareness we get from Flexing is trusting our inner guidance to let us know how we feel. With that, we can communicate openly and honestly with the people who populate our future. Once we've Flexed and learned to Connect with our own emotions, we can advance to connecting with others—"I feel you"—on a deeper level. When we can validate our own worth and give our feelings the respect they deserve, we can validate others—"I hear you"—from the heart, too.

Navigate conflict better. Three of the lowest-frequency emotions are shame, guilt, and anger, and these feelings regularly surface when we are in conflict with ourselves or others. They are so low vibration and have the capability to keep us *very* stuck, even for years or decades. So learning to navigate/Flex conflict is crucial to realizing our full future potential and charging forward motion and growth. Reframing conflict as a useful tool in helping us becoming more aligned with our values, wants, and desires is a super effective skill. "When you're open to learning in conflict, you learn new things about yourself and [the other person]. That newness can be useful even in keeping a relationship alive and evolving. It's not boring when you learn. They get boring when people are just stuck in their heads, in their wounded self," said author and psychologist Margaret Paul, PhD.

Seeing a conflict (like any challenge in life) as an opportunity to learn (Flex Step #4) and grow was a massive revelation for me because I've always been attached to the idea that all conflict is bad. Growing up, my parents never really fought in front of us, so I had few healthy examples of how conflict can actually strengthen relationships—with oneself and others—and make things better. I feared disagreements so much that I would rather suppress my needs over speaking my truth in fear of conflict creating separation forever. I believed one argument would result in immediate divorce or loss of friendship. Suppression turned into a ball of energy waiting to pop inside of me, and then I would burst like a firework over something unrelated. That was my past, though, where fear of conflict kept me in one place unable to evolve. My future, however, is one that nurtures full expression and understands that disagreement can provide useful information and a route to more self-knowledge for everyone involved.

The most important part of any conflict is the road to resolving it. The Flex provides an easy framework to break down what's really bugging you internally before engaging with external people. Psychologist and author Raj Persaud, MD, told me, "You should be able to resolve most conflicts within five minutes. There's no point in continuing an argument beyond that point. Ask the question, 'What do I need to say or do to make this relationship work?' So, the two of you (a couple, friends, colleagues, etc.), mutually decide that the disagreement is only a power struggle if you make it one. *(N.B.: This is not good advice if you are managing a narcissist, or in a toxic or abusive relationship. Don't just resolve the conflict and gaslight yourself. Instead, focus on Flex Step #3, making the Choice to step into love for yourself and away from fear of separation. Conflict can show us that current situations are not nutrient-filled environments for our future best selves to evolve in.*

Flex Step #4 asks you to consider how you would advise a friend experiencing what you are now. From that third-party perspective, greater wisdom and confidence can be found to resolve conflict and that may very well mean walking away.)

Reframe heartbreak. Heartbreak has the ability to completely knock us off our future journey and turn the forest from an adventure-filled magical expedition to a dark and lonely place in a flash. In hindsight, I used to unnecessarily torture myself after breakups large and small and I can now see just how stiff my thinking became. I blocked connection, used distraction and avoidance, was in WFML and couldn't listen or begin to practice compassion for anyone. I was so cruel to myself and allowed my brain to turn the whole thing into concrete evidence that my toxic core beliefs were accurate. My inner critic Regina screamed, "Seeee?! You *are* worthless! He was just saying what I've been telling you all along!"

The emotion spectrum that usually followed:

Sadness: *Oh, no, another loss.*

Self-hate: *I'm clearly not good enough and so unspecial.*

Anger: *That little shit!*

Shame: *I am so embarrassed, I opened up my heart and he didn't want it.*

Fear: *Am I going to be alone and single forever?*

Disappointment: *I thought this time was going to be different…*

I've focused on romantic heartbreak here but any form of it can be all-consuming, like painful friend breakups. Heartbreak is so intense, it can unravel all the progress we've made to be flexible, be self-assured, and manage our thoughts. I spoke to psychologist and Happy Not Perfect guide Dr. Sophie Mort about why heartbreak can be so derailing, and she explained, "While heartbroken, your body treats it as if you're in actual physical danger."

I wanted to know why heartbreak can have the potential to knock us off course into Gloomsville even when we haven't even been dating that long #askingforafriend. "When you break up with someone you haven't been dating for that long, you also are breaking up with your imagination, *the person you thought that person was*," said Dr. Mort. "You don't know this person well enough yet, so you create a fantasy around them. Our imaginations fill in the blanks with our ideals, desires, and wishes and we begin to project what we want to see, not what actually might be there in reality. When those kinds of relationships end, they're devastating because you're losing the *idea* of the perfect person you've created, and your future hopes and dreams are shattered. That's very, very distressing.

"On the other hand, when you've been dating someone for a while, we've incorporated them into our sense of identity," Dr. Mort said. "The other person may have become a mental representation of who we are, too. So the breakup feels like a part of our identity has been ripped out. Suddenly, there's an actual hole in our representation of ourselves, which leaves us feeling lost, confused, often quite uncertain of who we are now and what our future might hold. This unique mix of grief, physical and emotional pain, *plus* confusion and loss of identity can send us into a real tailspin."

As she said, "Oh, being human. Wow, what a ride." Yep, a ride to say the least! *insert terrified facial expression*

Practicing flexible thinking can help reframe potential heartbreak that our future might hold and reassure us that there's nothing to fear. When we have a plan to be ready for anything, we can maintain some emotional control. Ambi Kavanagh coaches people to trust that, just as the relationship—or a bad job, or an awkward friendship—came into your life for a reason, it left for a reason, too. "I feel very strongly that it is important to trust that the two of you played a divine role in each other's lives to teach you something and to be a great teacher to them."

Acceptance that someone is NOT madly in love with us, or a fan of our work, or a true friend who has our back, is liberating.

What's even more freeing and reassuring for the future is accepting that one person's feelings about us can have zero bearing on how we feel about ourselves and what happens to us next. "The tendency is to make what feels like a rejection mean something negative about us," said Kavanagh. Or the other tendency is for it to trigger bad emotional math when we assume *now* equals *always*, as in, "They don't love me, no one ever will!" We have to radically practice Flex Step #3 and choose to lean into love, self-appreciate, and embrace change, knowing it's here to propel us onto a better path forward. Steps #3 and #4 are excellent remedies for heartbreak as they guide us back to being in a flexible mindset that forgives and accepts all the different individuals who enter our lives, knowing there is always a gift to the roles we play in each other's journeys, however briefly.

I really don't say this lightly, but my Recovery Flex changed the game after my last breakup. It turned my recovery experience from excruciating into open admission to the School of Me. I Flexed every morning (for a few months—!—emotional injuries take time) but soon the heavy pangs faded, and I was left with an even brighter, liberated heart. The Flex took away my fear of future heartbreak, allowing me to live with an open heart now.

Flexercise: The Recovery Flex

I know this sounds strange, but I've come to realize heartbreak is the GREATEST gift. Especially if you're really, really broken, it's one of the few opportunities in life when you have the motivation to commit to new habits to take the pain away. For me, every heartbreak has accelerated my soul growth to a place I would have taken a lot longer to get to otherwise. Here's how I turned my breakup into a breakthrough.

CONNECTION. I sit with my feelings even when they're painful, allowing the 90-second waves to pass. Dr. Mort is a big proponent of journaling, which has been another key tool in my recovery box. "Get those emotions out onto paper. We know that journaling for twenty minutes a day changes your mood as it activates the computer side of your brain and it can boost your immunity," she said. Without negotiation, I upgrade the connection with my body through movement. Dance is my jam. When I move, I can feel trapped low-vibe energy in my hip flexors, shoulders, and back release into the air. I became a fan of Julianne Hough's classes at Kinrgy that combine movement and touch to release the feel-good chemical cocktail of oxytocin, serotonin, and endorphins. Just one song every morning does wonders. In case you need any more encouragement to get moving, daily exercise has been proven to be as effective as a low-grade antidepressant.[59] Dancing and journaling are major connection boosters.

CURIOSITY. Instead of the usual rundown of assuming my "not-enoughness" caused the breakup, I challenge all assumptions with Byron Katie's questions. Is it true I am not enough? *Yes?* Am I 100 percent sure it's true? *Well, no.* How do I react with these critical thoughts? *I feel terrible and have low confidence.* Who would I be without these thoughts? *I engage in freeing myself from unnecessary self-hate and look forward to the future.* I continue with curiosity to label and swat naughty ANTs away. *No, thank you, fortune-telling ANT, I have no idea what my future will hold. No, thanks, paralysis-by-analysis ANT, I cannot do anything about the should've, could've, would've scenarios, they are in the past.*

CHOICE. I choose to feed the Wolf of Love a steady, hearty diet of forgiveness. "Decide you're going to radically accept yourself and forgive yourself for anything that comes up," said Dr. Mort. "If your brain is going to go down the route of, 'Oh my God, I did this terrible thing,' you'll only be beating yourself up over something you can't change while you're already in survival mode. This is like taking a hammer to an already broken limb." Not a good idea, so forgive, forgive, forgive and have compassion. Choosing to lean into love allows me to take responsibility for myself by acknowledging any mistakes I might have made and radically accepting they happened for my future growth. We do the best we can with what we know at the time. I use the affirmation "Love is abundant. It's everywhere I look" to shift my confirmation bias to notice more love and "Everything is unfolding perfectly for my highest good" to stay committed to patience and optimism for the future.

COMMITMENT. I commit to self-compassion, to find the gifts by asking, "What am I learning?" and "What can I do differently next time when an even more fabulous situation arrives?" Recovery can be so heavy sometimes, it makes you forget what sassy and sexy feels like. So I use the third-person technique to ask, "What would Poppy do if she were past it by now and feeling great?" I start to imagine my future Wildest, sexiest, happiest, enacting self—going out, seeking fun and laughter, looking after herself, following her passions—and begin to do those things. I also used Flex mentors to inspire me. My great friend Misha transformed herself after a breakup and I wanted that transformation too. I followed her fitness plan, her diet, and her top tip of arranging lots of social time along with a strong-but-balanced work ethic. My heaviness began lifting, obsessive thoughts dissipated, and bizarrely my soul felt fuller than it was even before the relationship. The experience led me to an optimal state of emotional freedom as an individual where I felt loved and safe from the inside.

....

Up-level doubt and fear. A friend told me once that a man she'd fallen in love with told her in the early days, "I'm not sure I feel as deeply about you as you do about me." Oh, wow, *icy*! Her whole body went cold as she sat across from him, and as he searched her eyes for her reaction, she had a Flex breakthrough. "I looked at him and thought, *I've been here before, and survived. I'll probably be here again, and I'll survive that, too,*" she said. "And suddenly, I knew his words weren't about me but him. I knew I would be okay and I wasn't afraid of losing him. I told him, 'It's fine. You feel what you feel. I'm not going to argue with you about it.'" When he saw how unaffected she was by his declaration of not-sure, and her certainty in her worthiness, he suddenly lost whatever fear was holding him back. They decided to stay together and wound up getting married and having two kids. That conversation was a great example of (1) how the simple, brave act of expressing doubts and fears can dissipate them, (2) how vital it is for our self-worth to stay intact, and (3) not to assume a fixed outcome based on historical experiences. Both individuals stayed flexible and honest and elevated their relationship to build an amazing future together.

Our future is constantly changing because it depends on how we respond to the present. With a flexible mindset we can feel confident that any future challenges can be turned into growth nuggets that move us into greater alignment with our values and greater connection to our Wildest, most authentic selves.

Even experiences that *seem* like roadblocks are actually HUGE opportunities to propel ourselves forward . . . if we Flex them.

Think of triggers as gifts. Our future is created by the sum of our repeated actions and decisions. Changing habits is the surest way to get different outcomes. BUT it's difficult to "reset and forget" new habits and even harder sometimes to know what new habits we should be trying to incorporate in the first place!

Weakening strong neural pathways is a challenge. We have to be VERY kind when we're in the process of doing this. Think how difficult it is to stick to New Year's resolutions. As Dr. Mort explained, "Your brain does *not* want to create new habits. The moment you get tired or stressed, your rational brain switches off, it just sends you back into old habits." In other words, to stay on track with new habits, we need to sleep, move, and eat well. If we have the energy we need, we won't be as vulnerable to backsliding.

Does this ring true for you? When I'm tired, everything goes south for me. I don't want to exercise. I crave salt, sugar, and my couch. All my healthy habits go completely out the window. Sleep is the biggest factor for me to have the necessary fuel to look after myself (mind, body, soul, and thought health). Sleep deprivation cranks the volume on my ANTs and I find it harder to Flex and challenge them. In those moments, I don't even try. When I'm low energy and don't have the mental strength to Flex, I say to myself, "Before I think any more, go to bed and Flex in the morning." This stops the march of ANTs and by the time I wake up in the morning, they're usually a LOT quieter. If they *are* still banging around, I Flex over breakfast or over a morning walk. A busy mind is actually a GIFT, though, because it alerts us that we need more self-care ASAP.

Now, self-sabotage is a different animal. "Self-sabotage is any time you engage in a behavior consciously or unconsciously that gets in the way of your desired values and goals in life," said Dr. Mort. "It happens when people don't actually want the thing they think they want, and/or they don't think they deserve the thing they think they want."

For example, someone might talk about wanting to be in a relationship, but underneath that desire is an even bigger fear of losing one's independence. When the fear flares up, they panic and reactively do something like cheat or pick a fight or some other sabotaging behavior.

But even an act of self-sabotage is a gift. It gives us insight about what we *fear*. Just as envy, a low vibration if there ever was one, teaches us what we *do* want. I quite like feeling jealous now because it tells me what I really want. We're only envious about the things we wish we had. It acts as a great tool to work out what I should be putting on my action board.

If we're of flexible mind, we can turn our triggers into useful information in getting clearer on what we *really, really* want. "Very few of us check in and think, *What do I actually want from life?*" said Dr. Mort. "I don't mean [ego] goals. I mean *values*. For example, *What's really important to me?*"

Fuckups are gifts. Sabotage is a gift. Envy is a gift. Challenges are gifts. Emotions are gifts. They tell us what we want and provide personalized wisdom, if we have the openness to listen.

Take Choice Out of It

How to handle the paralysis of too many options for the future

We have more possible directions through the future forest than ever before and that can be stressful. We're constantly being seduced by different paths (jobs, partners, cities, to mention a few) and if you're like me, when you're afraid to make the wrong decisions, you don't make any at all and this creates stiff thinking and a stuck life.

The great thing is, there is no "wrong" or "right" decision. When we are in the habit of making decisions based on values that align with our greatest truth, we will only move in a direction that is approval-stamped by our core self. The scenery might look different, but the lessons and gifts will be the same.

A friend of mine was at a crossroads recently and she came to me for advice. She ran through her options and said, "I have no idea what to do!" Should she continue teaching? Go to grad school? Move across the country with her boyfriend? So many choices were laid at her feet. Any choice would alter her life for years to come. "What if I choose wrong?" she asked. "I don't know what I'm supposed to do."

What-Next Syndrome, or not knowing your life purpose, causes a lot of anxiety about the Future. When you don't know the answer to the Big Question—"What's my why?"—it's only natural to feel unmoored. The Future Forest most often doesn't have clear signposts.

Someone once told me that the definition of happiness was knowing you're on the right path. I believe that one of the main reasons we're in such a mental health crisis right now is because we face choice paralysis. It's deeply chaotic when we have so many decisions to make. Every choice has a consequence, so we're stuck overanalyzing everything, in WFML mode, triggering immediate overwhelm. Strategic planning isn't possible in that state of mind. When our monkey minds are screeching and jumping from synapse to synapse in our brain, how do we expect ourselves to find the peace of mind to figure it all out?

I asked Polly Bateman about how to advise the friend who was struggling with too many life choices and debating what to do.

She said, "Poppy, I've got a riddle for you. You have a bucket full of muddy water. Without pouring the water out or using any tools, how do you see what's at the bottom of the bucket?"

I thought for a moment. "I have no idea."

She replied, "You do nothing. In a few hours, the mud will settle, and you can see straight down to the bottom."

Love a riddle. Her point was clear: When we slow down, connect with our bodies—Step #1 of the Flex—and wait for clarity (not letting our impatient brains get the better of us) we can gather the insight and self-awareness and confidence we need to move forward on *any* path.

I was inspired by this quote in *Vogue* from activist Janaya Khan, aka Future: "It is never too late to become the person you always thought you could be...People have so much more to offer than what the world tells them. I have met some of the most incredible people in my life in this work, but no one starts out as remarkable."

It's important not to compare choices or purposes. Life is not a competition to have the BEST PURPOSE OF ALL TIME. Just making decisions that we can be proud of, that align with our truth, that contribute to a greater good, whether that be supporting our friends better or society, is enough. Keeping our plants alive. Doing stuff that lights us up will heal our souls and create wonderful futures.

Soul or ego. Love or fear. Soul desires don't change. They are traits, skills, like kindness, compassion, resilience. Ego manifestations (which we all have) for money, possessions, ownership always change depending on what we see externally and wind up being hollow on their own and leave us endlessly hungry for more. Only we can tell the difference between what our ego wants and what our soul longs for. But it's not easy, it requires us to slow down and Flex: (1) Connect to ourselves, (2) stay Curious in figuring it out, (3) Choose to lead with love and compassion, and (4) Commit to make decisions and take action in alignment with our truth.

Flexercise: "I Still Don't Know What I Want My Future to Look Like..."

We will all meet forks in the road and wonder which way to go. This is when your Flexi-Inspos can really help. Try to break down your future into different categories and assign a Flexi-Mentor to each. This person then acts as a model to help you decide the next step for that area.

So when I'm unsure where I should go next, I ask myself, depending on the category, "What would X person do now?" My mum is a fantastic adviser about self-care. For career, my best friend is better. My father is a pro at accounting. My friend Charlotte is my work

Flexi-Mentor for building impactful businesses. Jack is my social Flexi-Mentor because he's always the most enjoyable person to spend time with. I consider what decisions my Flexi-Mentors have made in their lives to create the skills they have. I think about how they allocate their time to help them be so good at the quality I admire about them.

Make a list of your go-to Flexi-Mentors for different areas of need in your life:

Who is your mentor in work? What do you admire about them? What's their daily routine like? _____

Who is your mentor for family? What qualities of theirs would you like to emulate? What decisions of theirs have helped them to be so good in this area? _____

Who is your friends mentor and why? How do they allocate their time? _____

Who is your relationships mentor and why? What decisions have they made to create what they have created? How do they allocate their time? _____

Housekeeping/decorating mentor and why? _____

Physical health mentor and why? _____

Fun mentor and why? _____

The next time you are making a decision, you can refer back to your Flexi-Mentors and what they have done to create the outcome you want to work toward. Cause and effect inspiration!

....

We'll Get There When It Gets There

Don't put a time stamp on it

Throughout the book, I've talked about tapping into our inner guidance system. When we do that, we "hear" what makes us feel good, what makes us excited, what lifts our energy—what lights us up (and also gain awareness of what and who makes us feel the opposite). It's a "feeling first" way to navigate life rather than headfirst. Being guided by what lights you up inside sets up an instinctual Wild life, the opposite of a conditioned life of living according to others.

As we stand at the shore of the future forest, it might seem forbidding, but when we are led by "what lights us up" into the darkness, our thoughts turn into LED beacons. Yes, looking to mentors for signposts is important. But our own inner guidance provides the truest direction. What makes us feel excited is our guiding lights and it is the most essential responsibility we have to ourselves to follow these feelings.

Just to clarify, those guiding lights are not "right" or "should" and cannot be planned ahead of time. They're not agreements we never made. Our lights are spontaneous messages that get brighter when we know our strengths, trust our instincts, respect our emotions, and replace still expectations with intention and flexibility.

What happens to me sometimes is that my lights take a while to flicker on and I get very impatient. I ask the stiff question, "When are things going to happen?" or "Why is this not happening?" And then my unconscious mind immediately starts Sherlocking for evidence to find reasons that it shouldn't happen. Cue the pressure, doubt, and anxiety.

This may seem counterproductive, but to create the future we want, we have to slow down the present. I learned this the hard way. I was so desperate to build my future, I blundered into trouble, latching on to the wrong people for the wrong reasons, and paying the price. Had I slowed down, and spent more time consciously thinking (Flexing) about how I was really feeling, what I was doing, I could have walked around potholes. But instead, I fell in them, and continued doing the same thing again and again (expecting a different result), staying stuck and frustrated for far longer than I needed to.

Slowing down, even just for a few minutes a day to run through the steps, ensures you are making decisions with your Wildest Self in mind, in the direction that is feeding the Wolf of Love, upgrading your energy but also letting go of what weighs you down. Like Rome, the future wasn't built in a day. As my friend always says, "What's the fucking rush? We just got here!"

The Forever Flex

Before I go, I want to leave you with my daily Flex ritual. This simple four-step framework has provided me with more self-trust, certainty, peace, and transformation than I ever thought possible. We are all works in progress navigating this crazy journey called life that is never linear. One step forward, two steps back, and just like a Snakes and Ladders board game, we can fall down a trap or jump ten spaces ahead at a moment's notice. Life is curvy but with flexible thinking, so can our thoughts be. I hope you will be able to turn the joy of flexible thinking into your default mindset as I have done and enjoy the endless benefits of daily mind reprogramming, thought bending, and energy upgrading. I begin every day with this Forever Flex.

I **connect** with my body, my powerful inner guidance system, by getting up and walking, or dancing to my favorite song of the moment. Three minutes of dancing or twenty minutes of walking/running to energize my body and feel my divine source of feminine energy awaken. As psychologist and relationship expert Michaela Boehm advises, this gets me in "flow" not just "go" mode and allows me to fully check in with my four brains.

I stay **curious** about how I'm feeling and instead of jumping to conclusions, I try to meet all new pieces of information and sensations with "that's interesting, let me find out more." When biases creep in, I question what's triggering them and if a naughty ANT is responsible for them. Labeling my faulty thought patterns diminishes their power instantly and even more so over time. When my ANTs are being managed, I am able to explore what wisdom and guidance my emotions are trying to give me.

I then consciously remind myself I always have a **choice** to either feed my Wolf of Love and step toward forgiveness, compassion, gratitude, unattachment, and positive intentions or step back into fearful thought loops. I choose the former.

And every day, I **commit** to finding the gifts my challenges bring me and celebrating my wins and emotional growth.

The Flex method is dynamic and constant; it's a framework to apply to any decision, situation, or daily reflection. I consciously ask different questions like "What can I give?" instead of "What can I get?" or "What am I learning from this?" instead of "Why is this happening to me?" Our mind will hunt whatever we tell it to find; use the Flex to ask for truffles, not turds. ☺

This is not to say that bad things won't happen or that the Flex will make us suddenly all better and we'll never suffer again. That would be a faulty and completely unrealistic *expectation* and a setup for disappointment. But remembering the human ability we all have to be bendy and adapt allows us to stay confident and ready to not just dodge curveballs but turn them into curve blessings.

When we focus on what we can give, how we can contribute joy, celebration, and happiness to the world, we take ownership of our lives from this proactive state. When we focus on what we're going to get, we give up agency and peace of mind as we wait reactively. We can be go-getters or go-givers.

With a flexible mindset, I know I can stretch all perspectives. There is no good or bad, just kind or mean narratives we tell ourselves. There is no right or wrong, just information for better future decisions. But what's most important is living full, being truly honest with what our soul desires, challenging the truth of our thoughts, and asking, "Who's speaking? Is this my bitchy inner critic, my wounded younger self just weaving another story to keep us 'safe' or trying to dig up the faulty core beliefs from my sponge years?"

Flexible thinking constantly gives me my awareness back to choose a new outlook; it keeps me curious and in a state of learning. We're all vulnerable, we all wonder whether we're enough, loved, or safe. There isn't a human I've met that doesn't question these things. But by staying connected to our Wildest, truest selves, we are reminded all fear is learned, emotions contain wisdom, and beneath insecurities and worries, an unlimited, passionate, loved and loving unique soul exists. In a world that often tells us otherwise, we have to become thought gymnastic experts!

So after all this, here's my truth: Being bendy has truly made me so much happier than perfection ever could.

ENDNOTES

1. Naomi Eisenberger et al., "Does Rejection Hurt? An fMRI Study of Social Exclusion," *Science* 302 (2003): 290–92, doi: 10.1126/science.1089134.

2. Kipling D. Williams and Steve A. Nida, "Ostracism: Consequences and Coping," *Current Directions in Psychological Science* 20, no. 2 (2011): 71–75, doi: 10.1177/0963721411402480.

3. Lisa Zadro et al., "How Low Can You Go? Ostracism by a Computer Is Sufficient to Lower Self-Reported Levels of Belonging, Control, Self-Esteem, and Meaningful Existence," *Journal of Experimental Social Psychology* 40, no. 4 (2004): 560–67, doi: 10.1016/j.jesp.2003.11.006.

4. Daryl B. O'Connor, Rory C. O'Connor, and Rachel Marshall, "Perfectionism and Psychological Distress: Evidence of the Mediating Effects of Rumination," *European Journal of Personality* 21, no. 4 (2007): 429–52, doi: 10.1002/per.616.

5. Martin M. Smith et.al., "The Perniciousness of Perfectionism: A Meta-analytic Review of the Perfectionism–Suicide Relationship," *Journal of Personality* 86 (2017): 522–42, doi: 10.1111/jopy.12333.

6. Gordon L. Flett et. al., "Components of Perfectionism and Procrastination in College Students," *Social Behavior and Personality* 20, no. 2 (1992): 85–94, doi: 10.2224/sbp.1992.20.2.85.

7. Thomas Curran and Andrew P. Hill, "Perfectionism Is Increasing Over Time: A Meta-Analysis of Birth Cohort Differences from 1989 to 2016," *Psychological Bulletin* 145, no. 4 (2019): 410–29, doi: 10.1037/bul0000138.

8. Elisabeth Kubler-Ross and David Kessler, *Life Lessons: Two Experts on Death and Dying Teach Us About the Mysteries of Life and Living* (New York: Scribner, 2000).

9. Julie Tseng and Jordan Poppenk, "Brain Meta-state Transitions Demarcate Thoughts Across Task Contexts Exposing the Mental Noise of Trait Neuroticism," *Nature Communications* 11, no. 1 (2020): 3480, doi: 10.1038/s41467-020-17255-9.

10. Stephen Maren, "Neurobiology of Pavlovian Fear Conditioning," *Annual Review of Neuroscience* 24, no. 1 (2001): 897–931, doi: 10.1146/annurev.neuro.24.1.897.

11. Y. Nir, T. Andrillon, A. Marmelshtein et al., "Selective Neuronal Lapses Precede Human Cognitive Lapses Following Sleep Deprivation," *Nature Medicine* 23, no. 12 (2017), doi: 10.1038/nm.4433.

12. Elaine Schmidt, "Spacing Out After Staying Up Late? Here's Why," UCLA Newsroom, November 6, 2017.

13. A. H. Maslow, "The Theory of Human Motivation," *Psychological Review* 50 (1943): 370–96.

14. David Rock, "SCARF: A Brain-Based Model for Collaborating and Influencing Others," *Neuroleadership Journal,* 2008.

15. Ditte Hoffmann et al., "Acceptance and Commitment Therapy for Health Anxiety," in *The Clinician's Guide to Treating Health Anxiety,* ed. Erik Hedman-Lagerlöf (London: Elsevier, 2019).

16. Evan Forma et al., "A Randomized Controlled Effectiveness Trial of Acceptance and Commitment Therapy and Cognitive Therapy for Anxiety and Depression," *Behavior Modification* 31, no. 6 (2007): 772–99, doi: 10.1177/0145445507302202.

17. Gareth Cook, "The Power of Flexible Thinking," *Scientific American,* March 21, 2018.

18. Tara Brach, *Radical Acceptance: Embracing Your Life with the Heart of a Buddha* (New York: Bantam, 2003).

19. J. Gutkowska et al., "Oxytocin Is a Cardiovascular Hormone," *Brazilian Journal of Medical and Biological Research* 33, no. 6 (2000): 625–33, doi: 10.1590/S0100-979X20000000600003.

20. Ichiro Kawachi et al., "A Prospective Study of Anger and Coronary Heart Disease," *Circulation* 95, no. 9 (1996): 2090–95, doi: 10.1161/01.1161/01. CIR.94.9.2090.

21. Jane Nelsen, "Connection Before Correction," *Positive Discipline* blog, https://www.positivediscipline.com/articles/connection-correction-0.

22. M. D. Lieberman et al., "Putting Feelings into Words: Affect Labeling Disrupts Amygdala Activity in Response to Affective Stimuli," *Psychological Science* 18, no. 5 (2007): 421–28, doi: 10.1111/j.1467-9280.2007.01916.x.

23. Sigrid Breit et al., "Vagus Nerve as Modulator of the Brain-Gut Axis in Psychiatric and Inflammatory Disorders," *Frontiers in Psychiatry,* March 2018, doi: 10.3389/fpsyt.2018.00044.

24. Erik Peper et al., "Increase or Decrease Depression: How Body Postures Influence Your Energy Level," *Biofeedback* 40, no. 3 (2012): 125–30, doi: 10.5298/1081-5937-40.3.01.

25. Philip Riley, "Research on Posture Yields Insight into Treating Depression," *SF State News,* October 2012.

26. Erik Peper et al., "Transforming Thoughts with Postural Awareness to Increase Therapeutic and Teaching Efficacy," *NeuroRegulation* 6, no. 3 (2019): 153–60, doi: 10.15540/nr.6.3.153.

27. Erik Peper et al., "Do Better in Math: How Your Body Posture May Change Stereotype Threat Response," *NeuroRegulation* 5, no. 2 (2018): 67–74, doi: 10.15540/nr.5.2.67.

28. Ruby Tandoh, "Work Sucks, I Know," WePresent, 2018, https://wepresent.wetransfer.com/story/work-sucks-i-know-ruby-tandoh/.

29. A. Larsson et al., "Using Brief Cognitive Restructuring and Cognitive Defusion Techniques to Cope with Negative Thoughts," *Behavioral Modification* 40, no. 3 (2016): 452–82, doi: 10.1177/0145445515621488.

30. Terese Eriksson et al., "Mindful Self-Compassion Training Reduces Stress and Burnout Symptoms Among Practicing Psychologists: A Randomized Controlled Trial of a Brief Web-Based Intervention," *Frontiers in Psychology* 9 (2018), doi: 10.3389/fpsyg.2018.02340.

31. Madeleine Ferrari et al., "Self-Compassion Interventions and Psychosocial Outcomes: A Meta-analysis of RTCs," *Mindfulness* 10 (2019): 1455–73, doi: 10.1007/s12671-019-01134-6.

32. Emma Seppälä et al., "Loving-Kindness Meditation: A Tool to Improve Healthcare Provider Compassion, Resilience, and Patient Care," *Journal of Compassionate Health Care* 1, no. 1 (2014), doi: 10.1186/s40639-014-0005-9.

33. Gallup 2019 Global Emotions Report, n.d., https://www.gallup.com/analytics/248906/gallup-global-emotions-report-2019.aspx.

34. L. S. Greenberg and W. Malcolm, "Resolving Unfinished Business: Relating Process to Outcome," *Journal of Consulting and Clinical Psychology* 70, no. 2 (2002): 406–16, doi: 10.1037/0022-006X.70.2.406.

35. E. J. Masicampo and R. F. Baumeister, "Consider It Done! Plan Making Can Eliminate the Cognitive Effects of Unfulfilled Goals," *Journal of Personality and Social Psychology* 101, no. 4 (2011): 667–83, doi: 10.1037/a0024192.

36. Josh Freed, "The Memory Image," *CBC Behind the Lens* blog, 2019.

37. E. F. Loftus and J. Palmer, "A Reconstruction of Automobile Destruction: An Example of the Interaction Between Language and Memory," *Journal of Verbal Learning and Verbal Behavior* 13 (1974): 585–89.

38. M. D. Ainsworth and S. M. Bell, "Attachment, Exploration, and Separation: Illustrated by the Behavior of One-Year-Olds in a Strange Situation," *Child Development* 41, no. 1 (1970): 49–67, doi: 10.2307/1127388.

39. D. Kahneman and A. Deaton, "High Income Improves Evaluation of Life but Not Emotional Well-Being," *PNAS* 107, no. 38 (2010): 16489–93, doi: 10.1073/pnas.1011492107.

40. S. Moscovici and M. Zavalloni, "The Group as a Polarizer of Attitudes," *Journal of Personality and Social Psychology* 12, no. 2 (1969): 125–35, doi: 10.1037/h0027568.

41. Brock Bastian et al., "Does a Culture of Happiness Increase Rumination of Failure?" *Emotion* 18, no. 5 (2018), doi: 10.1037/emo0000322.

42. Brock Bastian et al., "Perceiving Social Pressure Not to Feel Negative Predicts Depressive Symptoms in Daily Life," *Depression and Anxiety* 34, no. 5 (2017), doi: 10.1002/da.22653.

43. V. S. Ramachandran, *Phantoms in the Brain: Probing the Mysteries of the Human Mind* (New York: William Morrow and Co, 1998); *The Emerging Mind* (London: Profit Books, 2003); *A Brief Tour of Human Consciousness* (New York: PI Press, 2004).

44. Heather Gallivan, "Teens, Social Media and Body Image," Park Nicollet Melrose Center, Spring 2014.

45. Eric Stice and Heather E. Shaw, "Adverse Effects of the Media Portrayed Thin-Ideal on Women and Linkage to Bulimic Symptomatology," *Journal of Social and Clinical Psychology* 13, no. 3 (1994): 288–308.

46. Slavenka Kam-Hansen et al., "Altered Placebo and Drug Labeling Changes the Outcome of Episodic Migraine Attacks," *Science Translational Medicine* 6, no. 218 (2014): 218ra5, doi: 10.1126/scitranslmed.3006175.

47. "The Power of the Placebo Effect," Harvard Health Publishing, May 2017; updated August 9, 2019.

48. Robert K. Merton, "The Self-Fulfilling Prophecy," *Antioch Review* 8, no. 2 (1948): 193–210.

49. Marieke Jepma et al., "Behavioural and Neural Evidence for Self-Reinforcing Expectancy Effects on Pain," *Nature Human Behaviour* 2, no. 11 (2018), doi: 10.1038/s41562-018-0455-8.

50. John Sharp, *The Insight Cure: Change Your Story, Change Your Life* (New York: Hay House, 2018).

51. Charles H. Cooley, *Human Nature and the Social Order* (New York: Charles Scribner's Sons, 1902).

52. Jason S. Moser et al., "Third-Person Self-Talk Facilitates Emotion Regulation Without Engaging Cognitive Control: Converging Evidence

from ERP and fMRI," *Scientific Reports* 7, no. 1 (2017), doi: 10.1038 /s41598-017-04047-3.

53. J. Sakulku et al., "The Impostor Phenomenon," *International Journal of Behavioral Science* 6, no. 1 (2011): 73–92.

54. Pauline Rose Clance, *The Impostor Phenomenon: When Success Makes You Feel Like a Fake* (New York: Bantam, 1985).

55. Katerina Lup et al., "Instagram #instasad?: Exploring Associations Among Instagram Use, Depressive Symptoms, Negative Social Comparison, and Strangers Followed," *Cyberpsychology, Behavior, and Social Networking* 18, no. 5 (2015): 247–52, doi: 10.1089 /cyber.2014.0560.

56. Douglas LaBier, "To 'Win the Future,' We Need to Redefine 'Success' In Work and Life," *Psychology Today,* February 5, 2011.

57. J. Tseng and J. Poppenk, "Brain Meta-state Transitions Demarcate Thoughts Across Task Contexts Exposing the Mental Noise of Trait Neuroticism," *Nature Communications* 11 (2020), doi: https://doi .org/10.1101/576298.

58. Jade Scipioni, "Top Execs Use This Visualization Trick to Achieve Success—Here's Why It Works, According to a Neuroscientist," CNBC, November 22, 2019.

59. James A. Blumenthal et al., "Exercise and Pharmacotherapy in the Treatment of Major Depressive Disorder," *Psychosomatic Medicine* 69, no. 7 (2007): 587–96, doi: 10.1097/PSY.0b013e318148c19a.

ACKNOWLEDGMENTS

There aren't enough pages to adequately express my thank-yous. This book is the product of so many people.

Firstly, thank you to Matthew Benjamin and everyone at Harmony for the opportunity to write my first book. I've had no greater joy in my entire career than working on this. Nothing has ever made me feel as complete as being able to share my story and learnings so honestly with the world.

Thank you to Jennifer Weis for being the first one to suggest I write a book and helping make that happen. Also, thanks to Howard Yoon for his input and advice on the book proposal.

Thank you to Valerie Frankel for working around the clock to help me express myself and guiding me back after I got lost so many times. This book wouldn't be even 5 percent what it is now without you.

Thank you to my amazing mentors, teachers, interviewees, thought leaders, and contributors who shared their wisdom, knowledge, and experiences with me so generously.

A huge thank-you to one of my greatest idols, Dr. James Doty, for writing the foreword. To have your words open this book meant the world and your book *Into the Magic Shop: A Neurosurgeon's Quest to Discover the Mysteries of the Brain and the Secrets of the Heart* will always be one of my all-time favorites.

Thank you to my first investors for funding the Happy Not Perfect app creation when I had just a nugget of an idea and a big vision. I appreciate your patience as I learned how to navigate starting a business as well as understanding my own mental health at the same time.

Thank you to my friends for your patience with my late phone replies, missed birthdays, and missed parties when work for so many years took over. I love you all so much and I'm so grateful you stayed around.

Thank you to the best business partner, Suki Waterhouse. No one makes me laugh more or makes me enjoy working so much.

Thank you to my family for being the best teammates I could ask for. My brothers, Thomas and Edward, I adore you. As for my parents, there's no way I can thank you enough for what you've done for me. You taught me to fight for my dreams and that anything is possible.

Lastly, thanks to the readers. The time you have invested in yourself by reading this makes every minute of writing it worthwhile. I hope, forevermore, the FLEX can help you.

ABOUT THE AUTHOR

Credit: Adam Brazier

Poppy Jamie is an entrepreneur, influencer, and rising star in the mental health and mindfulness space. She launched the *Not Perfect* podcast and the Happy Not Perfect app after four years of aggregating behavioral studies and developing the app with neuroscientists, researchers, and her neurotherapist mom. She has been featured by the *New York Times, Wired, Fast Company, Refinery29, Forbes, Vogue, Bustle, Cosmopolitan,* E!, NBC News, and MTV.